OCCASIONAL PAPER 257

Economic Growth and Integration in Central America

Edited by Dominique Desruelle and Alfred Schipke

INTERNATIONAL MONETARY FUND
Washington DC
2007

Production: IMF Multimedia Services Division
Typesetting: Bob Lunsford
Figures: Bob Lunsford

Cataloging-in-Publication Data

Economic growth and integration in Central America / edited by Dominique Desruelle and Alfred Schipke — Washington, DC : International Monetary Fund, 2007.

p. cm.—(Occasional paper ; 257)

Includes bibliographical references.
ISBN 978-1-58906-616-8

1. Central America — Economic conditions. 2. Central America — Economic policy. 3. Debts, Public — Central America. I. Desruelle, Dominique. II. Schipke, Alfred 1959- III. Series: Occasional paper (International Monetary Fund) ; 257

HC141 .E266 2007

Price: US$30
(US$28 to full-time faculty members and students at universities and colleges)

Please send orders to:
International Monetary Fund, Publication Services
700 19th Street, N.W., Washington, D.C. 20431, U.S.A.
Tel: (202) 623-7430 Telefax: (202) 623-7201
E-mail: publications@imf.org
Internet: http://www/imf.org

Contents

Boxes

Tables

Figures

The following conventions are used in this publication:

- In tables, a blank cell indicates "not applicable," ellipsis points (. . .) indicate "not available," and 0 or 0.0 indicates "zero" or "negligible." Minor discrepancies between sums of constituent figures and totals are due to rounding.

- An en dash (–) between years or months (for example, 2005–06 or January–June) indicates the years or months covered, including the beginning and ending years or months; a slash or virgule (/) between years or months (for example, 2005/06) indicates a fiscal or financial year, as does the abbreviation FY (for example, FY2006).

- "Billion" means a thousand million; "trillion" means a thousand billion.

- "Basis points" refer to hundredths of 1 percentage point (for example, 25 basis points are equivalent to ¼ of 1 percentage point).

As used in this publication, the term "country" does not in all cases refer to a territorial entity that is a state as understood by international law and practice. As used here, the term also covers some territorial entities that are not states but for which statistical data are maintained on a separate and independent basis.

Foreword

There is substantial optimism about Central America's investment and growth potential, reflecting continuing political and economic stability, and deepening global and regional integration to achieve sustainable employment growth and poverty reduction. This optimism has already led to increased investment in the region, and was echoed by a diverse group of investors who, at a High-Level Conference on Investment on February 1–2, 2007, in Costa Rica, expressed a strong interest to start or expand operations in Central America.

Given the increased international focus in Central America, policymakers have an opportunity to make the region even more attractive for investment by accelerating reforms to reach higher levels of economic growth and by fostering integration. These issues are at the center of this publication, which highlights the region's progress and discusses—in light of the international experience—a number of key areas where further reforms are needed. International experience reveals, for example, that strengthening institutions and improving the business environment can substantially improve Central America's growth potential, and thereby reduce still-high levels of poverty. It also argues that there is substantial scope to further develop capital markets, which would not only improve access to financing and facilitate growth but also reduce vulnerabilities and strengthen the effectiveness of monetary policy. Additional important topics covered in this publication include pension reform, monetary policy frameworks, and sovereign debt structures.

As Central America advances, the IMF will continue to assist the authorities in their reform efforts through policy advice and technical assistance with the aim of improving the living conditions of all citizens.

Rodrigo de Rato
Managing Director
International Monetary Fund

Central America is moving forward with its integration efforts. Clear indications of this are the free trade agreement between the United States, Central America, and the Dominican Republic (CAFTA-DR), the initiation of negotiations on a partnership agreement with the European Union, and increasing integration among the Central American economies, including the establishment of a customs union. However, these efforts need to move hand-in-hand with reforms in other areas to ensure that the benefits of integration materialize and that the region is in a better position to face adverse shocks.

This publication covers a number of policy priorities, including measures to increase the region's growth potential to narrow the income gap with more developed countries, ensure the sustainability of public pension systems, improve the structure and functioning of public debt markets, and increase the effectiveness of monetary policy. The currently benign global environment provides a unique opportunity for policymakers in the region to press ahead with these reforms.

This publication is the second volume on Central America coordinated by our team in the Western Hemisphere Department and reflects our increased focus on issues that are common across countries or directly related to Central America's integration process.

Anoop Singh
Director, Western Hemisphere Department
International Monetary Fund

Preface

Reflecting our increased focus on cross-country issues and topics related to integration, this is the second publication on Central America produced by the IMF's Western Hemisphere Department, complementing Occasional Paper 243. The production of this publication is the result of a team effort that included staff from a number of departments led by Dominique Desruelle and Alfred Schipke.

The authors would like to thank Anoop Singh and David Robinson for their comments and guidance. The authors would also like to acknowledge the comments and suggestions from the Central American authorities and the participants at the Fifth Annual Regional Conference on Central America, Panama, and the Dominican Republic in Punta Cana (June 28–29, 2006).

Special thanks go to Carmen Sanabia, who worked extremely hard to ensure the timely submission of the manuscript. Also, the authors would like to thank Cleary Haines and Ewa Gradzka for their outstanding research support. David Einhorn of the External Relations Department coordinated production of the publication.

The opinions expressed in this paper are solely those of its authors and do not necessarily reflect the views of the International Monetary Fund, its Executive Directors, or the authorities in the respective Central American countries, Panama, and the Dominican Republic.

I Overview

Dominique Desruelle and Alfred Schipke[1]

Central America has made substantial progress in regaining macroeconomic stability and has continued to integrate further both globally and at the regional level.[2] The challenge now is how to entrench these gains, improve growth performance to significantly reduce poverty, and reduce vulnerabilities, including those that are associated with increased integration. This paper addresses some of these important issues. After reviewing recent developments, this chapter provides an overview of key policy issues facing Central America: economic growth, fiscal issues related to pension reform and sovereign debt structures, the development of capital markets, and monetary policy. It also briefly discusses the progress that has been made with integration and regional policy coordination.[3] The subsequent chapters analyze these key issues in more depth.

Recent Developments

Over the past two years, a series of presidential and congressional elections in Central America have demonstrated that democracies are functioning well and that transfers of power occur smoothly. While the governments in the region continue to embrace macroeconomic stability, the ability of the countries in the region to move economic reforms forward will depend critically on their ability to build alliances, since many governments lack majority support in congress.

Benefiting from a continued favorable global environment, the region has recently improved its growth performance, reaching on average 5 percent in 2005 and around 6 percent in 2006. Growth in Costa Rica, the Dominican Republic, and Panama has been particularly impressive in recent years (Table 1.1). Exports from countries in the region grew by 11 percent in dollar value terms in 2005 and 2006.

Despite the uptick in inflation that followed the oil price shock, external positions remained strong. As a result of the oil price hike, inflation in the region rose to 8 percent in 2005, but fell to around 6 percent in 2006. At the same time, the regional current account deficit did not deteriorate notably and remained stable at about 5 percent of GDP in both 2005 and 2006, aided by strong export growth and rising remittances. In addition, strong capital flows to the region have led to further accumulation of foreign exchange reserves.

Authorities in the region have maintained robust fiscal policies, but public finances remain vulnerable, and more is to be done to reduce debt levels and finance priority spending (Figure 1.1). With Guatemala the notable exception, public debt levels in the rest of region remain high (an average of about 53 percent of GDP at end-2005), despite debt relief delivered to Nicaragua and Honduras under the Heavily Indebted Poor Countries (HIPC) Initiative. The need for urgent increases in priority spending in many of the countries in the region will require raising revenue, reducing exemptions, and reorienting spending.

Financial sector intermediation is increasing, but financial dollarization, weaknesses in supervision, and rapid credit growth remain sources of vulnerability. With the exception of Panama, financial systems in the region are still shallow. In that light, the rise in credit growth is a welcome development, but, with increases in credit of 3½ percentage points of GDP or higher in Costa Rica, Nicaragua, and Panama during 2006, risks need to be closely monitored.[4] The proliferation of foreign currency lending is a potential source of currency-induced credit risk for banks, even in countries where

[1]This chapter has benefited from comments by Ivanna Vladkova Hollar.

[2]Unless otherwise stated, Central America refers to Costa Rica, El Salvador, Guatemala, Honduras, and Nicaragua, as well as Panama and the Dominican Republic. The inclusion of the latter two countries reflects their membership in a number of regional institutions such as the Central American Integration System.

[3]This paper complements Occasional Paper 243 (Rodlauer and Schipke, 2005), which covered the macroeconomic implications of the Central America-Dominican Republic Free Trade Agreement with the United States, trade liberalization and tax coordination, fiscal sustainability, regional integration and exchange rate arrangements, financial system issues, and issues related to the political economy of reforms and macroeconomic statistics.

[4]Rapid rises in credit raise questions about the capacity of the banking system to assess risk and to allocate credit efficiently. However, the current credit expansion does not so far appear to qualify as a "lending boom" (Gourinchas, Valdes, and Landerretche, 2001; Borio and Lowe, 2002). Furthermore, fiscal consolidation has likely played a role in "crowding in" the private sector.

Table 1.1. Central America: Real GDP Growth

	2004	2005	2006
Central America	**4.0**	**5.1**	**6.0**
Costa Rica	4.1	5.9	7.5
Dominican Republic	2.0	9.3	10.1
El Salvador	1.8	2.8	4.2
Guatemala	2.7	3.2	4.6
Honduras	4.6	4.2	5.5
Nicaragua	5.1	4.0	3.7
Panama	7.5	6.4	6.5

Source: IMF, *World Economic Outlook*.
Note: 2006 numbers are preliminary.

net foreign currency positions of banks are roughly balanced. Weaknesses in supervision, particularly of the offshore banking sector and nonsupervised deposit-taking institutions, pose significant additional risks. Recent banking failures in Guatemala, including the failure of the fourth largest bank (Banco del Café) as a result of problems in an affiliate offshore and of Banco del Comercio related to lending to an unregistered deposit-taking institution, have brought to the fore the need to improve supervision and bank resolution frameworks at both the national and regional levels.

Key Policy Issues

Economic Growth

Central America's biggest challenge is how to reduce still widespread poverty and narrow the income gap with more developed countries. Despite Central America's improved record of macroeconomic stability and recent recovery in economic activity, average growth rates over the past decade have fallen short of the records achieved in the 1960s and 1970s. Furthermore, the region scores less favorably when compared against the growth performance of the more dynamic emerging market economies in the world, especially emerging Asia. Given that poverty levels remain extremely high (except in Costa Rica) and are well above the Latin American average, addressing issues of economic growth will be paramount to lift people out of poverty and significantly raise living standards. Only three countries (Costa Rica, Panama, and the Dominican Republic) have succeeded in raising GDP-per-capita levels above their levels in the late 1970s. A growth accounting exercise at the regional and country level reveals that, from 1960–2005, increases in output per worker almost exclusively reflected capital deepening as opposed to productivity growth, and that variations in growth within subperiods and across countries were closely associated with differences in productivity growth.

Improving growth performance in Central America will depend to a large degree on the countries' abilities to implement productivity-enhancing reforms. Both the recent growth literature and the empirical evidence for Central America presented in Chapter II suggest that the region would benefit substantially by improving the quality of institutions, including those related to business activity and governance. Bringing institutional quality up to Chile's level, for example, could raise growth by 0.5 percentage points per year in countries with relatively strong institutions (Costa Rica) and by 3 percentage points or more per year in countries with relatively weak institutions (Honduras and Nicaragua). A concerted effort to improve institutions and the business environment in Central America is also paramount to ensuring that implementation of the Central America-Dominican Republic Free Trade Agreement with the United States (CAFTA-DR) and potential trade agreements with the European Union will lead to the expected productivity improvements and tangible benefits for all.

Fiscal Issues: Pension Reform and Sovereign Debt Structures

Creating sustainable debt dynamics is another key policy challenge for countries in the region. As shown in Chapter III, a key element in a strategy to reduce fiscal vulnerabilities is putting Central America's pension systems on a sound footing. Although Central America has more favorable demographics than countries with low or even declining birth rates, its population will age substantially in the coming decades. The ratio of the working age population to the elderly will fall from about eight today to less than three in 2050. In addition, by international standards, the countries in the region have very generous benefits relative to contributions and low retirement ages, even when taking into account differences in life expectancy. As a result, the real internal rate of return of the defined-benefit systems in the region is about 10 percent on average, that is, more than twice the growth rate of the real wage bill or the average growth performance over the past decades.

While some countries have started to introduce pension reforms, more needs to be done. Pension reform is warranted both in countries with pay-as-you-go, defined-benefit systems and those that have shifted to defined-contribution systems through privatization. Although there is no one-size-fits-all solution, sustainability requires some combination of increased contribution rates, higher retirement ages, and lower

Figure 1.1. Central America: Selected Macroeconomic Indicators

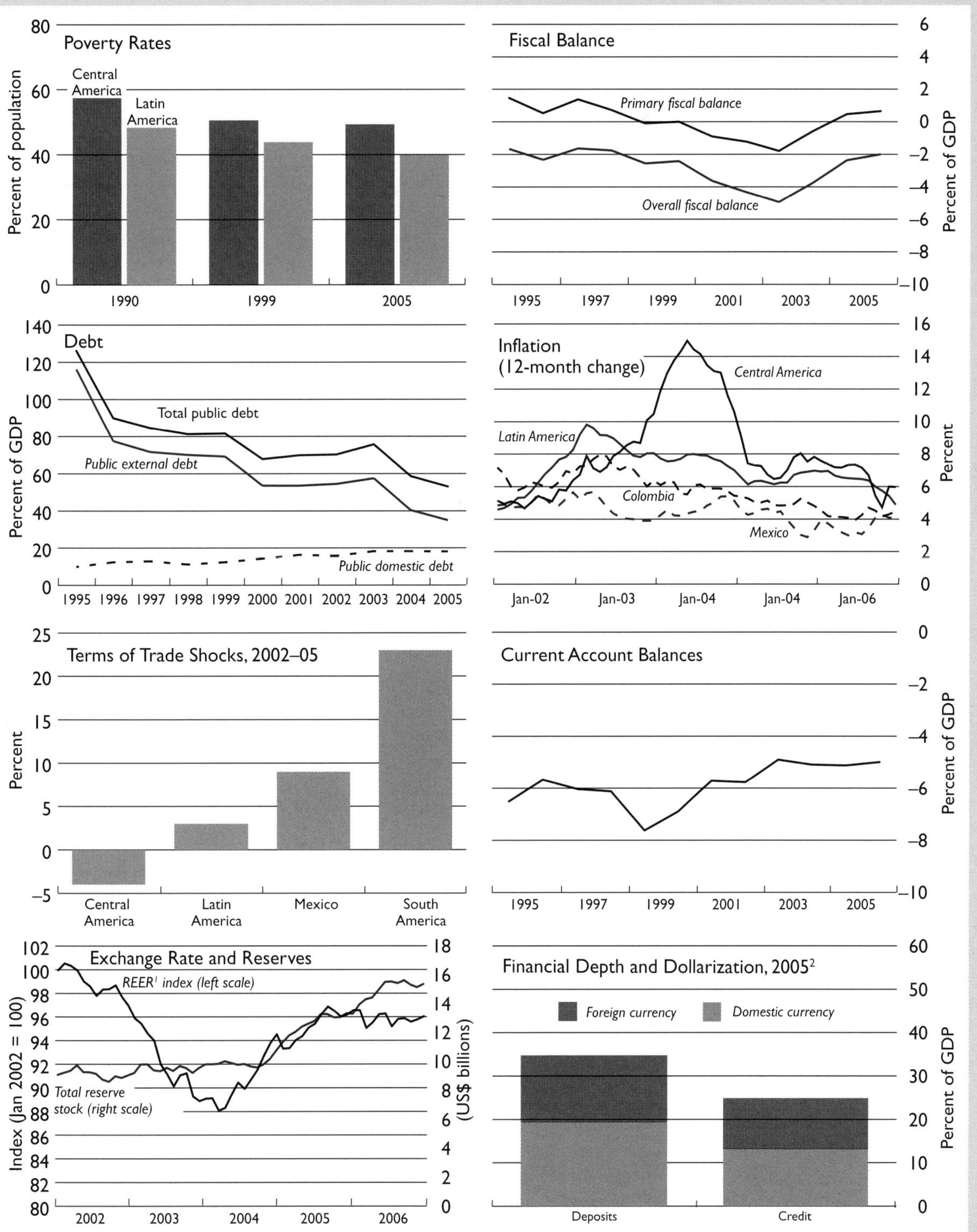

Sources: IMF, *World Economic Outlook*; IMF, *International Financial Statistics*; IMF, Information Notification System; and Economic Commission for Latin America and the Caribbean.

[1]REER = Real effective exchange rate.

[2]Excludes Panama.

benefits in most countries. Also, the link between contributions and benefits should be strengthened. Countries that have privatized their pension system still need to make additional parametric reforms to their old defined-benefit system to reduce transition costs. Success in implementing pension reforms in Central America will depend not only on the design of the reforms themselves, but also on the authorities' ability to mobilize the necessary political support. As experience both in the region and in other countries has shown, successful pension reform requires broad-based consensus in society.

Another key element in reducing vulnerability is moving toward "safer" debt structures. Sustainable debt dynamics are a function not only of the level of debt, but also of its structure. Currency denomination, maturity composition, capital structure, and solvency play an important role in the likelihood of a crisis. The public sector balance sheets often exhibit significant mismatches along those dimensions. The analysis in Chapter IV of Central America's sovereign debt structures reveals that the region not only has relatively high public debt levels (except Guatemala), but also a higher share of foreign currency debt in total debt (except Costa Rica) than the rest of Latin America. At the same time, Central America compares favorably to other Latin American countries in terms of its share of short-term debt, with the exception of Costa Rica and the Dominican Republic. In line with broader developments in emerging markets, Central America more recently has been able to reduce its foreign currency exposure and modestly lengthen its maturity structure.

While Central America's debt structure is endogenous to past policies and institutions, economic policies can help further improve structures and therefore reduce vulnerabilities. As the empirical evidence in Chapter IV shows, stronger institutions, for example, go hand-in-hand with the ability of Central American countries to issue debt domestically. The chapter also reveals that the more financially developed a country, the lower the share of foreign currency and short-term debt. Strengthening institutions will therefore be important to reducing vulnerabilities.

Financial Sector Issue: Development of Public Debt Markets

Central America's financial system is largely bank-based. With the exception of Panama, which has a bank-asset-to-GDP ratio of 250 percent, there is substantial scope for further development in the region.[5] Guatemala and the Dominican Republic, in particular, have relatively low levels of financial sector penetration, with bank-asset-to-GDP ratios of around 35 and 40 percent, respectively. Capital markets in turn are underdeveloped and dominated by public debt markets. The number of equity and corporate bond listings are generally in the single digits (except in Panama). Institutional investors (pension funds, mutual funds, and insurance companies) intermediate only a small share of national savings.

The development of capital markets would not only be important to reduce vulnerabilities stemming from limited diversification and improve access to financing, but would also allow the authorities to conduct monetary policy more effectively. Chapter V shows that there is substantial scope for institutional and operational improvements. To aid the establishment of liquid public debt markets and a unified sovereign yield curve, the quasi-fiscal debts of central banks need to be transferred to the government, thus dealing directly with the problem of dual sovereign debt issuers.[6] Central America has a large stock of nonstandard and nontradable debt that should be restructured. In most countries, it will also be important to develop and implement a medium-term debt management strategy and improve the technical capacity of debt management units. In that respect, Costa Rica, El Salvador, and Panama have made some improvements over the past few years.

A regional public debt market may help overcome the size and scale limitations of the individual Central American countries. This can, however, only be accomplished in the medium to long term, after improvements in local markets provide the foundation on which such an integrated regional market could be built. The Central American Monetary Council, in collaboration with the Central American Committee of Finance Ministers, is working to harmonize the technical standards of public debt issuance.

Monetary Policy Issues

Bringing inflation down to the level of trading partners generally remains a challenge for the region. The conduct of monetary policy in the nondollarized economies in Central America is further tested by regional integration with the United States, record levels of remittance flows, and in some cases increasing integration into global capital markets. Given theses challenges for monetary policy, some countries (for example, Costa Rica and Guatemala) are reviewing their policy regimes to make them more effective.

Chapter VI shows that all the countries in the region have made substantial progress in strengthen-

[5]For a discussion of financial sector issues, see Morales and Schipke (2005) and Brenner (2006).

[6]These quasi-fiscal debt stocks are substantial: 11 percent of GDP in Costa Rica and 18 percent in the Dominican Republic.

ing the institutional underpinnings for formulating and executing monetary policy. New central bank legislation has given the monetary authorities enhanced autonomy. As a result, the mandate of central banks is more clearly focused on preserving price stability, even though some attention is still given to the competitiveness of the tradable sector. Central banks have also benefited from increased de jure political autonomy.

Despite these advances, substantial shortcomings remain. Trying to maintain price stability while, at the same time, preserving the external value of the domestic currency raises concerns about objectives, causes policy conflicts (for example, in the case of strong capital inflows), and undermines the credibility of central banks. Also, while direct political intervention and the financing of fiscal deficits has been curtailed, there is still, in practice, a potentially strong link between the political business cycle and monetary policy decisions. Indeed, since the executive branch continues to have substantial leeway to remove central bank governors and other members of central bank boards of directors. Furthermore, central banks still generally lack financial autonomy, as there are often no legal provisions to protect the integrity of central bank capital.

Integration and Policy Coordination

Trade Liberalization and Bilateral Trade Agreements

The region continues to move toward greater trade liberalization and is negotiating additional regional and bilateral trade agreements. Of course, these should be intermediate steps toward greater multilateral opening and the completion of the Doha trade round, which are still the most important vehicles for promoting strong global growth and sustained poverty reduction. In 2006, CAFTA-DR became effective in El Salvador, Guatemala, Honduras, and Nicaragua. The Dominican Republic followed in 2007. Ratification in Costa Rica is pending; the new government of Oscar Arias in Costa Rica, however, has made ratification of the agreement a priority. Panama, which was not part of CAFTA-DR, has concluded, on a technical level, negotiations on a separate agreement with the United States (Table 1.2.). In addition, Central America is set to begin negotiations for an Association Agreement with the European Union in early 2007, which would create a free trade area between the two regions.

Increased Regional Coordination

With the private sector and financial institutions increasingly operating regionally, the challenge will be to maximize the benefits that integration will bring and to reduce integration-related vulnerabilities. This implies that government policies, regulation, and supervision follow suit. In particular, more needs to be done to standardize norms and regulations (e.g., customs), improve the flow of information among government agencies (e.g., financial sector supervisors), and improve policy coordination in certain areas (e.g., tax policies). At the center of this coordination effort is the Central American System of Integration, which brings together heads of state as well as regional councils and committees of ministers, central bank presidents, and superintendents.

Association Agreement Negotiations with the European Union

The framework of negotiations for an Association Agreement between Central America (including Panama) and the European Union could further accelerate policy coordination and integration among the Central American economies. Based on the Declaration of Vienna (May 2006), the respective countries committed themselves to implementing the decisions adopted at the presidential summit in Panama, ratifying the Central American Treaty on Investments and Services, and developing a legal framework to ensure that commercial and economic regulation is applied uniformly within the region. Furthermore, the format of negotiations with the European Union, employing a single regional spokesperson,[7] would go substantially beyond the setup of CAFTA-DR negotiations, where country-specific schedules and exemptions were negotiated bilaterally.

Tax Coordination

Implementation of CAFTA-DR and the establishment of the planned customs union will provide additional benefits to the region. At the same time, increased economic integration will be associated, at least in the short-term, with custom revenue losses. It could also lead to further tax competition at a time when the countries in the region need to raise tax revenue to address social needs, fight poverty, and reduce vulnerabilities by bringing down relatively high debt-to-GDP ratios.

Initial steps have been taken over the past year to overcome these risks. In addition to efforts aimed at improving tax administration and raising taxes in some countries (notably in Guatemala, Costa Rica, Nicaragua, and the Dominican Republic), the ministers of

[7]It is expected that while each country will have its own negotiation team, discussions with the European Union will be headed by a single spokesperson, with that position being held on a rotating basis by a representative of each of the Central American countries.

Table 1.2. Central America: Regional and Bilateral Free Trade Agreements

Country	Agreement and Date
Guatemala	Regional, CAFTA-DR (2006)[1] Regional, Central America–Dominican Republic (1999) Taiwan, Province of China (2006) Regional, Northern Triangle, Mexico (2001)[2] Regional, Central America–Chile (negotiating) Regional, Central America–Panama (negotiating)
El Salvador	Regional, CAFTA-DR (2006)[1] Regional, Central America–Dominican Republic (1999) Regional, Northern Triangle, Mexico (2001)[2] Regional, Central America–Chile (negotiating) Regional, Central America–Panama (negotiating)
Honduras	Regional, CAFTA-DR (2006)[1] Regional, Central America–Dominican Republic (1999) Regional, Northern Triangle, Mexico (2001)[2] Regional, Central America–Chile (negotiating) Regional, Central America–Panama (negotiating) Colombia and Taiwan (negotiating)
Nicaragua	Regional, CAFTA-DR (2006)[1] Regional, Central America–Dominican Republic (1999) Mexico (1998) Regional, Central America–Chile (negotiating) Regional, Central America–Panama (negotiating)
Costa Rica	Regional, CAFTA-DR (2006),[1] not ratified Regional, Central America–Dominican Republic (1999) Canada (2002) Mexico (1995) Caribbean Community (2004)[3] Regional, Central America–Chile (negotiating) Regional, Central America–Panama (negotiating)
Dominican Republic	Regional, CAFTA-DR (2007)[1] Regional, Central America–Dominican Republic (1999)

Source: http://www.sieca.org.gt.
[1]Free trade agreement between Central America, the Dominican Republic, and the United States.
[2]Free trade agreement between Mexico, Guatemala, and Honduras.
[3]Free trade agreement with the Caribbean Community.

finance of the region have identified a number of areas to achieve greater coordination of their tax policies. Key measures in that respect are: (1) increasing transparency by compiling a matrix of current tax incentives in the respective countries and making the information available to the seven countries; (2) reducing the risk of a "race to the bottom" and further proliferation of tax incentives by seeking an agreement on a code of conduct on good practices for fiscal incentives for investments; (3) protecting the corporate tax base by defining clear rules on transfer pricing and thin capitalization; (4) increasing cooperation between tax and customs administrations through a systematic exchange of information, which will be even more necessary given the stated goal of creating a customs union; and (5) improving international taxation by establishing treaties to avoid the double taxation of income and capital.

Furthermore, institutionally, countries in the region strengthened their coordination efforts through the establishment of a regional Committee of Finance Ministers and a supporting technical secretariat. Creation of this committee closes an important gap in the regional institutional structure, which already has regional coordination mechanisms such as the Central American Monetary Council and the Council of Ministers of Economy and Trade.

Coordination of Financial Sector Regulation and Supervision

The regionalization of financial services is accelerating, with more and more banks establishing offices and subsidiaries in different countries. While Central America's financial sector integration allows for a reduction in funding costs and risk diversification for companies and households alike, it requires the adoption of appropriate regulation and supervision arrangements to minimize regulatory gaps, arbitrage, and cross-border contagion. Given these challenges, the Central American Council of Financial Sector Superintendents is strengthening its efforts to improve the coordination of financial sector regulation and supervision. It has initiated a regional project that aims to (1) strengthen understanding of the current operations of regional financial groups and the regulatory system governing their activities; (2) devise an adequate regulatory framework for cross-border consolidated supervision by improving the flow of information and enhancing collaboration between the supervisory authorities of the region; (3) adopt minimum regulatory standards and harmonize them at a regional level; and (4) create mechanisms to monitor progress.

In 2006, Panama, Costa Rica, and El Salvador signed an agreement to establish a regional exchange for equity and corporate bonds with the objective of creating a regional capital market. Superintendents of security exchanges also initiated efforts to increase coordination. At their first regional meeting in the Dominican Republic in 2006, the security superintendents started the process of creating a Central American Council of Security Regulators.

Harmonization of Macroeconomic Statistics

Deepening economic integration and increasing policy coordination require reliable and comparable data across countries. While Central America has made significant progress in improving data quality and provision, the quality of data remains heterogeneous and the region lacks a coordinated, consolidated, and harmonized statistical system.

As a first step, the authorities in the region have embarked on a project to improve and harmonize monetary and finance statistics, which at a later stage could be followed by the harmonization of fiscal statistics. The aim is to facilitate cross-country comparison and regional analysis and provide reliable and comprehensive data to the private sector and policymakers. The project will (1) improve existing monetary and financial statistics compilation systems; (2) expand coverage by gathering data from all the major financial institutions in the region, including offshore banks and other financial intermediaries such as pension funds, insurance companies, and investment funds; and (3) define common classification and valuation criteria for financial instruments and economic sectors. The project is expected to be completed in 2008.

Moving Forward

Reflecting both sound economic policies and a benign global environment, Central America has experienced an improved economic performance over the past few years. It is in a good position to build on progress that has been made. Its political and economic institutions are maturing and there is a broad-based consensus on maintaining macroeconomic stability, taking advantage of the benefits that globalization brings, and strengthening regional cooperation. In this context, the challenge is how to reduce poverty, improve the living standards of all citizens, and increase the region's resilience against adverse shocks. The following chapters address these issues in more depth.

References

Borio, Claudio, and Phillip Lowe, 2002, "Asset Prices, Financial and Monetary Stability: Exploring the Nexus," BIS Working Paper No. 114 (Basel, Switzerland: Bank for International Settlements, July).

Brenner, Patricia, 2006, *Central America: Structural Foundations for Regional Financial Integration* (Washington: International Monetary Fund).

Gourinchas, Pierre-Olivier, Rodrigo Valdes, and Oscar Landerretche, 2001, "Lending Booms: Latin America and the World," NBER Research Working Paper No. 8249 (Cambridge, Massachusetts: National Bureau of Economic Research).

Morales, R. Armando, and Alfred Schipke, 2005, "Regional Integration and Financial System Issues," in *Central America: Global Integration and Regional Cooperation*, edited by Markus Rodlauer and Alfred Schipke, IMF Occasional Paper No. 243 (Washington: International Monetary Fund).

Rodlauer, Markus, and Alfred Schipke, eds., 2005, *Central America: Global Integration and Regional Cooperation*, IMF Occasional Paper No. 243 (Washington: International Monetary Fund).

II Growth Performance

José Brambila Macías, Guy Meredith, and Ivanna Vladkova Hollar

During the period of reforms that began in the early 1990s, economic growth in Central America recovered from the poor performance of the 1980s.[1] Yet, in spite of the region achieving a welcome degree of macroeconomic stability, growth in the 1990s still fell short of the record achieved in the 1960s and 1970s. It also fell short of more dynamic emerging market countries, notably in Asia. Despite the more recent stronger performance, there continue to be concerns about the region's ability to grow at a pace that will significantly raise living standards and reduce poverty.[2] Underscoring this challenge, even while the incidence of poverty edged down in the region during the 1990s, it remained well above that of Latin America as a whole at the end of the decade (Figure 2.1).

This chapter first reviews the stylized facts regarding the growth performance in Central America since the 1960s. It then analyzes the proximate sources of growth over this period using a standard growth-accounting framework, both for the region as a whole and for individual countries. The chapter then reviews some of the explanations for the region's relatively unsatisfactory growth performance in the context of the broader literature on growth across countries, focusing on shortfalls in institutions and, in particular, on business regulations. Empirical support for the role of weak institutions is then presented in a panel regression framework, illustrating the possible importance of such effects for Central America.

Figure 2.1. Poverty Rates, Nationally Defined Poverty Line
(Percent of population)

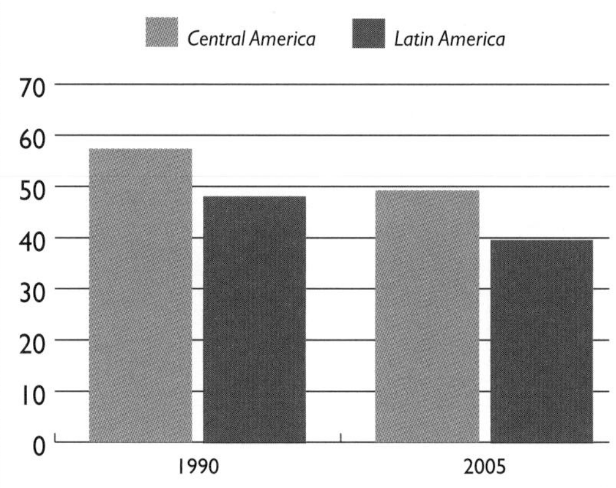

Source: Economic Commission for Latin America and the Caribbean, *Social Panorama of Latin America, 2006.*

Stylized Facts

Central America, and Latin America as a whole, experienced relatively rapid growth during the 1960s and 1970s. Real GDP growth in Central America averaged about 5½ percent during the two decades as a whole (Table 2.1 and Figure 2.2). Growth was similar across countries during the 1960s, ranging from Nicaragua at the high end with 7½ percent to the Dominican Republic at the low end with 4¾ percent. The positions of the best and worst performers reversed in the 1970s, however, and the dispersion increased sharply, as the Dominican Republic grew by 8¼ percent on average, while Nicaragua's growth plunged to zero. Developments were more stable in other countries in the region during the 1960s and 1970s, with most witnessing relatively robust growth.

The picture changed dramatically in the 1980s, as the region was adversely affected by armed conflicts and external shocks, combined with poor policy responses, as in much of Latin America. The negative external shocks included the oil and debt crises, soaring inflation, and steep declines in the prices of coffee and fruits, which are among the region's leading exports to the developed world. Consequently, Central America experienced a widespread economic downturn, with

[1]Covers the countries that form part of the Central America-Dominican Republic Free Trade Agreement (CAFTA-DR) with the United States: Costa Rica, the Dominican Republic, Guatemala, Honduras, Nicaragua and El Salvador.

[2]These concerns are underscored by the evidence in Berg and others (2006) that Latin American countries in general have experienced difficulties in sustaining growth over longer periods of time.

Table 2.1. Central America: Long-Term Real GDP Growth by Country
(In percent a year)

	1960–69	1970–79	1980–89	1990–99	2000–05	1960–2005
Costa Rica	5.9	6.3	2.1	5.4	3.7	4.7
Dominican Republic	4.8	8.2	3.8	4.6	4.3	5.1
El Salvador	6.0	3.9	–2.1	4.9	2.2	3.0
Guatemala	5.5	5.9	0.9	4.1	2.7	3.8
Honduras	4.9	5.8	2.5	2.8	3.9	4.0
Nicaragua	7.4	0.0	–0.9	3.0	3.3	2.6
Central America	5.7	5.3	1.2	4.4	3.4	3.9

Sources: World Bank, *World Development Indicators* (2005); and IMF, *World Economic Outlook* (2005).

growth averaging only 1¼ percent in the 1980s. Nicaragua witnessed a particularly spectacular collapse, as political turmoil led to a sharp decline in real per capita GDP in 1979, followed by stagnation through the 1980s (Figure 2.3).[3] El Salvador was also hard hit, experiencing a cumulative decline in output of almost 30 percent during 1979–83. Costa Rica, Guatemala, and Honduras had contractions in output in the early 1980s, albeit less severe than in Nicaragua and El Salvador. The Dominican Republic presents an interesting exception to the weak performance during this period, as growth continued at a relatively robust pace during the early 1980s before slowing later in the decade.

After the "lost decade" of the 1980s, the 1990s ushered in signs of recovery in most Central American countries. Democratic changes, structural reforms, and global economic stability enabled the region to achieve modest but sustained increases in output, with real GDP growth averaging about 4½ percent during the

[3]In 1979, the Somoza government was overthrown and a new governing coalition dominated by the Frente Sandinista de Liberacion Nacional (FSLN) assumed power.

Figure 2.2. Central America: Long-Term Real GDP Growth
(In percent)

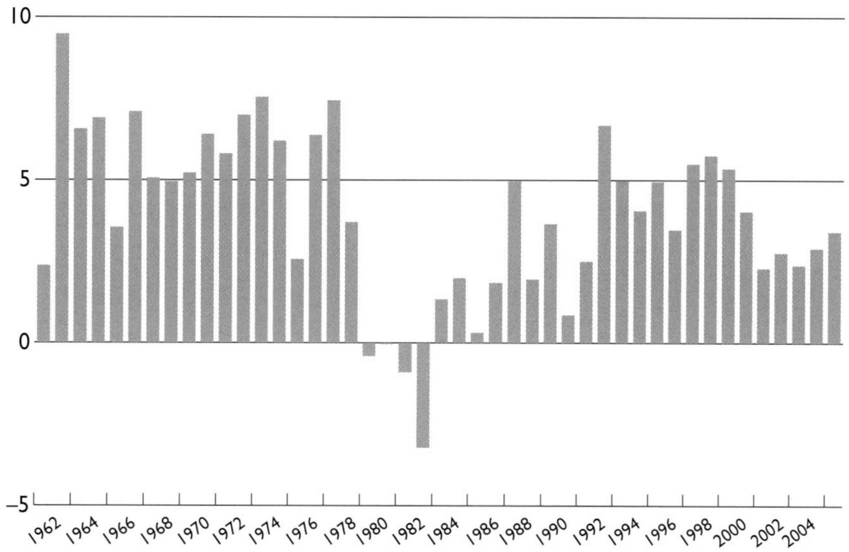

Sources: World Bank, *World Development Indicators* (2005); and IMF, *World Economic Outlook* (2005).

Figure 2.3. Real Per Capita GDP by Country
(In constant 2000 U.S. dollars)

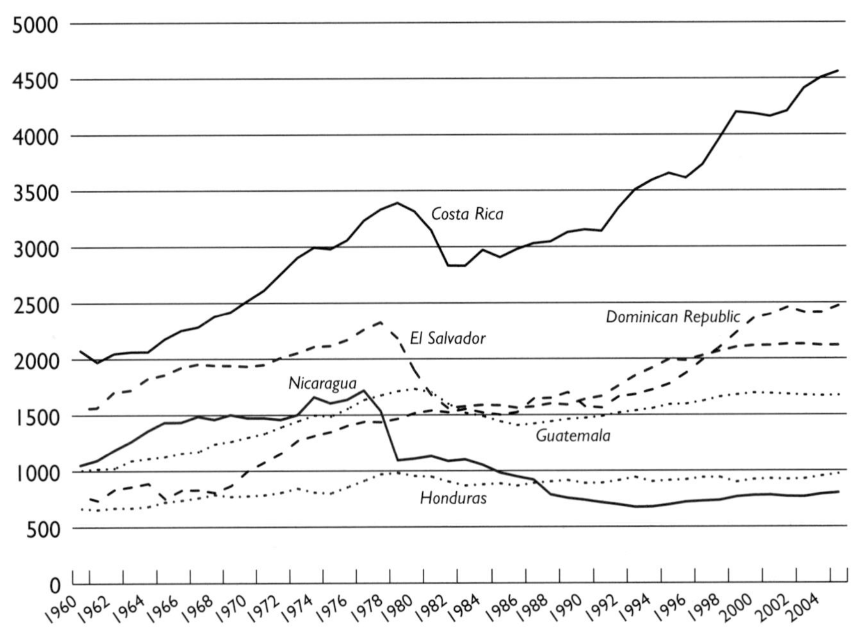

Sources: Penn World Table Version 6.1; and IMF, World Economic Outlook database.

decade. Even with this recovery, however, growth was a full percentage point below the average of the 1960s and 1970s, with only El Salvador approaching the rate achieved during those decades. During the first five years of the current decade, there were some renewed declines in growth in the region, with the pace on average falling to 3 percent. El Salvador experienced a particularly sharp reduction in growth to slightly less than 2 percent during this period, while Honduras was the only country in the group to witness some improvement in growth relative to the 1990s. By 2005, the level of real per capita GDP was higher than that in the late 1970s in only two countries—Costa Rica and the Dominican Republic (Figure 2.3).

The slowing of GDP growth during 2000–05 raises the question of how much of the improved performance in the 1990s was transitory. In particular, the performance in the 1990s may have partly reflected temporary rebounds from the recessions of the 1980s. In addition, the durability of the region's expansion during the past decade is in question given that it was primarily fueled by rising *maquila* exports to the United States that have been subject to increasing competition from other countries, particularly in Asia. To better understand the factors that have underpinned the changing growth fortunes of the region since the 1960s, the next section looks at the historical experience from the point of view of a growth-accounting framework, before turning to structural explanations for why growth in the region has not been stronger.

Growth Accounting

To assess the proximate determinants of the shifts in growth in the region since the 1960s, a growth-accounting exercise was performed that decomposed changes in output into the contributions of the factor inputs, leaving the unexplained component of growth as a residual (Box 2.1). In line with the terminology originally adopted by Solow (1957), we refer to this residual as total factor productivity (TFP). Over the longer term, TFP captures intangible aspects of human and technological progress that allow capital and labor to increase their productivity. Longer-term productivity is also influenced by the efficiency of the allocation of resources, as an inefficient allocation can take a country inside its production frontier even if labor and capital are fully utilized.

Over the period from 1960–2005, the growth-accounting framework suggests that TFP made virtually no contribution to output growth in Central

Box 2.1. Growth Accounting Framework

We decompose output growth using the neoclassical Cobb-Douglas production function:

$$Y = AK^{\alpha}L^{1-\alpha},$$

where A corresponds to total factor productivity, K to the physical capital stock, L to labor, and α to the share of capital. Taking logs and time derivatives gives the traditional equation for the estimated growth rate of total factor productivity (TFP):

$$\frac{d\log A}{dt} = \frac{d\log Y}{dt} - \alpha\frac{d\log K}{dt} - \left(1-\alpha\right)\frac{d\log L}{dt}$$

*TFP growth = Output growth - (Capital share)*Capital growth - (Labor share)*Labor growth.*

Labor input is measured using the size of the labor force. The capital stock series were built using the perpetual-inventory method:

$$K_{t+1} = (1-\delta)K_t + I_t,$$

with an annual depreciation rate δ of 4 percent, while α was set to 33 percent, in line with typical estimates (see Loayza, Fajnzylber, and Calderon, 2005). The initial capital stock was calculated as

$$K_0 = Y_0\left[\frac{g1}{\delta + g}\right]\left(\frac{I}{Y}\right),$$

where Y_0 is output in 1960, I is gross fixed investment in 1960, δ is the assumed depreciation rate, and g is average output growth during the 1960s.

America. Real output per worker in the region rose by an average of about 1¾ percent annually, but all of the increase reflected capital deepening as opposed to productivity growth (Table 2.2). This lack of productivity growth was characteristic of Latin America as a whole, although real output per worker grew even less quickly in Latin America due to a lower contribution of capital accumulation. In East Asia, by way of comparison, growth in real output per worker averaged 3¾ percent over this period, with both capital and TFP making significant contributions. The example of China is particularly notable, with a contribution of TFP to growth of close to 3 percentage points per year.

Looking at the experience in Central America by subperiods, changes in the contribution of TFP have been the main factor explaining shifts in output growth over time (Figures 2.4 and 2.5).[4] During the 1960s, the favorable growth performance reflected a contribution of TFP of slightly over 1 percentage point per year. While output continued to grow at a relatively rapid pace in the 1970s, its underpinnings changed, as TFP growth came to a halt while the contribution of capital accumulation increased. This unbalanced combination of capital accumulation without productivity growth proved unsustainable, however, and the shocks in the late 1970s and early 1980s led to both a collapse in TFP and weak investment. The recovery in the region during the 1990s was primarily associated with a return to positive productivity growth, albeit at a somewhat slower pace than in the 1960s, combined with some increase in the capital contribution. In terms of the experience over 2001–05, the slowing in growth was associated with a renewed decline in TFP, albeit at a more moderate pace than during the 1980s.

There are interesting similarities and differences in the experiences of countries within the region using the growth-accounting framework. As is the case for the region as a whole, it is evident that variations in real per capita GDP, both across countries and over time, are closely associated with movements in TFP (Figure 2.6).[5] From the early 1960s through the late 1970s, TFP rose in almost all of the countries in this group—the exception being Nicaragua, where pro-

[4]This is characteristic of the findings of Easterly and Levine (2001) for a wider range of countries. See also Faal (2005) for evidence on Mexico, and Cabrera Melgar, Fuentes, and Morales (2005) for El Salvador.

[5]The results of the growth accounting exercise for each individual country are shown in Appendix Figure 2A.1.

Table 2.2. Growth Accounting Across Regions, 1960–2003

		Contributions of:	
	Growth in Output per Worker	Capital	TFP
Central America (1960–2005)	1.8	1.8	0.0
Latin America	1.0	0.9	0.1
East Asia (excluding China)	3.8	2.8	1.0
China	5.0	2.2	2.7

Sources: IMF staff calculations; and Singh and Cerisola (2006, Table 1).
Note: TFP = total factor productivity.

Figure 2.4. Central America: Growth Accounting
(Contribution in percentage points)

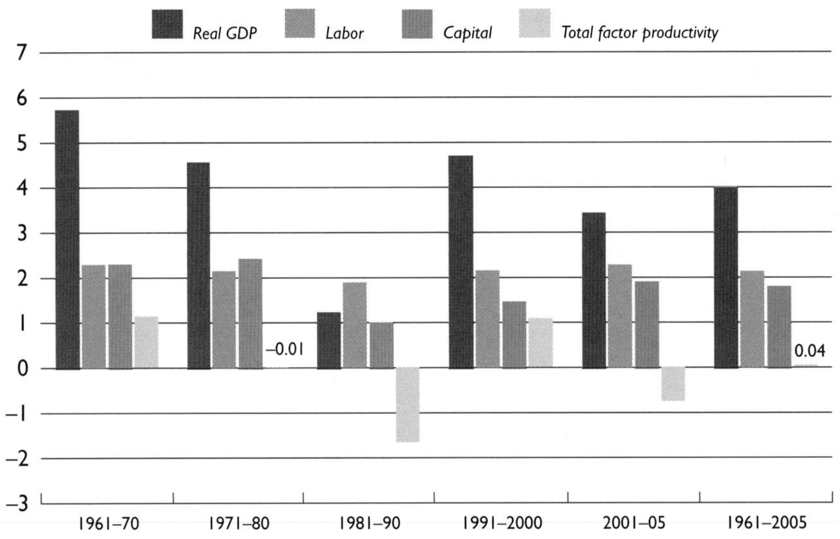

Source: IMF staff estimates using World Bank, *World Development Indicators* (2005) and IMF, *World Economic Outlook* (2005).

ductivity stagnated from the mid-1960s on. There was also a notable flattening of productivity growth in El Salvador in the 1970s. It is interesting that these two countries experienced the sharpest drops in output when conditions deteriorated at the end of the 1970s, suggesting that weak "fundamentals," as reflected in the absence of sustained productivity growth, left them particularly exposed to unfavorable shocks.

The early 1980s witnessed sharp declines in TFP and output in most of the other countries in the region, but they were generally less severe than those in Nicaragua and El Salvador. In Honduras, Guatemala, and Costa Rica, the recessions of the early 1980s were fairly short-lived, and renewed growth in productivity and output was evident by the middle of the decade (albeit at a subdued pace in Honduras). The only country to avoid a significant shock to output in the early 1980s was the Dominican Republic, although even its performance was relatively lackluster, as the downward trend in TFP that began in the mid-1970s continued through the 1980s.

The 1990s were characterized by a return to rising productivity levels in most of the region. Together with the Dominican Republic, the countries that recovered most quickly from the crises of the early 1980s—Costa Rica and Guatemala—also experienced the steadiest productivity growth during the 1990s. El Salvador and Nicaragua also witnessed some recovery in productivity in the 1990s, but the growth phases were shorter

Figure 2.5. Central America: Per Capita GDP and Total Factor Productivity
(Logarithms)

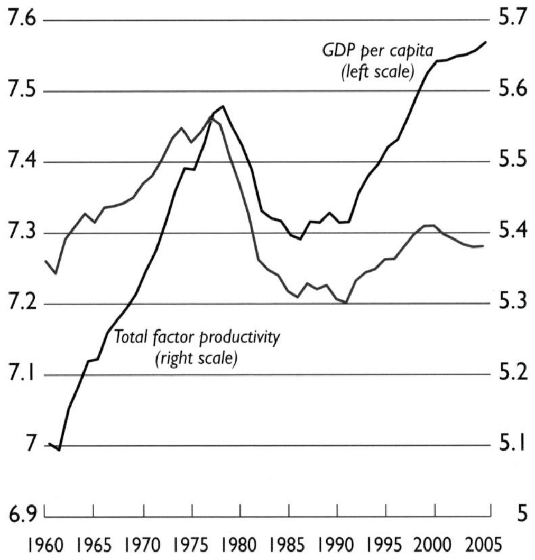

Source: IMF staff estimates using World Bank, *World Development Indicators* (2005) and IMF, *World Economic Outlook* (2005).

Figure 2.6. Real Per Capita GDP and Total Factor Productivity by Country
(In logarithms)

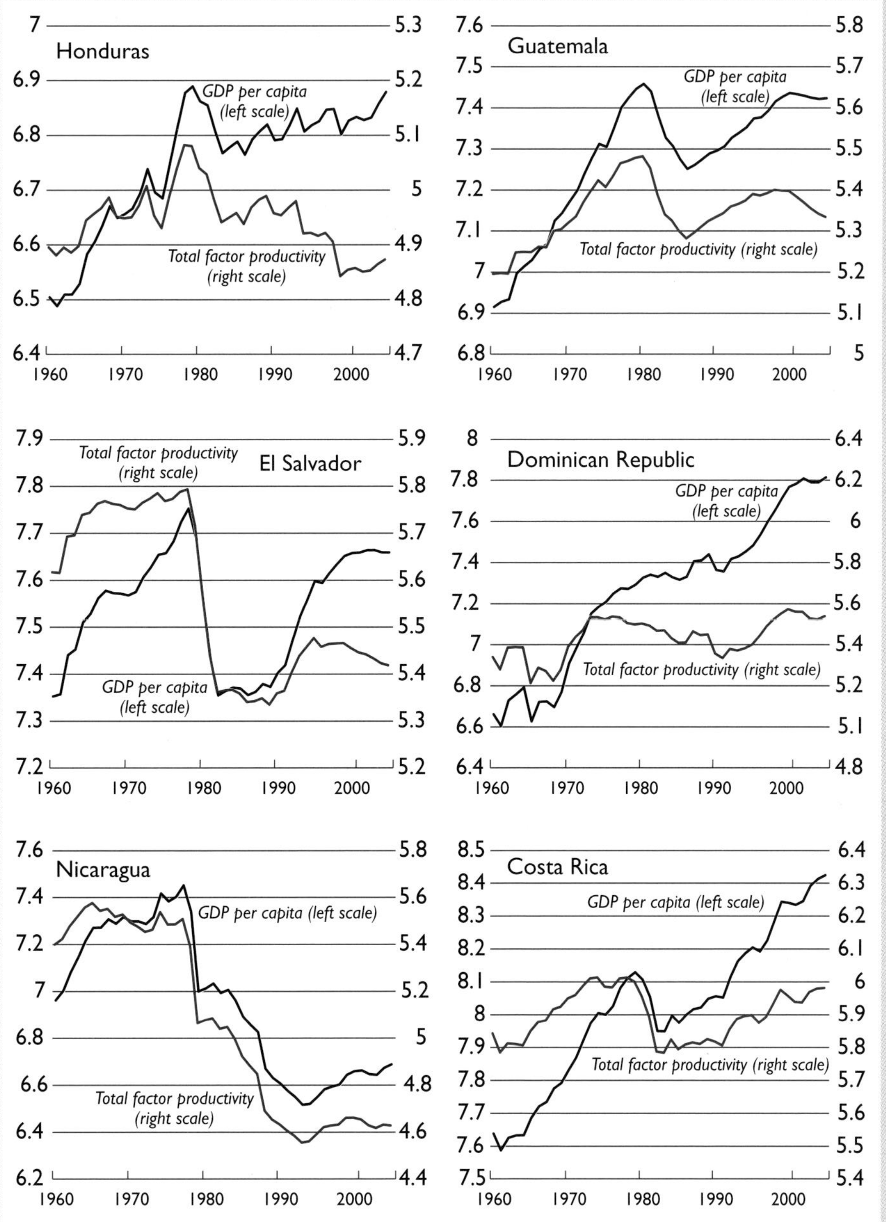

Sources: World Bank, *World Development Indicators* (2005); and IMF, *World Economic Outlook* (2005).

lived. Honduras was a notable exception to the picture of improvement in the 1990s, as productivity fell steadily throughout the decade.[6]

The more recent experience during 2000–05 indicates that the slowing in output growth in the region has

[6]Recent revisions of the national accounts in Costa Rica and Nicaragua introduced breaks in 1991 and 1994, respectively, with improvement in the coverage focused principally on the services and informal sectors. Thus, the increases in the contribution of total factor productivity to growth for Costa Rica in 1992 and Nicaragua in 1995 at least partly reflect a break in the coverage of the GDP series.

been associated with renewed declines in productivity in several of the countries that experienced recoveries in the 1990s. This group includes Guatemala, El Salvador, the Dominican Republic, and Nicaragua. Productivity in Honduras appeared to have bottomed out in this period after the declines of the 1990s, but without signs of a meaningful recovery. This leaves Costa Rica as the only country in the group that has experienced steadily rising productivity levels since the shocks of the early 1980s. The weak productivity performance in most of these countries over the past five years underscores concerns about medium-term prospects in the absence of productivity-enhancing reforms. To better understand the underlying factors that may be holding back growth in the region, the next section reviews the evidence on structural impediments to growth, followed by an empirical analysis of the role of institutions in the context of Central America.

Figure 2.7. Central America: Real Per Capita GDP
(Logarithm)

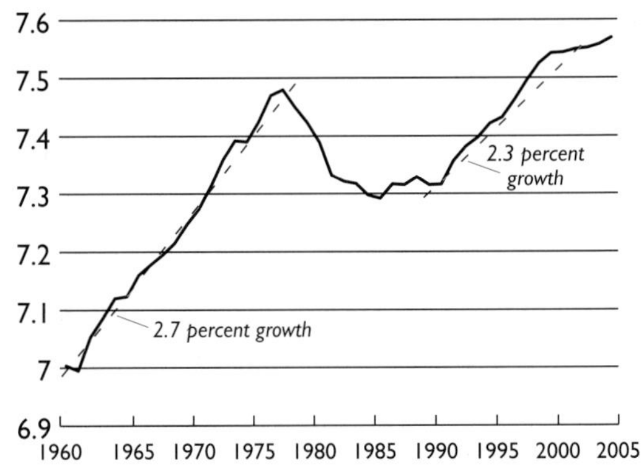

Sources: World Bank, *World Development Indicators* (2005); and IMF, *World Economic Outlook* (2005).

Bottlenecks to Productivity Growth

There is, of course, an extensive literature on the sources of growth in developing countries, and the factors that hold back progress in some countries, while encouraging it in others. Zettelmeyer (2006) surveys the evidence for Latin America, which is particularly relevant given that the experience in Central America has been similar to that in the rest of the region, at least in terms of GDP and productivity growth. He observes that the weak performance in Latin America has been associated with macroeconomic volatility, relatively high income inequality, and a low degree of external openness compared with other regions.[7]

In terms of macroeconomic volatility, the historical record for Central America appears to be typical of the rest of Latin America. The evidence presented in Sahay and Goyal (2006) indicates that the role of factors such as external growth, terms-of-trade shocks, and policy reversals has been similar in Central American countries to elsewhere, and that volatility in these factors has been associated with low growth throughout Latin America. The most dramatic example, of course, is the debt crisis of the early 1980s. As shown in Figure 2.7, real GDP per capita for the region as a whole declined by close to 20 percent from the late 1970s to the mid-1980s, and the growth path appears to have subsequently shifted down permanently. This shift is perhaps not surprising in light of the historical evidence on the effects of major shocks on long-term growth, indicating that some of the output loss tends to be permanent.[8] But it is more notable that, after a period of stagnation, the subsequent slope of the growth path was flatter than prior to the "lost decade," even as one might have expected partial recovery from the output losses of the 1980s, and also as the region regained macroeconomic stability (Sahay and Goyal, 2006).

The evidence, then, suggests that factors beyond the historical record of macroeconomic volatility have been holding back growth in the region, at least since the beginning of the 1990s. Of the other two characteristics noted by Zettelmeyer (2006), income inequality in Central America is typical of that in Latin America as a whole (Sahay and Goyal, 2006), and thus would be expected to play a similar role. In contrast, regarding the third factor—trade openness—Central America has typically had higher trade shares than the rest of Latin America, and has also had more trade with the United States—although both gaps have closed somewhat in recent years (Figures 2.8 and 2.9).[9] On this basis, one would expect trade to have positively affected growth in Central America in light of the extensive cross-country evidence linking trade and growth, and also the finding of Arora and Vamvakidis (2005) that income levels benefit positively from trading with faster-growing, more developed countries.

Part of the reason why trade has not provided a greater boost to growth in Central America may relate to the

[7]See also Easterly, Loayza, and Montiel (1997) and Solimano and Soto (2005) for discussions of the growth performance of Latin America.

[8]Cerra and Saxena (2005) use panel data to analyze how fast economies recover after a shock, finding that output losses during recessions are followed by partial but not full recovery phases, such that some of the output loss is permanent.

[9]Since the Caribbean Basin Initiative in 1983, Central American countries have benefited from trade preferences in U.S. markets that have allowed duty-free access for a wide range of products.

Figure 2.8. Trade Openness: Total Exports Plus Imports
(In percent of GDP)

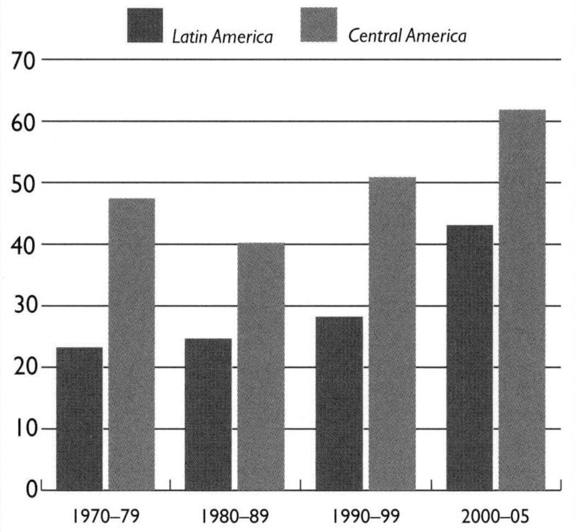

Sources: IMF, *Direction of Trade* database; and *World Economic Outlook* (2005).

Figure 2.9. Exports to the United States
(In percent of GDP)

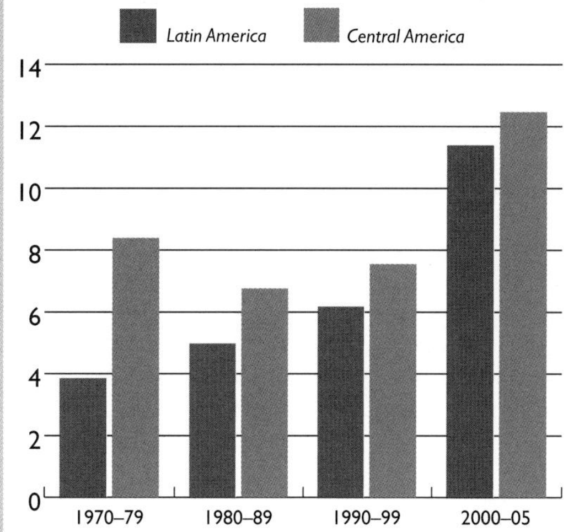

Sources: IMF, *Direction of Trade* database; and *World Economic Outlook* (2005).

structure of trade in the region. Lederman and Maloney (2003) focus on factors specific to the composition of trade in Central America, such as resource abundance, export concentration, and the structure of intra-industry trade. They find that export concentration has been a significant factor hampering growth in the region—a critical conclusion, since more than 50 percent of the region's exports are comprised of *maquilas*, which are exposed to direct competition from China and Mexico. Yet, studies of this nature do not explain why the structure of trade has evolved in a particular direction, and in particular why the region has not proven to be more dynamic in adjusting to changing trade opportunities, and in diversifying its export industries toward higher value-added activities.

The lack of dynamic adaptation in Central America's trade raises the issue of the role that market flexibility and entrepreneurship play in translating the advantages of trade opportunities into economic growth. In this regard, Dollar and Kraay (2002) analyze the effects of both institutions and trade on growth, finding a joint role for trade and institutions in the long run. A possible interpretation is that sound institutions create the appropriate incentives for reallocating resources productively in the face of new trading opportunities. In the same vein, Bolaky and Freund (2004) examine the effects of trade openness on growth, arguing that trade does not stimulate growth in economies with excessive regulation because bureaucratic red tape prevents resources from moving into more productive sectors.[10] Consequently, increases in trade are more likely to occur in the wrong sectors, amplifying existing distortions. Similarly, Chang, Kaltani, and Loayza (2005) find strong complementarities between institutional reforms and trade liberalization in enhancing growth.

The literature, then, suggests an important link between the quality of the institutional framework and the benefits of trade openness. This is a key point for Central America, where business regulation is notably burdensome (Table 2.3), and institutional quality tends to be weak. The implications of this finding are particularly important as the region enters a new period of trade liberalization with the entry into effect of the CAFTA-DR with the United States and prospective trade negotiations with the European Union. Benefiting from the opportunities associated with this agreement can provide a fundamental stimulus to a more satisfactory growth performance in the region in the appropriate institutional environment.[11]

[10]Djankov, McLiesh, and Ramalho (2005) also analyze how regulations affect growth in a cross-country context, finding that improving its index of business regulations from the worst to the best quartile can result in a 2½ percentage point increase in a country's average annual growth. Loayza, Fajnzylber, and Calderon (2005) also find a strong relationship between regulations and growth.

[11]See World Bank (2005a) for a discussion of the opportunities presented by CAFTA-DR.

Table 2.3. Ranking of Ease of Doing Business

Country	Rank
Costa Rica	105
Dominican Republic	117
El Salvador	71
Guatemala	118
Honduras	111
Nicaragua	67
Panama	81
United States	3
Canada	4
Chile	28
Mexico	43

Source: World Bank (2005b).

Empirical Analysis

This section analyzes the empirical evidence on the effects of institutions, as well as other factors, on growth in Central American countries. The above discussion points to the lack of improvements in productivity as the proximate factor restraining growth in the region, notwithstanding its relative openness to trade. The absence of comparable international data on factors that might directly affect productivity, such as research and development and patent activity, precludes an analysis at the microeconomic level. In any case, these activities are likely to be endogenous to the institutional environment in a given country, defined to include the legal system, business regulations, etc. It seems more useful, then, both in terms of understanding deeper determinants of the factors driving productivity and the policy actions that could affect these factors, to focus on the role of such institutions in promoting growth. The empirical analysis examines the role of institutions as proxied by two widely used measures, and takes both a more recent cross-country perspective, as well as a longer-term dynamic perspective. Using a broad cross-country dataset[12] and controlling for the key determinants identified in the extensive growth literature, we estimate a growth model whose coefficients allow us to verify that institutions matter for growth and to quantify the effect of improving institutions in Central America to levels attained by strong performers in Latin America, such as Chile.

The analysis begins with an examination of the effect of institutions on growth during the period beginning in the mid-1990s. Focusing on this more recent period has the advantage of abstracting from the effects on Central America the events of the 1980s and their immediate aftermath. Developments since the mid-1990s may be more reflective of the underlying productivity performance of these countries and its implications for future growth. The dependent variable is defined as average growth in real per capita GDP during 1995–2003. As a measure of the quality of institutions, we use the governance indicators of Kaufmann, Kraay, and Mastruzzi (2003). Two indexes are built with these indicators: Index 1 is the average of all the dimensions[13] of their indicators, while Index 2 is the average of the two components most directly associated with business activity—i.e., regulatory burden and rule of law. We compare the explanatory power of these two indexes to determine how broadly the institutional environment should be defined for the purpose of assessing its impact on growth. We also introduce the political risk rating of the widely used International Country Risk Guide (ICRG) rating system as an additional robustness check.[14] A potential criticism of the use of institutional indicators is that they are endogenous to other factors that may affect growth, biasing their estimated impact using ordinary least squares. To control for potential endogeneity, instrumental variables regressions were also performed, using legal origin and the English-speaking percentage of the population from the Dollar and Kraay (2002) dataset as instruments.[15]

Table 2.4 shows the results for the cross-section regressions using alternative definitions of the institutions index as the explanatory variable. The results are shown using ordinary least squares (OLS), as well as two-stage least squares (TSLS) using the instruments described above for the institutions variable. The signs of the parameter estimates are as expected in all of the regressions, although those on trade (trading partner growth and openness) and inflation are statistically insignificant. The coefficients on all of the institutions' variables are significant, and of a similar magnitude in the regressions using OLS (Models 1 and 2) and TSLS (Models 3 and 4), suggesting that endogeneity is not a major problem. There is no clear "winner" between the broad and narrow definition of institutions—the coeffi-

[12]The country list is provided in Appendix 2.1.

[13]The dimensions consist of government effectiveness, control of graft or corruption, political instability and violence, regulatory burden, voice and accountability, and the rule of law.

[14]The overall political risk rating reflects risk ratings of the following components: government stability, socioeconomic conditions, investment profile, internal conflict, external conflict, corruption, military in politics, religion in politics, law and order, ethnic tensions, democratic accountability, and bureaucratic quality.

[15]Acemoglu, Johnson, and Robinson (2001) explore the role of colonial history in determining institutions. They find that high mortality rates led European settlers to establish "extractive states." In other regions, where mortality rates were lower, they were more likely to establish European-style institutions where the rule of law prevailed and investment was encouraged. Hence, early Latin American colonies were endowed with institutions and regulations that favored exploitation, empowering a narrow elite and restricting other economic activity.

Table 2.4. Cross-Country Growth Regressions
(t-statistics in parentheses)

	(1) OLS	(2) OLS	(3) 2SLS	(4) 2SLS	(5) OLS	(6) OLS	(7) OLS	(8) OLS
Log of initial GDP per capita (1995)	−1.26	−1.35	−1.55	−1.38	−1.07	−1.42	−1.43	−1.12
	(−5.58)	(−6.14)	(−3.09)	(−2.69)	(−4.59)	(−6.31)	(−5.30)	(−4.28)
Institutions KKM Index 1	1.91	...	2.46	...	1.79	1.49		
	−5.68	...	−2.53	...	−5.45	−4.05		
Institutions KKM Index 2	...	2.09	...	2.07				
	...	−6.61	...	−1.83				
Institutions ICRG Index							0.19	0.17
							−5.21	−4.74
Inflation	−0.02	−0.03	−0.02	−0.03	−0.02	−0.01	0.00	0.01
	(−1.10)	(−1.53)	(−0.96)	(−1.65)	(−1.29)	(−1.31)	−0.23	−0.36
Education	0.04	0.04	0.04	0.04	0.02	0.05	0.04	0.02
	−3.60	−3.49	−3.28	−3.05	−1.80	−5.83	−2.90	−1.31
Government consumption	−0.10	−0.08	−0.10	−0.09	−0.06	−0.06	−0.05	−0.01
	(−3.08)	(−2.88)	(−2.67)	(−2.76)	−1.67	(−1.94)	(−1.37)	(−0.20)
Growth in trading partners	0.22	0.04	0.34	0.05	−0.08		0.37	0.05
	−0.44	−0.07	−0.72	−0.09	(−0.17)		−0.73	−0.10
Openness						0.00		
						(−0.30)		
Investment					0.13	0.12		0.13
					−4.27	−3.94		−3.56
Constant	9.78	10.52	11.7	10.83	6.61	8.03	−2.85	−4.87
	−5.42	−6.04	−3.03	−2.63	−3.82	−4.81	(−1.46)	(−2.58)
Number of observations	91	91	84	84	84	119	84	80
R-squared	0.40	0.41	0.40	0.42	0.51	0.43	0.41	0.50

Note: KKM = Kaufmann, Kraay, and Mastruzzi (2003); ICRG = International Country Risk Guide; OLS = ordinary least squares; 2SLS = two stage least squares.

cient on the latter is somewhat larger and more significant in the OLS regressions, while the reverse is true in the TSLS regressions.[16] We interpret this as showing that both aspects of institutions—i.e., those directly affecting the business environment and those dealing with broader governance considerations—can affect the environment for growth, although the business environment institutions could be somewhat endogenous to other factors affecting growth. Furthermore, separating the "pure" effect of institutions from the effect that they may have on growth through their effect on investment (Models 5, 6, and 8 in Table 2.4) shows that the coefficient on institutions remains highly significant, and its magnitude does not decline substantively.

The next set of robustness checks allow for exploring the time variation that is left unexplored through averaging the data. A panel of three five-year non-overlapping averages of the dependent and explanatory variables was constructed.[17] The estimation of a fixed-effects panel regression[18] shows that the coefficient on the quality of institutions as measured by the ICRG political index is robust in magnitude, and continues to be significant (Models 9 and 10 in Table 2.5).[19] Similarly unchanged is the coefficient on investment. The coefficient on the openness variable is significant, and its effect is in line with that estimated in other papers such as Arora and Vamvakidis (2005). The coefficient on inflation[20] is also significant and negative in this specification.

Overall, the results from the empirical analysis suggest an important link between the quality of the institutional framework and growth. Institutional quality,

[16]Nesting the hypothesis of which is more important by including both definitions in the same regression yields a similar conclusion—neither is highly significant due to multi-collinearity, but the narrow definition is more significant using OLS and the broad definition using TSLS.

[17]In order to construct the panel, the original estimation period of 1995–2003 was extended to 1990–2004.

[18]The choice of a fixed-effects versus a random-effects specification is justified by a Hausman test.

[19]The governance indicators employed in the cross-section regressions above have only been available since the mid-1990s and thus could not be used in this specification.

[20]Measured as the log of (1 + inflation).

Table 2.5. Fixed-Effects (FE) Panel Regressions
(t-statistics in parentheses)

	(9) FE	(10) FE
Log of initial GDP per capita (1995)	–5.92	–7.40
	(–4.91)	(–6.02)
Institutions ICRG Index	0.18	0.13
	–5.41	–3.46
Inflation	–1.34	–1.09
	(–2.97)	(–2.47)
Education	0.00	–0.16
	–0.11	–0.33
Government consumption	–0.10	–0.16
	(–3.08)	(–2.28)
Openness	0.03	0.02
	–3.07	–2.42
Investment	0.11	0.15
	–1.90	–2.64
Time dummies		
1990–94		–1.53
		(–3.12)
1995–99		–1.11
		(–3.63)

Note: ICRG = International Country Risk Guide.

both broadly and more narrowly defined, is found to have a significant and robust impact on growth, above and beyond its effect through investment. Some direct tests of the hypothesis that benefits of trade openness to growth are linked to the quality of the institutional framework provide tentative support—the coefficient on an interaction term of institutional quality and openness is positive and significant, suggesting that greater benefits to trade accrue to countries with better institutions, but the empirical evidence is not robust.[21]

How do institutions in Central America fare? Figure 2.10 and Table 2.6 show the scores for the Central American countries on the indices of institutional quality, along with those for Chile, which has the highest scores in the Latin American region, and the average score for the overall sample of countries. Only Costa Rica has institutional scores above the sample mean, but they still fall notably short of Chile's scores. El Salvador and the Dominican Republic are in the middle of the rankings for Central America, with Guatemala, Honduras, and Nicaragua lagging.

The question, then, is how much improvements in institutional quality could contribute to higher growth rates in the region? Table 2.7 addresses this issue by hypothetically assuming that the institutional scores of the countries in Central America were raised to Chile's level, and then calculating the resulting change in the fitted value for growth using the parameter estimates

[21]The interaction term is significant and positive in the cross-sectional regressions using both the ICRG and the Kaufmann, Kraay, and Mastruzzi indices, but is not significant in the fixed-effects panel regression.

Figure 2.10. Comparison of Institutional Ratings

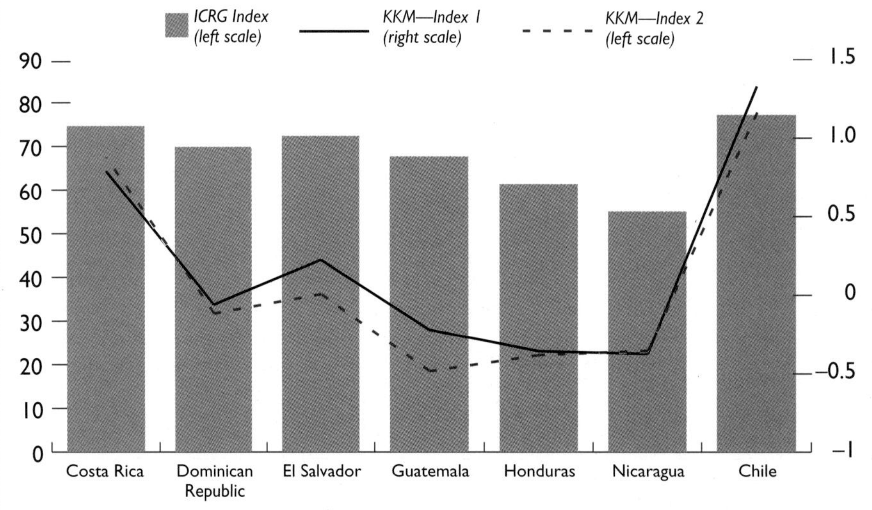

Note: ICRG = International Country Risk Guide; KKM = Kaufman, Kraay, and Mastruzzi (2003).

Table 2.6. Scores of Institutional Quality
(Average of dimensions)

Country	Index 1—"Broad"	Index 2—"Narrow"
Average of 91 countries	0.28	0.34
Chile	1.16	1.33
Costa Rica	0.88	0.80
Dominican Republic	–0.12	–0.05
El Salvador	0.01	0.23
Guatemala	–0.48	–0.21
Honduras	–0.38	–0.35
Nicaragua	–0.35	–0.37

Source: Kaufmann, Kraay, and Mastruzzi (2003).

Table 2.7. Estimated Impact on Growth of Improving Institutions
(Percentage points, change in predicted value)

Country	Model 1	Model 2	Model 5	Model 7	Model 8
Costa Rica	0.6	1.1	0.5	0.5	0.4
Dominican Republic	2.5	2.9	2.3	1.4	1.2
El Salvador	2.3	2.3	2.1	0.9	0.8
Guatemala	3.1	3.2	3.0	1.8	1.6
Honduras	3.0	3.5	2.8	3.0	2.6
Nicaragua	2.9	3.5	2.7	4.2	3.7

Source: IMF staff calculations.

from the regression framework.[22] The effects would be significant, pointing to improvements in growth ranging from around 0.5 percentage points per year in Costa Rica to 3 percentage points or more in the countries with the weakest institutional scores.[23] Of course, transformations in institutions of this magnitude would take a considerable amount of time to realize. But the results indicate that institutional reforms could play a major role in putting Central American countries on more satisfactory growth paths.[24]

Conclusions

While the recovery in growth in Central America in the 1990s provided a welcome contrast to the "lost decade" of the 1980s, the record was still not fully satisfactory, and the more recent performance raises concerns about long-run prospects. The region has failed to regain the high productivity and growth rates observed in some previous periods, such as the 1960s. Growth has also been insufficient to decisively reduce poverty and narrow the income gap with more developed countries. In most countries in Central America, the level of productivity is below that observed in the late 1970s. In addition, the slowing of output growth and weak productivity during the 2000–05 period raises questions about the prospects for the region to enter a period of sustained rapid growth, even with the

[22]The fit of the regression models for the Central American countries is shown in Table 2A.1.

[23]Given the robustness of the coefficient on institutional quality, the estimated impact of raising the quality of institutions is shown in Table 2.7 only for a representative subset of all the estimated specifications. These cover the use of three different institutional measures (the narrow and broad definitions of the Kaufmann, Kraay, and Mastruzzi index and the International Country Risk Guide political risk index), and the inclusion of investment levels as a control variable.

[24]A nice overview of the nature of institutional change, desirable features of market economies, and the role for policies in fostering institutional development can be found in a *World Economic Outlook* study of growth and institutions (IMF, 2003).

Figure 2A.1. Growth Accounting, by Country
(Contribution in percentage points)

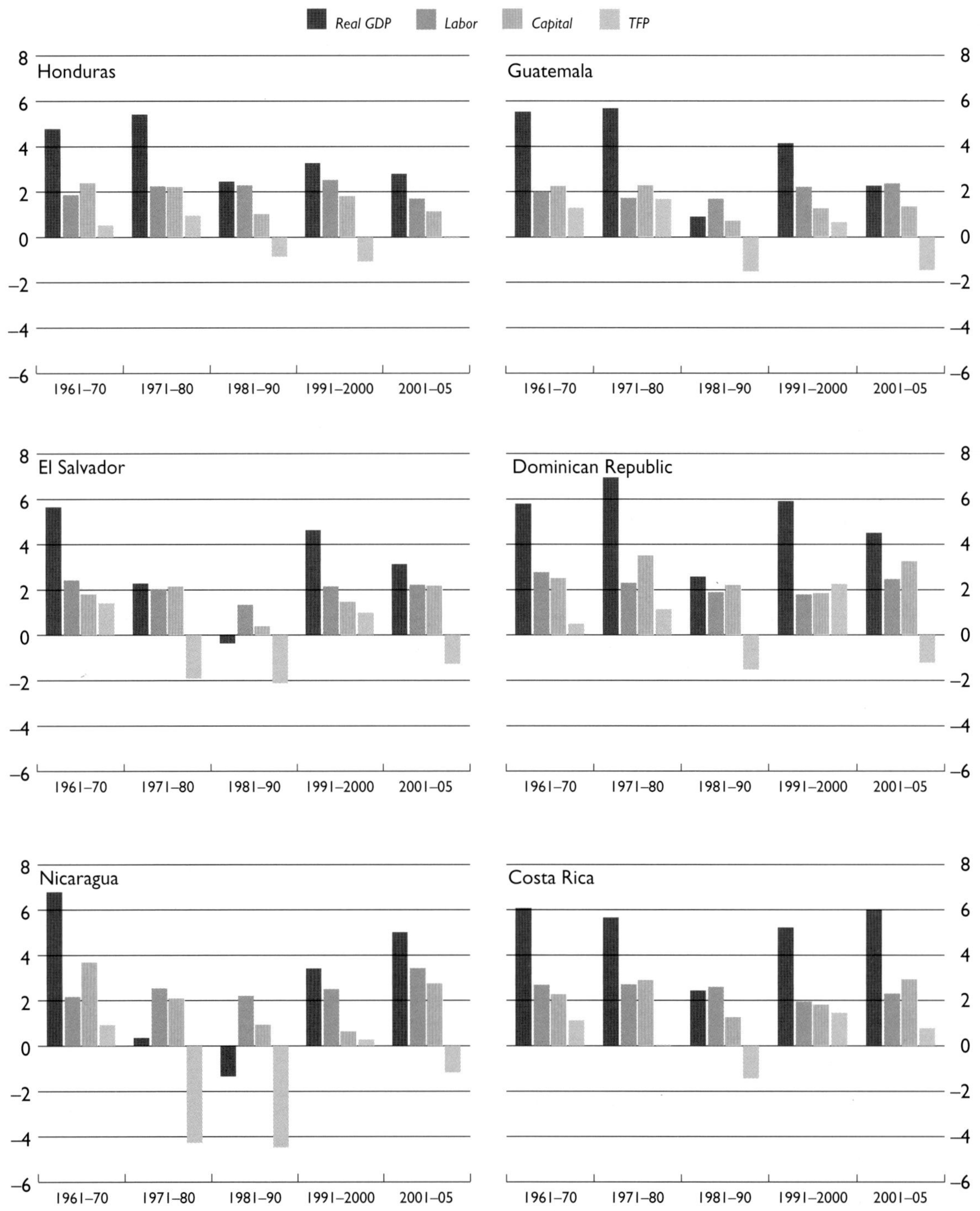

Source: IMF staff estimates using World Bank, *World Development Indicators*, and IMF, *World Economic Outlook*.
Note: TFP = total factor productivity.

Table 2A.1. Actual and Predicted Growth, Cross-Sectional Regressions, 1995–2003

Country	Actual Growth	Model 1	Model 2	Model 5	Model 6	Model 7	Model 8
Costa Rica	2.3	1.8	1.5	1.7	1.4	1.6	1.4
Dominican Republic	3.8	1.3	1.2	0.9	1.0	1.9	1.4
El Salvador	1.2	1.3	1.7	0.9	1.0	2.0	1.6
Guatemala	0.8	0.3	0.6	0.2	0.0	1.0	0.9
Honduras	0.3	0.7	0.6	1.6	1.7	0.6	1.5
Nicaragua	1.4	1.1	1.0	2.2	2.4	-0.3	1.0
Average	**1.6**	**1.1**	**1.1**	**1.2**	**1.3**	**1.1**	**1.3**

opportunities that arise given the implementation of CAFTA-DR.

Both the growth literature and the empirical evidence for Central America suggest that the quality of institutions, including those related to business activity and governance more generally, significantly affect growth performance. This is an area in which there is scope for considerable improvement in most Central American countries—indeed, weaknesses in institutions may explain why these countries have failed to fully capitalize on the trading opportunities offered by proximity to developed markets and a relatively high degree of trade openness. The evidence suggests that the beneficial effects of trade are only likely to be realized in an environment where sound institutions promote an efficient allocation of resources and a dynamic business environment. The estimated impact of improving institutions on growth is large, and suggests that changes in this area could play an important role in putting Central America on a higher sustained growth path.

Appendix 2.1. Countries Included in the Sample

Specifications with 91 countries: Argentina, Australia, Austria, Bangladesh, Barbados, Belgium, Benin, Bolivia, Brazil, Burkina Faso, Cameroon, Canada, Central African Republic, Chad, Chile, China, Colombia, Republic of Congo, Costa Rica, Cyprus, Denmark, Dominican Republic, Ecuador, Egypt, El Salvador, Fiji, Finland, France, Gambia, Germany, Ghana, Greece, Guatemala, Guyana, Honduras, Hong Kong SAR, Hungary, Iceland, India, Indonesia, Ireland, Israel, Italy, Jamaica, Japan, Jordan, Kenya, Korea, Madagascar, Malawi, Malaysia, Mali, Mauritania, Mexico, Morocco, Mozambique, Nepal, the Netherlands, New Zealand, Nicaragua, Niger, Nigeria, Norway, Pakistan, Panama, Papua New Guinea, Paraguay, Peru, the Philippines, Poland, Portugal, Saudi Arabia, Senegal, Sierra Leone, Singapore, South Africa, Spain, Sri Lanka, Sweden, Switzerland, Syria, Togo, Tunisia, Turkey, Uganda, United Kingdom, United States, Uruguay, Venezuela, Zambia, Zimbabwe.

Appendix 2.2. Fit of the Regression Model for the Central American Countries

Table 2.A.1 compares the actual growth rates of the Central American countries with the predicted values obtained from the regression models. In general, the models tend to underpredict growth in the Central American countries, with the exception of Honduras, for which the models consistently overpredict growth, and El Salvador, for which all specifications predict growth relatively well. In addition, the predicted values from the specifications that include investment ratios (Models 5, 6, and 8) substantially overestimate the growth rates in Honduras and Nicaragua, where the predicted growth rates are about 1 percentage point higher than the average actual growth rate. Honduras and Nicaragua both have average investment levels above the sample median of 21 percent of GDP (at 25 and 27 percent, respectively).

References

Acemoglu, Daron, Simon Johnson, and James Robinson, 2001, "The Colonial Origins of Comparative Development: An Empirical Investigation," *American Economic Review*, Vol. 91, No. 5 (December), pp. 1369–401.

Arora, Vivek, and Athanasios Vamvakidis, 2005, "How Much Do Trading Partners Matter for Economic Growth?" *Staff Papers*, International Monetary Fund, Vol. 52, No. 1.

Berg, Andy, Carlos Leite, Jonathan Ostry, and Jeromin Zettlemeyer, 2006, "What Makes Growth Sustained?" (unpublished; Washington: International Monetary Fund).

Bolaky, Bineswaree and Caroline Freund, 2004, "Trade, Regulations and Growth," World Bank Policy Research Working Paper No 3255 (Washington: World Bank).

Cabrera Melgar, Oscar Ovidio, Julieta Fuentes, and Hada Desiree de Morales, 2005, "Hechos estilizados en el crecimiento económico de El Salvador 1978–2004: Una propuesta de acciones de política económica en el corto y mediano plazo," Departamento de Investigacion Economica y Financiera, Banco Central de Reserva de El Salvador.

Cerra, Valerie, and Chaman Saxena, 2005, "Growth Dynamics: The Myth of Economic Recovery," IMF Working Paper 05/147 (Washington: International Monetary Fund).

Chang, Roberto, Linda Kaltani, and Norman Loayza, 2005, "Openness Can Be Good for Growth: The Role of Policy Complementarities," World Bank Policy Research Working Paper No. 3763 (Washington: World Bank).

Djankov, Simeon, Caralee McLiesh, and Rita Ramalho, 2005, "Regulation and Growth," Social Science Research Network Electronic Papers. Available via the Internet: http://ssrn.com/abstract=893321.

Dollar, David, and Aart Kraay, 2002, *Institutions, Trade and Growth* (Washington: World Bank).

Easterly, William, and Ross Levine, 2001, "It's Not Factor Accumulation: Stylized Facts and Growth Models," Social Science Research Network Electronic Papers. Available via the Internet: http://ssrn.com/abstract=269108.

Easterly, William, Norman Loayza, and Peter Montiel, 1997, "Has Latin America's Post-Reform Growth Been Disappointing?" *Journal of International Economics,* Vol. 43 (November): 287–311.

Faal, Ebrima, 2005, "GDP Growth, Potential Output, and Output Gaps in Mexico," IMF Working Paper 05/93 (Washington: International Monetary Fund).

International Monetary Fund (IMF), 2003, *World Economic Outlook*, World Economic and Financial Surveys (Washington, April).

Kaufmann, Daniel, Aart Kraay, and Massimo Mastruzzi, 2003, "Governance Matters III: Governance Indicators for 1996–2002" (Washington: World Bank).

Lederman, Daniel, and William Maloney, 2003, "Trade Structure and Growth," World Bank Policy Research Working Paper No. 3025 (Washington: World Bank).

Loayza, Norman, Pablo Fajnzylber, and Cesar Calderon, 2005, *Economic Growth in Latin America and the Caribbean. Stylized Facts, Explanations, and Forecasts* (Washington: World Bank).

Sahay, Ratna, and Rishi Goyal, 2006, "Volatility and Growth in Latin America: An Episodic Approach" (unpublished; Washington: International Monetary Fund).

Singh, Anoop, and Martin Cerisola, 2006, "Sustaining Latin America's Resurgence: Some Perspectives from the Historical Experience," paper prepared for the IMF-World Bank Annual Meetings Seminar (September).

Solimano, Andrés, and Raimundo Soto, 2005, "Economic Growth in Latin America in the Late 20th Century: Evidence and Interpretation," ECLAC Economic Development Division Macroeconomía del desarrollo series No. 33 (Santiago, Chile: Economic Commission on Latin America and the Caribbean).

Solow, Robert M., 1957, "Technical Change and the Aggregate Production Function," *Review of Economics and Statistics*, Vol. 39, pp. 312–20.

World Bank, 2005a, "DR-CAFTA: Challenges and Opportunities for Central America," Central America Department and Office of the Chief Economist, Latin America and Caribbean Region. Available via the Internet: http://lnweb18.worldbank.org/LAC/LAC.nsf/ECADocByUnid/ 3D4B4F71AE8214FE8525702D0071 0E58?Opendocument.

———, 2005b, Doing Business in 2005: Removing Obstacles to Growth (Washington: World Bank, International Finance Corporation, and Oxford University Press).

Zettelmeyer, Jeromin, 2006, "Growth and Reforms in Latin America: A Survey of Facts and Arguments," IMF Working Paper 06/210 (Washington: International Monetary Fund).

III Pension Reform

Kevin Fletcher and Alfred Schipke[1]

Public pension systems are coming under increasing financial pressure around the world. As populations age, the number of pensioners is rising relative to the number of workers in many countries, resulting in increasing pension system deficits as spending on benefits rises relative to contribution revenue.

Although Central America has more favorable demographics than many countries with low or even declining birth rates, its population will still age substantially in the coming decades. This, together with generous benefits relative to contributions and low retirement ages, makes many of Central America's public pension systems unsustainable over the long run under their current parameters. If not addressed, these rising pension system deficits will crowd out private sector activity and may threaten macroeconomic stability.

Reforming public pension systems has been politically challenging both in Central America and the rest of the world. Pension reforms often face substantial political opposition, causing either delays in reforms—and therefore higher adjustment costs in the future—or reforms that are insufficient to put the system on a sound footing. Mobilizing broad political support for reforms can therefore be as important as the design of the reforms themselves.

Nonetheless, some countries in Central America have implemented significant reforms in recent years, ranging from the establishment of funded, defined-contribution systems in El Salvador and the Dominican Republic to the creation of multipillar systems in Costa Rica and Panama.

However, the region's pension systems still face substantial challenges. Many of the region's defined-benefit systems have large unfunded liabilities over the long run, while countries that switched to funded, defined-contribution systems face high transition costs and potentially large implicit liabilities due to minimum pension guarantees. Coverage also remains low, with less than 25 percent of the labor force contributing to the main pension system on a regular basis in most countries.

This chapter analyzes Central America's pension systems, taking stock of recent changes and discussing options for future reform. To provide background for this analysis, the chapter first reviews the structure of the systems and assesses their sustainability. Given that almost all governments are currently considering pension reforms, the chapter also provides an overview of recent reform efforts. The chapter then highlights a number of options and directions for future reform, drawing on international experience with pension systems.

Basic Structures of Public Pension Systems

Central America has an increasingly wide range of public old age pension systems. Most of the region's systems were started between the 1940s and 1970s as traditional pay-as-you-go, defined-benefit systems. In Guatemala, Honduras, and Nicaragua, the public pension systems still retain this basic structure. In contrast, El Salvador and the Dominican Republic both recently closed their traditional defined-benefit systems to new entrants, replacing them with defined-contribution systems of privately-invested individual accounts. In the middle of the spectrum are Costa Rica and Panama, both of which recently added second pillar defined-contribution systems while keeping their traditional defined-benefit systems as the first pillar of their pension systems. The main features of these various systems are summarized in Table 3.1 and described further below.

Defined-Benefit Systems

The traditional defined-benefit systems in Central America are run by social security agencies that administer an array of benefits. Typically, these social security systems are divided into a long-term branch that provides old age, disability, and survivor pensions and a short-term branch that provides sickness, maternity, and work injury benefits. Old age pensions are the primary focus of this chapter, since they are the largest single social security expenditure item and the main source of long-run unfunded liabilities.

[1]The authors would like to express their appreciation to Cleary Haines for her excellent research support.

Table 3.1. Main Characteristics of Mandatory Public Old Age Pension Systems

Country	Contribution Rate[1] (in percent of employees' wages)				Eligibility Requirements			Calculation of Benefits				
					Standard retirement age		Minimum years of contributions	Pension base	Replacement rates by years of contributions (in percent of pension base)			
	Employee	Employer	Total	Government	Men	Women			15 years	25 years	35 years	Max
Defined-benefit systems												
Costa Rica—first tier[2]	5.5	4.75	10.25	0.25	62	60	38 (falls gradually to 25 by age 65)	Average real wage over the last 20 years	60	65	75	...
Guatemala	1.83	3.67	5.5	25 percent of benefit cost	60	60	15	Average wage over last 5 years	55	65	75	80
Honduras	1.0	2.0	3.0	0.5	65	60	15	Average wage over last 3 or 5 years (whichever is higher)	50	60	70	80
Nicaragua[3]	4.0	6.0	10.0	0.0	60/55	60/55	14.4	Average wage over last 3–5 years (depends on years of service)	57/65	71/82	80/98	80/100
Panama—first tier[4]	9.25	4.25	13.5	1.04	62	57	20	Average wage over best 10 years	...	66.25	78.75	100
Defined-contribution systems												
Costa Rica—second tier[5]	1.0	1.75	2.75	0.0	61.9	59.9	Must be eligible for first-tier benefits	Amount in individual account at retirement is annuitized or periodically withdrawn				
Costa Rica—second tier[5]	1.0	1.75	2.75	0.0	61.9	59.9						
Dominican Republic[6]	2.88	7.12	10.0	0.0	60	60	30	Amount in individual account at retirement is annuitized or periodically withdrawn				
El Salvador[7]	6.25	6.75	13.0	0.0	60	55	25	Amount in individual account at retirement is annuitized or periodically withdrawn				
Panama—second tier[8]	5.75	4.25	10.0	0.0	62	57	20	Amount in individual account at retirement is periodically withdrawn				

Sources: Country authorities; and U.S. Social Security Administration, 2003, *Social Security Programs Around the World: The Americas*.

Note: The table reflects current mandatory old age pension systems once any approved reforms have been fully phased in.

[1]For old age, disability, and survivors insurance.

[2]Once system is fully phased in in 2035. Replacement rates will be lower for high-income individuals.

[3]Retirement age is 55 for miners, teachers, and the physically or mentally impaired. Workers with average earnings less than twice the minimum wage receive higher replacement rates (e.g., with 15 years of service, a worker earning below twice the minimum wage receives a 65 percent replacement rate, while a worker earning over twice the minimum wage receives a 57 percent replacement rate).

[4]Once reforms are fully phased in in 2013. Applies only to monthly wages up to $500. Wages over this amount are taxed at a rate of 3.5 percent to help fund the scheme. In addition to its contribution, the government earmarks a variety of other taxes to help fund the system.

[5]Contribution rate excludes administrative fees and 1.5 percent for a mandatory severance pay scheme.

[6]Refers only to the contributory regime (see Appendix 3.1 for a description of the different regimes). Contribution rates will rise to these levels by 2008. Workers can retire at age 55 if they have accumulated enough assets to purchase an annuity equal to 150 percent of the minimum pension. Includes 1.6 percent for disability and survivor insurance and administrative fees.

[7]Contributions include 1.3 percent of wages for disability and survivor insurance and 1.4 percent of wages for administrative fees. Retirement is permitted at any age if the insured has 30 years of contributions and the pension equals at least 60 percent of basic earnings or 160 percent of the current minimum pension.

[8]Only applies on monthly wages over $500. On earnings over this amount, workers make an additional contribution of 3.5 percent to the defined-benefit scheme (the "solidarity contribution").

Old age pensions in Central America's defined-benefit systems are determined as a percentage of pre-retirement income. At retirement, an individual's average wage is calculated over some period of years (anywhere from three to 20 years, depending on the system). The individual's pension is then set as a percentage of the individual's average wage. This percentage, or *replacement rate*, generally rises with an individual's years of contributions and varies from 50 to 100 percent (Table 3.1). In most countries, minimum and maximum pensions are also set in nominal terms. Once an individual's pension is set at retirement, it is adjusted periodically through ad hoc, discretionary increases.

The defined-benefit systems are primarily financed by a payroll contribution that is split in some proportion between the employer and employee. These contributions are typically divided into portions that are earmarked for the long-term (old age, disability, and survivor pensions) and short-term (maternity, sickness, and work injury) branches of the social security system. The contributions for old age, disability, and survivor insurance vary by country from 3 to 13.5 percent of an employee's wages.

In several countries, the central government also subsidizes the social security system directly. For example, in Guatemala the government pays 25 percent of benefits, while in Costa Rica, Honduras, and Panama, the government provides subsidies equal to 0.25 percent, 0.5 percent, and 1.04 percent of an employee's covered wages, respectively. The Costa Rican and Panamanian governments also make a variety of additional transfers to their social security funds, including the proceeds of an earmarked alcohol tax (Panama) and profits of some state-owned enterprises (Costa Rica).

Most of the region's defined-benefit systems have a weak link between contributions and benefits. In most cases, an individual's pension is calculated as a percentage of his or her average wage over just the three to five years immediately before retirement. (Costa Rica, which calculates the average wage over 20 years, is the notable exception.) Such systems thus discourage individuals from earning and reporting high incomes during most of their career, since higher contributions outside of the years immediately before retirement do not affect one's pension and are therefore a pure tax. Conversely, individuals have a strong incentive to earn and report very high amounts in the years immediately before retirement in order to boost their pensions. Short averaging periods are also inequitable in that they favor individuals with steep lifetime earnings profiles (typically higher-income individuals) over those who have flatter earnings profiles (typically lower-income individuals).

The defined-benefit systems operate largely on a pay-as-you-go basis. That is, current contributions primarily pay for current pension benefits, rather than being invested to fund current workers' future pensions. However, all of the systems are partially funded in that they have built up at least some reserves.

Defined-Contribution Systems

In contrast, the Dominican Republic and El Salvador are in the process of switching to funded, defined-contribution systems. Both countries used to have traditional defined-benefit systems. However, El Salvador closed its defined-benefit system to new entrants in 1998, with a view to phasing it out. Workers under the age of 36 were automatically transferred into a new defined-contribution system of individual accounts. The vast majority of workers between ages 36 and 55 (for men) or 50 (for women) also voluntarily chose to switch to the new system. The Dominican Republic instituted a similar reform in 2003, with age 45 being the cut-off above which transfer to the new scheme was optional rather than mandatory.

Costa Rica and Panama have also introduced systems of mandatory individual accounts, but as supplements to, rather than replacements for, their defined-benefit systems. These countries thus have true multipillar systems. In Costa Rica, this system was adopted in 2000, while Panama's system was approved in December 2005 and will be phased in over several years.

As with defined-benefit schemes, the defined-contribution schemes in Costa Rica, the Dominican Republic, and El Salvador are financed by payroll contributions divided between the employer and employee. However, instead of going to pay current benefits, the payroll contributions are invested in individual accounts with private pension funds, known as pension fund administrators (*Administradoras de Fondos de Pensiones–AFPs*). Upon retirement, individuals choose either to make programmed withdrawals from the account or use the account to purchase a private annuity (or some combination of the two).[2] Both the Salvadoran and Dominican systems guarantee that the resulting pensions will be at least at some minimum level. In the Dominican Republic, the minimum pension is equal to the minimum wage and funded by 0.4 percent of the payroll contribution. In El Salvador, the minimum pension is determined each year in the annual budget (in 2006, it was $114 per month, or 72 percent of the minimum wage) and paid by the central government. A portion of an individual's payroll contributions pays for the AFPs' administrative

[2]It remains to be seen whether an adequate annuity market will actually be available when individuals in the privatized systems begin to retire in large numbers. Individual annuity markets have had difficulties developing in some countries due to adverse selection problems.

expenses. In the Salvadoran and Dominican systems, a portion of the contribution is also used to purchase private life and disability insurance, since there is no first-pillar social security system that provides these benefits. In all countries, the AFPs are regulated by a superintendent of pensions.

In Panama, the defined-contribution scheme will apply only to workers with monthly wages over $500. These workers will be affiliated with the first-pillar defined-benefit scheme on the first $500 of their monthly wages, together with workers earning less than $500 (approximately the average wage). On earnings over this amount, workers will contribute 3.5 percent to the first pillar (as a "solidarity contribution"), with the remainder of their contributions (10 percent of wages) going into individual investment accounts that will be managed by the social security agency. Individuals will be able to withdraw the amount in these accounts gradually upon retirement. In the very long run, only the individual investment accounts, which are expected to be sustainable, will remain as the $500 per month limit shrinks in real terms, assuming the government sticks to its intention to keep the $500 limit fixed in nominal terms (see Appendix 3.1 for more details on this recent reform).

Figure 3.1. Pension Coverage: Number of Contributors as a Share of the Labor Force, 2003
(In percent)

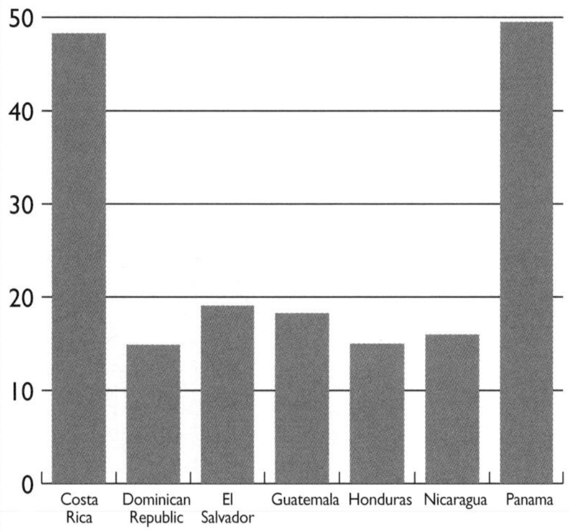

Sources: Country authorities; World Bank, *World Development Report* database; and IMF staff estimates.

Comparison of Key Parameters

Coverage

Most Central American pension systems cover a relatively small portion of workers. Only about 15 to 20 percent of the labor force contributes to the main pension system in El Salvador, the Dominican Republic, Guatemala, Honduras, and Nicaragua (Figure 3.1). These low numbers partly reflect the large informal sectors in these countries, as well as the fact that public sector workers are covered by separate, special regimes in some countries. The notable exceptions to low pension coverage are Costa Rica and Panama, which have achieved coverage rates of approximately 50 percent due to their larger formal labor markets.

Because coverage applies mainly to the formal sector (where incomes are higher than for the population as a whole), pension beneficiaries tend to be relatively high-income individuals. Consequently, government subsidies to pension systems (such as those mentioned in the previous subsection) tend to be quite regressive. For example, one study finds that, in Guatemala, 80 percent of net pension subsidies (government transfers to pension systems to fill gaps between contributions and benefits) accrue to the richest 20 percent of the population, while the poorest 20 percent receive less than 2 percent of net pension subsidies (Lindert, Skoufias, and Shapiro, 2006).

Contribution Rates

Contribution rates in Central America are somewhat low by international standards, but have been rising recently in some cases. Contribution rates in the region for old age, disability, and survivor insurance range from 3 percent of earnings in Honduras to 13.5 percent in Panama,[3] a range that is somewhat lower than the Latin American average (excluding Central America) of 15 percent and well below the average of 19 percent for member countries of the Organization for Economic Cooperation and Development (OECD) (Figure 3.2). However, the trend is toward higher rates—Costa Rica, the Dominican Republic, and El Salvador all effectively raised their total contribution rates in the process of introducing defined-contribution systems; Nicaragua raised its contribution rate from 5.25 to 10 percent in 2000; and Panama recently adopted reforms that will raise its contribution rate from 9.5 percent in 2006 to 13.5 percent by 2013.

Some pension systems also place a ceiling on earnings that are subject to contributions. The application of this ceiling varies across countries. For example, in Honduras it is relatively low at only about twice average earnings, while in Nicaragua it is largely nonbinding

[3]Once recent reforms are fully phased in by 2013.

Figure 3.2. Contribution Rates for Mandatory Old Age, Disability, and Survivor Pensions
(In percent)

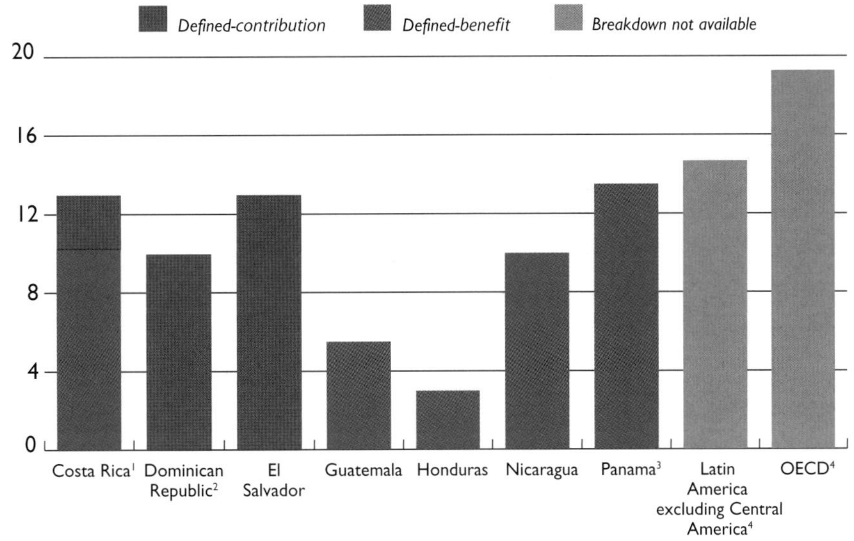

Source: U.S. Social Security Administration, 2003, *Social Security Programs Throughout the World.*
Note: OECD = Organization for Economic Cooperation and Development.
[1]Rates gradually rising to this level by 2035.
[2]Rates gradually rising to this level by 2008.
[3]Rates when recent reforms are fully phased in in 2013. Contributions on monthly wages over $500 also have a defined-contribution element.
[4]Simple average.

at nearly 10 times average earnings.[4] In Costa Rica, there is no ceiling at all. Since ceilings are placed on maximum pensions, the absence of a ceiling on earnings effectively taxes the earnings of very high-income workers to subsidize the rest of the system.

Retirement Ages

Like contribution rates, retirement ages in Central America are somewhat low by international standards. Standard retirement ages range from 55 to 65, with 60 being the most common (Table 3.1). Costa Rica, El Salvador, Honduras, and Panama have lower retirement ages for women than for men, despite women's longer life expectancy. Average retirement ages for the region are similar to the averages for the rest of Latin America, but well below the OECD average (Figure 3.3). This is true despite the fact that average life expectancy at age 60 in Central America is basically the same as in OECD countries for men and only somewhat lower for women (larger differences in life expectancy at birth are mainly due to differences in infant and child mortality).[5] However, the minimum contribution requirements—15 to 39 years, depending on the country (Table 3.1)—mean that some workers have to work beyond the standard retirement age before becoming eligible for old age pensions, especially given the large informal sector that results in many workers contributing only during a portion of their working career.

Benefits

Average pensions in the region are comparable to international averages, despite the relatively low contri-

[4]Unless otherwise noted, "average earnings" in this chapter refers to the average of earnings on which social security contributions are due.

[5]While commonly used, it is unclear whether life expectancy is the proper basis for setting retirement ages. If the rationale for mandatory public pension systems is to provide for elderly persons who cannot work (and to preclude the moral hazard arising from the provision of such benefits), then the appropriate metric for determining the retirement age may be morbidity (the degree to which poor health at a given age prevents work) rather than life expectancy. However, cross-country morbidity data are less readily available.

Figure 3.3. Standard Retirement Age and Life Expectancy at Age 60
(In years)

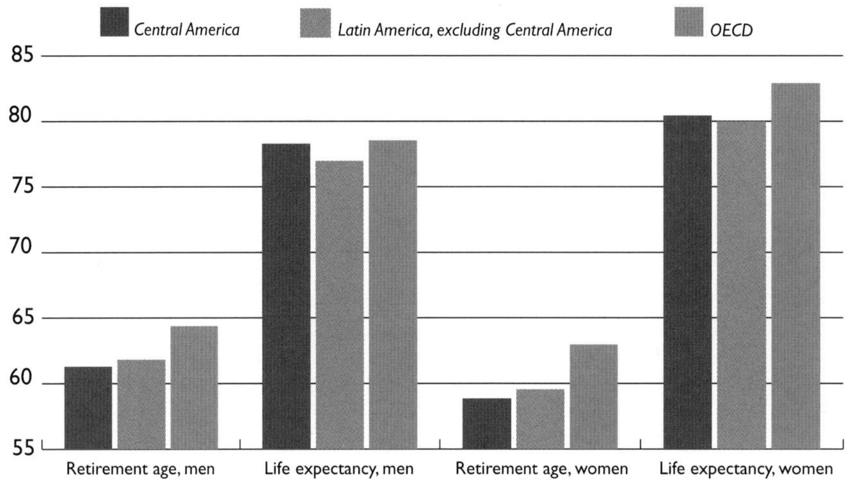

Sources: U.S. Social Security Administration, 2003, *Social Security Programs Throughout the World*; United Nations, 1999, *Population Aging*; and country documents.

Note: Simple averages for each group. Life expectancy is expressed in terms of age 60 plus the expected remaining years of life, given that an individual has reached age 60. OECD = Organization for Economic Cooperation and Development.

bution rates and retirement ages. In the defined-benefit systems, average old age pensions range from 38 to 86 percent of average earnings (Table 3.2), levels that are broadly similar to the average of 57 percent across OECD countries.

However, there is substantial variation in average pensions across countries. Panama's pensions are the high-end outlier at 86 percent of average earnings, a ratio that may be due in part to Panama's high minimum pension (41 percent of average earnings).

There is also substantial variation across age groups within countries, with average pensions typically falling with age. For example, in 2001, the typical 65 year old in Costa Rica had a pension equal to 67 percent of the economy-wide average wage, while the typical 78 year old had a pension that was only 34 percent of the economy-wide average wage. These differences across age groups reflect some combination of pensions growing more slowly than wages once they are set at retirement and recent retirees having more years of contributions and therefore higher replacement rates. These factors also explain why average pensions in most countries are only 40 to 50 percent of average earnings, despite statutory replacement rates of 50 to 100 percent (Table 3.1). More years of contributions for more recent retirees may imply, however, that average pensions will rise over time. In any event, the mix of low contribution rates, low retirement ages, and relatively high benefits is feasible in most of Central America's defined-benefit systems only as a result of

Table 3.2. Defined-Benefit Systems: Average and Minimum Old Age Pensions
(Percentage of economy-wide average earnings)

	Average Old Age Pension	Minimum Old Age Pension
Costa Rica	48	19
Guatemala	44	22
Honduras	38	None
Nicaragua	59	32
Panama	86	41
OECD average	57	...

Sources: Country authorities; Organization for Economic Cooperation and Development (2005); and IMF staff estimates.

Note: Data are for 2003, except for Honduras (2002). Economy-wide average earnings are calculated as total annual covered earnings divided by the number of active contributors. OECD = Organization for Economic Cooperation and Development.

the currently favorable demographics. Over the longer run, this combination is unsustainable.

Sustainability

Defined-Benefit Systems

Most of the region's defined-benefit systems have run moderate cash flow surpluses and built up reserves in recent years (Table 3.3). These surpluses are due to the region's relatively young population (Table 3.4), which results in a high ratio of contributors to pensioners. The one exception is Panama, which has already begun to run cash flow deficits due to its more generous benefits.

In the future, the systems' demographics will deteriorate significantly. Over the coming decades, the ratio of contributors to pensioners will fall dramatically in Central America as the population ages. In particular, if contributors and pensioners remain constant fractions of the age 20–59 and 60+ populations, respectively, then the number of contributors supporting each pensioner would fall by about threefold in most countries (Table 3.4). Moreover, the share of elderly that are pensioners is likely to rise as pension systems mature. For example, in Guatemala old age pensioners currently constitute only about 5 percent of the population age 65+, whereas contributors constitute 18 percent of the working age population. As current contributors age, it is likely that the pensioner share of the elderly population will rise closer to 18 percent. While the low coverage of the labor force also leaves room for expanding the share of the working age population that contributes, this would probably only offset the rising pensioner share of the population, at best, under current policies.

The effect of a worsening ratio of contributors to pensioners can be seen by looking at the basic arithmetic of pay-as-you-go systems. In a pure pay-as-you-go system, sustainable pension parameters must satisfy the following condition: $r = cX$, where r = the average gross replacement rate (the average pension benefit divided by the average wage), c = the contribution rate, and X = the ratio of contributors to pensioners.[6] From this expression, one can see that, if X falls on average from 7.8 to 2.8 as projected, then either contribution rates would have to be raised threefold or average pen-

Table 3.3. Defined-Benefit Systems: Balances and Reserves, 2004
(In percent of GDP)

	Balance	Reserves
Costa Rica	1.2	7.5
Guatemala	0.2	2.6
Honduras	0.6	...
Nicaragua[1]	0.4	2.2
Panama	–0.3	11.5

Sources: Country authorities; and IMF staff estimates.
Note: For old age, disability, and survivor insurance.
[1]Estimated out-turn for 2005. Reserves are total assets in investment accounts for the entire social security system times the portion of earnings on these assets that are allocated to the old age, disability, and survivor's branch.

[6]This expression can be derived as follows: total contributions = cCw (where C = the number of contributors and w = the average wage) and total benefits = pB (where p = the average pension and B = the number of beneficiaries). Setting total benefits equal to total contributions in each period (as in a pure pay-as-you-go system) yields $pB = cCw$. Rearranging yields $(p/w) = c\ (C/B)$. Defining r (the replacement rate) = p/w and X (the ratio of contributors to pensioners) = C/B yields $r = cX$. Note that this equation ignores administrative costs.

Table 3.4. Projected Population Aging
(In percent)

	Ratio of Population Ages 20–59 to Population Age 60+					
	2003	2010	2020	2030	2040	2050
Costa Rica	6.6	5.9	4.3	3.1	2.5	2.0
Guatemala	8.1	8.1	7.6	6.3	4.8	3.6
Honduras	8.6	8.4	7.3	5.8	4.5	3.4
Nicaragua	9.9	9.7	7.7	5.6	3.9	2.7
Panama	5.8	5.2	4.3	3.3	2.7	2.4
Average	7.8	7.5	6.2	4.8	3.7	2.8

Source: U.S. Census Bureau international database: http://www.census.gov/ipc/www/idbnew.html.

Table 3.5. Defined-Benefit Systems: Real Internal Rates of Return on Contributions
(In percent)

	Costa Rica	Guatemala	Honduras	Nicaragua	Panama
Men	8.3	9.0	11.3	8.4	5.2
Women	9.3	9.8	13.5	9.0	6.8

Source: IMF staff estimates.

Note: For old age benefits once all approved reforms are fully phased in. Based on a stylized individual who contributes for 30 years, spread out evenly over the individual's working career before retirement at the standard retirement age. Assumes that the old age benefit share of contributions is proportional to the old age benefit share of expenditure and that pensions-in-payment grow with inflation. Mortality rates are based on Nicaraguan data. Results do not differ significantly if Costa Rican mortality rates or an alternative number of years of contributions are used.

sions would have to be cut threefold to maintain the current balance. While the pension systems' current surpluses and reserves give them some cushion against such a demographic shock, significant changes to the parameters of the systems—either higher contribution rates, lower benefits, or higher retirement ages to improve the ratio of contributors to pensioners—will nonetheless be required eventually, especially considering that population aging will likely strain the survivor (mainly elderly widows and widowers) and disability portions of social security systems as well.

Another way to see the systems' unsustainability is to examine their internal rates of return. The internal rate of return is the discount rate that equates the present discounted value of an individual's expected contributions and pension benefits. In other words, the internal rate of return is the rate of return that an individual effectively receives on his or her contributions. In a pure, steady-state, pay-as-you-go system, the sustainable real internal rate of return is the real growth rate of the wage bill (perhaps 4 percent over the long run, assuming labor force growth of 1.5 percent and real wage growth per worker of 2.5 percent).[7,8] In a fully-funded system, the sustainable internal rate of return is equal to the real return on investments (perhaps 3 to 6 percent, depending on how much risk the system is willing to bear).

The parameters of Central America's current defined-benefit systems entail real internal rates of return that are unsustainable. Real rates of return for stylized cases are shown in Table 3.5. The rates range from 5½ to 13½ percent, with the recently-reformed Panamanian system being the outlier on the low end. In general, these internal rates of return are quite high and will only grow over time as longevity improves. Such rates of return are clearly unsustainable, indicating that current contribution rates are insufficient to fund the promised replacement rates and retirement ages over the long run.

To fully assess the sustainability of pension systems, however, proper actuarial analyses are required. Such analyses project future cash flows based on detailed data on the profile of existing contributors and pensioners, together with assumptions regarding the future path of economic and demographic variables. Unfortunately, such thorough actuarial analyses are not readily available for all countries. Moreover, the results of actuarial analyses can be sensitive to assumptions regarding long-run growth rates, interest rates, and increases in longevity, as well as the time horizon chosen, which makes direct comparisons across analyses for different countries difficult.

Nonetheless, available actuarial analyses confirm that many of Central America's defined-benefit systems are unsustainable. For example, recent analyses indicate that Nicaragua's old age, disability, and survivor pension system will begin running cash flow deficits around 2017–18. Panama's defined-benefit system is already in deficit, although recent reforms are expected to gradually phase out the system (and therefore its deficit) over the very long run. Costa Rica's system was projected to go into deficit by 2018, but the 2005 reforms extended this date to 2040 according to the government's actuarial analyses (Superintendencia de Pensiones, 2005).[9]

[7]While this result is a close approximation for many pay-as-you-go systems, it strictly applies only for pure pay-as-you-go systems (no reserve fund) that are in a steady-state (the difference between the average age of contributors and pensioners is constant). See Settergren and Mikula (2006).

[8]In the very long run, 4 percent wage bill growth is likely to be optimistic, since labor force growth in many developed countries is approaching zero and real wage growth per worker is closer to 2 percent.

[9]See Appendix 3.1 for more information on these recent reforms.

Defined-Contribution Systems

The region's funded, defined-contribution systems are generally sustainable by construction, except to the degree that low pensions trigger government guarantees. Two countries have defined contribution systems as a first pillar—the Dominican Republic and El Salvador. In theory, these systems should be self-funding, with each beneficiary simply receiving whatever retirement benefits can be purchased by his or her accumulated savings. However, if this level of benefits is very low, the government will be required to subsidize pensions to bring them to the guaranteed minimums that exist in both countries.

The magnitude of future government liabilities arising from minimum pension guarantees will depend on the rates of return that contributors earn on their savings and their years of contributions. Table 3.6 shows the replacement rates (pension benefits as a share of pre-retirement earnings) that retirees would be able to achieve in the Dominican and Salvadoran systems in certain stylized cases, depending on the rate of return that individuals earn on their investments and their years of contributions. The estimates indicate that real rates of return of less than 5 percent in the Dominican Republic and 4 percent in El Salvador are likely to lead to low replacement rates (10 to 30 percent) that will likely trigger significant fiscal costs to fund minimum pension guarantees. The size of fiscal liabilities generated by these first-pillar, defined-contribution systems will thus depend crucially on investment performance.

The Dominican Republic and El Salvador also face significant legacy costs from their old defined-benefit systems. When these countries changed their systems, most workers switched to the new defined-contribution systems and stopped contributing to the old systems. However, the old defined-benefit systems retained their obligations to pay pension benefits to current retirees and older workers who opted to remain in the old system. Moreover, in 2003 a government decree in El Salvador guaranteed that individuals who opted to move to the new defined-contribution system (those between ages 36 and 50/55 at the time of the reform in 1998) would receive a pension at least equal to what they would have received under the old system (despite the fact that these individuals' contribution rate in the new system is 1 percentage point lower than for those who opted to stay in the old system). The vast majority of pensioners in this cohort will need a significant top-up at retirement in order to meet this guarantee, since the returns on their individual accounts will almost certainly be less than the very high implicit internal rates of return that they would have received under the old system. This guarantee will thus significantly increase the legacy costs of old system.

These old systems will run substantial deficits during the transition due to these legacy costs. For example, El Salvador's old system currently requires transfers from the central government of nearly 2 percent of GDP, a figure that is projected to rise to 2.7 percent of GDP by 2018, before gradually declining to near zero by 2040. In the Dominican Republic, transfers from the central government to the legacy system were 0.8 percent of GDP in 2005.

Administrative Costs

Central America's defined-benefit systems vary somewhat with regard to their administrative costs.

Table 3.6. Replacement Rates under Different Rates of Return in First-Pillar, Defined-Contribution Systems
(In percent)

	Real Rate of Return on Investments			
	3	4	5	7
Dominican Republic				
(8 percent contribution to accounts)				
30 years of contributions	13	18	28	46
40 years of contributions	18	24	33	61
El Salvador (10.3 percent contribution to accounts)				
30 years of contributions	18	24	36	60
40 years of contributions	23	31	42	79

Source: IMF staff estimates.

Note: For a male beginning work at age 20 and retiring at age 60; estimates assume that contributions are spread out evenly over the individual's working career, that current mortality rates will apply by the time the individual retires, and that the annuity mark-up over actuarial value is 15 percent.

Costs range from 3 to 11 percent of total contributions (Table 3.7). Overall, administrative costs are significantly higher than in some developed countries. For example, administrative costs in the United States are only 0.5 percent of contributions. Such differences may reflect economies of scale and other country-specific factors. However, they may also indicate an opportunity to lower administrative costs in some Central American systems.

Administrative costs in the privately-administered, defined-contribution systems are somewhat higher than in the publicly-administered, defined-benefit systems. In Costa Rica, roughly half of AFPs charge the maximum allowable for administrative fees—4 percent of contributions and 8 percent of returns—although fees on contributions go as low as 2.5 percent for some AFPs. In the Dominican Republic, administrative fees are set at 0.6 percent of an individual's wages (0.5 percent for AFPs and 0.1 percent for the pension supervisor), plus a certain percentage of returns over benchmark yields. In El Salvador, the maximum allowable fee is 1.4 percent of wages. These fee levels reduce effective contributions (and therefore balances at retirement) by roughly 13, 8, and 11 percent in Costa Rica, the Dominican Republic, and El Salvador, respectively.[10]

Investment Policies

Available data indicate that both defined-benefit and defined-contribution plans invest the vast majority of their assets in domestic government securities and bank deposits. For example, 70 percent of the assets in Costa Rica's defined-benefit plan were invested in government bonds at end-2003. The defined-contribution plans (AFPs) have similar portfolios—for example, government and central bank securities account for 89 and 83 percent of investments in the defined-contribution systems in Costa Rica and El Salvador, respectively. In some cases, such portfolios may be due in part to regulatory limits on other types of investments. In the Dominican Republic, investments are primarily with banks, since AFPs are not allowed to invest directly in government paper. However, banks in turn invest a significant portion of the AFPs' deposits in government securities.[11] The real rate of return on AFPs' investments has varied from 1 to 15 percent in recent years because of macroeconomic volatility (especially in the Dominican Republic due to the recent banking crisis).

[10]Assuming a 30-year contribution history, 4 percent annual wage growth, and 8 percent nominal returns. The estimate for the Dominican Republic assumes an average charge on returns of 2 percent.

[11]Allowing AFPs to invest directly in government securities may improve their returns, since capital market imperfections and intermediation costs may prevent banks from fully passing on the return on government securities to their depositors.

Table 3.7. Administrative Costs in Defined-Benefit Systems

	Percent of Contributions	Percent of Benefits
Costa Rica	2.8	3.7
Guatemala[1]	4.7	5.6
Honduras[2]	10.8	32.6
Nicaragua	5.3	5.9
Panama[3]	6.8	4.8
United States	0.5	0.6

Sources: Country authorities; and IMF staff estimates.

Note: For old age, disability, and survivor portion of social security schemes in 2004, unless otherwise noted.

[1]For 2003.

[2]For 2001.

[3]For complete social security system.

Special Regimes

Many Central American countries have special pension systems for civil servants and uniformed personnel. The basic structure of these systems is similar to that of the regular defined-benefit systems, but typically with even more generous benefits (lower retirement ages, higher replacement rates, etc.) relative to contributions. The importance of these special systems varies across countries. For example, in Honduras the unfunded liabilities of these special systems are much larger than those of the regular system. In contrast, the special pension system in El Salvador for government employees is being phased out as part of the transition to the new private defined-contribution system. Special regimes are not the main focus of this chapter, in part due to a lack of detailed actuarial analysis and publicly available information. However, the fundamental issues facing these systems, particularly the unsustainability of benefits, are in many cases similar to—or more severe than—those facing the regular pension systems.

Several countries also have special noncontributory regimes for low-income groups. Noncontributory, means-tested pensions are provided to the elderly poor and other vulnerable groups in Costa Rica (financed by a 5 percent employer payroll tax and 20 percent of sales tax revenue), the Dominican Republic (financed by the government), and Nicaragua (financed by the regular pension system).

Recent Reform Developments

The need for pension reform has been recognized by all governments in Central America. While reform efforts cover a wide spectrum, they are uneven across countries. As pointed out above, some countries (the Dominican Republic and El Salvador) are in the process of privatizing their systems—that is, switching to a fully-funded, defined-contribution system of privately-managed individual accounts. Others (Costa Rica and Panama) have recently chosen to adopt multipillar systems. These countries are now considering or undertaking second-generation reforms to address ongoing unsustainable initial pillars (in multipillar systems) or high transition costs and potentially large contingent liabilities (in privatized systems).

Some countries have started to address unsustainability through parametric reform (reform of pension system parameters such as contribution rates and benefit formulas). A number of countries (Costa Rica, the Dominican Republic, and Panama) have started to raise retirement ages, increase contribution rates, tighten eligibility requirements, or change a combination of parameters. Appendix 3.1 provides a country-by-country overview of such recent reform efforts. Despite these reforms, however, further reforms are necessary.

The experience of reform efforts in Central America also demonstrates how difficult it is to move pension reform forward and generate or sustain sufficient public support. Fractured or polarized political landscapes and elections in Nicaragua (2006) and Guatemala (2007), for example, have delayed reforms. The experience of Panama and El Salvador, in turn, demonstrates how public opposition can lead to weaker reforms. In Panama, a strong parametric reform to address the system's actuarial imbalance was ultimately withdrawn as a result of public opposition, despite passage by the assembly in mid-2005. To address public concerns, the government engaged in a five-month consultative process with civil society, which ultimately resulted in passage of a revised but somewhat weakened reform in December 2005. In El Salvador, authorities tried to ensure popular support of the privatized system by offering costly guarantees to those who chose to switch to the new privatized system.

Pension Reform and Development of Local Capital Markets

At present, financial systems in Central America are largely bank-based, and capital markets remain underdeveloped. In particular, equity and corporate bond markets are limited to a handful of companies (except in Panama). Instead, public debt markets account for the lion's share of market-based financing in Central America, and much of this is in foreign currency (Panama and El Salvador officially adopted the U.S. dollar as legal tender). Furthermore, local markets in domestic currency tend to be short term.

Some argue that privatizing parts of the pension system (as in Costa Rica, El Salvador, and the Dominican Republic) can have the positive side effect of fostering capital market development, especially through the creation of pension funds and an increase in institutional investors.[12] In particular, such proponents suggest that decentralizing and increasing the number of managers of pension assets can promote development of "institutional capital" and competitive pricing of financial assets.[13]

Pension reforms that reduce fiscal liabilities could also contribute to the development of capital markets in Central America by reducing macroeconomic vulnerabilities and increasing national savings. The lack of developed capital markets in the region reflects in part persistent and relatively high levels of fiscal deficit and debt. In the absence of reform, rising pension system deficits may thus further undermine capital market development. Conversely, pension reforms that reduce unfunded liabilities (e.g., by raising retirement ages and contribution rates and reducing replacement rates) could promote capital markets by reducing fiscal deficits and associated macroeconomic vulnerabilities. Such reforms may also increase national savings, which in turn could be associated with positive externalities such as the deepening of financial markets, increased liquidity, and lengthened maturities. The establishment of benchmark yield curves, in turn, provides the foundation for the development of corporate debt markets.

To date, however, privately-managed pension pillars have had limited success in promoting capital markets in Central America or Latin America overall (World Bank, 2006), perhaps in part because reforms have not been sufficiently aimed at reducing unfunded pension liabilities, there has been a lack of complementary reforms to security laws and regulations, and pension funds have been very tightly regulated (Roldos, 2004). The decentralization of pension asset management may also have come at the cost of reducing administrative economies of scale.

Moreover, requiring pension funds to invest in underdeveloped domestic markets can lead to distortions and potential asset price bubbles. It also heavily exposes pension systems to country-specific risk. Indeed, the experience from Latin America demonstrates that most pension funds are not well diversified and are highly exposed to sovereign risk (World Bank, 2006). However, rapidly relaxing restrictions on foreign investment could lead to capital outflows that could undermine

[12]See, for example, Walker and Lefort (2002) and Holzmann (1997).

[13]In the Dominican Republic, domestic capital market development has been curtailed by the portfolio restrictions imposed on pension funds.

macroeconomic management. Such relaxations should thus be managed gradually.

Reform Options

Pension reform in Central America needs to be tailored to each country's specific circumstances and preferences. However, some common features of reform approaches can be identified, given the commonality of issues across many of the region's pension systems. In particular, policymakers may wish to consider the suggestions that follow in terms of reform.

Parametric Reform of Defined-Benefit Systems to Make Them Sustainable

As noted earlier, many of the region's defined-benefit systems are unsustainable due to the aging of populations and to benefit formulas that are very generous relative to contributions. Some combination of higher contribution rates, higher retirement ages, and lower replacement rates is therefore needed to balance contributions and benefits over the long run. Such adjustments should be the first priority of pension reform.

How such adjustments are allocated among contribution rates, retirement ages, and replacement rates will vary according to country-specific circumstances and preferences. In countries where contribution rates are relatively low (e.g., Honduras and Guatemala), contribution rates could be increased somewhat. In many countries, however, the scope for raising contribution rates may be limited, given the adverse consequences that higher rates may have on development of the formal sector.[14] In contrast, there is scope in many countries to scale back replacement rates (which reach up to 100 percent) to more moderate levels and to raise retirement ages to reflect increased longevity. Retirement ages for men and women could also be equalized in some countries.

Parametric reforms will likely need to be phased in over time to allow individuals to adjust their retirement planning to the new rules and make such reforms politically palatable. However, if reforms are delayed, unfunded liabilities will continue to accumulate, necessitating more dramatic and abrupt reforms in the future. Policymakers should thus take early action to allow a smooth and gradual adjustment process.

Parametric reforms could either be done on their own or as part of a shift to a defined-contribution system. Shifts to defined-contribution systems in Central America typically result in implicit benefit cuts, since rates of return on investments are lower than internal rates of return on existing defined-benefit systems. Shifts to defined-contribution plans can therefore be one way to introduce parametric reforms. This approach may be appealing to policymakers, since the change in systems can make implicit benefit cuts less transparent and therefore more politically acceptable. For example, many Salvadorans appeared not to realize the implicit benefit cuts involved in such a shift, since most voluntarily chose to shift from the generous defined-benefit system to the less generous defined-contribution system. However, such "stealth" parametric reforms entail risks—in El Salvador, those who chose to switch eventually realized that they would be getting a lower pension. They then lobbied the government to issue the 2003 decree guaranteeing that those who switched would get at least as large a pension as they would have gotten under the old defined-benefit system, expanding the transition costs and undoing much of the initial reform.

It should be stressed that shifting to a defined-contribution system reduces a pension system's unfunded liabilities only to the degree that it reduces expected benefits, increases contributions, or increases the return on the system's assets. Reforms that simply move from a defined-benefit to a defined-contribution system without altering these underlying parameters do little to solve the sustainability problem. Indeed, privatizations that attempt to shift from an unfunded, defined-benefit system to a funded, defined-contribution system without addressing the underlying imbalance between contributions and benefits in the old system can actually worsen the overall system's finances by transforming implicit unfunded liabilities (which typically have no legal guarantee and therefore can be altered) into explicit government liabilities (that have a legal guarantee and therefore cannot be altered without triggering a default), as evidence suggests happened with Argentina's pension reform (Cuevas and others, 2006).

For those countries that shifted to a defined-contribution system, further parametric reform of their old defined-benefit systems would help reduce transition costs. As noted earlier, El Salvador and the Dominican Republic have shifted to defined-contribution systems but still face substantial transition costs because of payments of pensions to those who remain in the old systems. These old systems still offer relatively high replacement rates and low retirement ages; gradually adjusting these parameters to more internationally comparable levels would substantially reduce transition costs.

[14]If individuals receive a market rate of return on their contributions, then contributions are in theory savings rather than a pure tax. However, in most cases, weak and nontransparent links between contributions and benefits, together with high discount rates (i.e., myopia), result in contributions having or being perceived as having a high taxation element, with all of the associated labor market distortions.

Tightening the Link between Contributions and Benefits to Reduce Labor Market Distortions

In most of the region's defined-benefit systems, benefits are only weakly linked to contributions. As a result, contributions in many systems are largely a pure tax, with all of the associated labor market distortions.

One way to tighten the link between contributions and benefits in defined-benefit systems would be to increase the number of years over which an individual's average wage is calculated. As noted earlier, in most systems, an individual's pension is calculated as a percentage of his or her average salary only over the three to five years immediately before retirement. To reduce the resulting distortions and inequities, the region's systems could move to the common international practice of basing pensions on average earnings over 25 to 40 years, with missing years counted as zeroes and wages from past years typically converted into current dollars using an index of the average economy-wide wage. Costa Rica recently adopted such a reform, gradually expanding the wage-averaging period from four to 20 years.

Another way to tighten the link between contributions and benefits would be to move to a defined-contribution system; however, this may come at the cost of increased financial market risk for participants.[15] As noted above, defined-benefit systems often have a poor link between contributions and benefits either because benefit formulas are poorly designed (e.g., with the short wage-averaging periods discussed above) or poorly understood due to their complexity. In contrast, defined-contribution systems have a clear link between contributions and benefits—individuals can easily see that each dollar contributed adds to their account. However, the volatility of investment returns in defined-contribution systems creates significant volatility in the replacement rates that any individual or generation receives. For this reason, countries may prefer to maintain a defined-benefit system for their first-pillar, universal public pension system, but improve the tightness and transparency of the system's link between contributions and benefits.

One system that tries to create a tight and transparent link between contributions and benefits while insuring pensioners against financial market volatility is the notional defined-contribution (NDC) system. NDC systems mimic defined-contribution systems in that they credit contributions in individual accounts that earn a rate of return. Upon retirement, the amount in the account is paid out through some combination of annuitization, programmed withdrawals, or lump sum distributions. NDC systems are thus technically defined-contribution systems and have a very clear link between contributions and benefits. However, NDC systems are like defined-benefit systems and unlike most defined-contribution systems in that the return that the individual accounts earn is not determined by investments in financial markets, but is set and guaranteed by the government, thereby reducing the volatility of replacement rates. Typically, the rate of return is tied in some way to the government's ability to pay benefits. For example, the return may be set equal to the growth rate of the economy or the wage bill covered by the system. NDC systems are typically unfunded in that current benefits are paid out of current contributions, but such systems could also build up reserves so that they are funded.

NDC systems can be phased in through a variety of mechanisms. One of the simplest is to calculate pensions as a weighted average of what benefits would be under current law and what they would be if the individual had been in an NDC system all along, with the weights varying by birth cohort. For example, to phase in an NDC system over 10 years, those turning 65 next year would receive a pension equal to 10 percent of the NDC pension and 90 percent of the current law pension; those turning 65 in the year after that would receive a pension equal to 20 percent of the NDC pension and 80 percent of the current law pension, and so forth until the NDC pension is fully phased in. Such a transition mechanism is being used in Sweden.[16]

Strengthening Social Protection

Indexing pensions-in-payment to consumer prices (after replacement rates have first been reduced to sustainable levels) would strengthen pensions' income protection function. Currently, most of the region's defined-benefit systems adjust pensions-in-payment annually largely on an ad hoc basis, which has several drawbacks:

- The discretionary nature of ad hoc increases makes systems vulnerable to political pressures;
- The erratic nature of ad hoc adjustments raises pensioners' uncertainty regarding the future path of their pensions in real terms, reducing the system's insurance value; and
- Ad hoc adjustments create inequities, since pensioners with similar contribution histories can receive different rates of return on their contributions due to differences in ad hoc adjustments that may occur during their retirement years.

[15]Defined-benefit systems also subject participants to some risk, including political risk and the risk that permanent economic shocks will eventually force an adjustment of benefits (Shoven and Slavov, 2006).

[16]Fully fledged NDC systems are also being introduced in Italy, Latvia, and Poland. For more on NDC systems, see Holzmann and Palmer (2006).

These problems could be avoided by automatically indexing pensions to consumer prices (as in most OECD countries), thereby fixing pensions in real terms and removing discretion for any additional upward adjustment.[17] In countries where pensions-in-payment would have otherwise been increased in real terms, such indexation would reduce pension costs. However, indexation will increase costs in countries that rely on nonindexation to reduce the real value of pensions that are set at unsustainably high levels at retirement. In these cases, it may be necessary to first reduce replacement rates to sustainable levels before indexing pensions-in-payment to consumer prices. To safeguard the government's fiscal flexibility in times of financial stress, it may also be useful to include "safety valves," such as setting a limit (e.g., 5 percent) on the increase that can occur automatically in any given year, with adjustments for inflation over this amount dependent on government approval based on an assessment of the system's finances.

It may also be possible to strengthen pension systems' social protection objectives by reducing the systems' redistributive elements and using the proceeds to finance well-targeted transfers to the poor outside of the systems themselves. Most public pension systems have some redistributive element, whether it be via minimum pensions or providing relatively higher internal rates of return to pensioners with fewer years of contributions. However, recipients of minimum pensions may not necessarily be poor, due to nonpension income, and pensioners with fewer years of contributions may still have high pensions due to high earnings and short wage-averaging periods. Moreover, the vast majority of the poor are likely to fall outside of the pension system altogether, since they are not heavily involved in formal sector employment. Consequently, pension systems' redistributive mechanisms may result in substantial leakage to the nonpoor, and subsidization of pensions from general revenue is likely to be poorly targeted and even regressive. Governments may thus wish to consider whether poverty (old age and otherwise) could be more effectively combated by reducing some of the current redistributive elements in pension systems, scaling back general pension subsidies, and using the proceeds to fund better-targeted transfers to the poor outside of the contributory pension system. Costa Rica, the Dominican Republic, and Nicaragua have begun reforms along these lines by establishing noncontributory, means-tested pensions.

[17]In some systems, pensions are indexed to wages rather than consumer prices, which requires lower initial pensions at retirement (assuming positive real wage growth). However, indexation to consumer prices is generally viewed to be preferable, as it is unclear why pensioners would want rising real consumption profiles in retirement. Moreover, even if pensioners prefer such profiles, they could still achieve them under price indexation by saving a portion of their initial pensions.

Expanding coverage would also provide better protection against poverty among the elderly and improve short-term cash flows. As noted earlier in this chapter, most Central American pension systems cover less than 20 percent of the labor force. Expanding coverage through better enforcement of mandatory contributions will therefore be critical to ensuring that pension systems provide adequate protection against poverty among the elderly. Expanding the contribution base will also improve short-term cash flows. However, long-term imbalances will grow as coverage expands, since more individuals will enter systems that promise unsustainably high internal rates of return. Parametric reform is thus critical to place defined-benefit systems on a sustainable footing before expanded coverage magnifies the long-run imbalance between contributions and benefits.

Reducing the Contingent Liabilities of Defined-Contribution Systems

As noted earlier in this chapter, the defined-contribution systems in the Dominican Republic and El Salvador both guarantee minimum pension levels. As a result, these governments may incur significant liabilities to fund these minimum pensions, especially if real returns on private accounts are modest. These contingent liabilities could be reduced by measures such as raising the minimum age at which one can retire with a minimum pension to 65 or by modestly increasing contribution rates.

Improving Investment Performance

Investment performance could be improved by gradually facilitating more international diversification. Most Central American pension plans (both defined-benefit and defined-contribution) invest almost all of their assets domestically, mainly in government securities and bank deposits. As a result, these plans are highly exposed to risks specific to Central America. These risks could be reduced by increasing investment in well-diversified, professionally-managed, and well-regulated portfolios of international assets. Diversification into international assets should be done gradually, however, in order to minimize any macroeconomic disruptions that may be caused by a shift in capital flows.

Governments should also avoid directing pension plans (whether defined-benefit or defined-contribution) to lend to social and politically-favored projects. While such projects may be worthy, these should be funded from the budget rather than through pension funds in order to ensure that the costs of such projects are transparent and that they compete with other priorities for public funding. Governments may also wish to preclude public defined-benefit plans from investing their reserves in domestic assets other than government securities or bank deposits, since investments in domestic equities or real estate run the risk of becoming politicized. Public pension institutions are also not generally well placed to actively manage and operate commercial enterprises and real estate.

Controlling Administrative Costs

The efficiency of both the region's public defined-benefit systems and the private defined-contribution systems could be enhanced by controlling and reducing administrative costs, especially in cases where these costs are particularly high (e.g., Honduras). For the public defined-benefit systems, this may mean re-engineering pension institutions to streamline employment costs and enhance use of information technology. For private defined-contribution systems, governments may wish to investigate whether the prescribed level of AFP fees could be lowered and whether regulations adequately promote competition on the basis of administrative costs. Lower AFP fees could perhaps be facilitated by restricting (as El Salvador recently did) how often workers can change AFPs and by limiting marketing costs.

Better Integrating Special Regimes and the Regular Systems

Several countries could achieve significant efficiency and equity improvements by better integrating special regimes (e.g., for civil servants) with the regular system. For example, in Honduras an array of special systems for different types of government employees remain. In these cases, integrating these special systems into the regular pension system could provide more uniformity of treatment, facilitate mobility across sectors (currently hindered because moving from one sector's plan to another can reduce benefits), and cut administrative costs through economies of scale.

Repealing Excessively Generous Tax Treatments for Pensions

The fiscal cost of pension systems could be reduced by repealing the excessively generous tax treatment that pensions sometimes receive. The commonly-recommended international practice is to tax income placed into pension plans once (but only once), either by making pension contributions nondeductible or by taxing withdrawals from pension accounts.[18] However, in some Central American countries (e.g., El Salvador), pension contributions are tax deductible when made, earn interest and dividends tax-free, and are tax-free upon withdrawal. As a result, the original earnings escape the income tax net altogether, giving the pension preferential treatment relative to other forms of income. Repealing this preferential treatment (i.e., by taxing pension withdrawals in countries where contributions are tax deductible) would reduce the tax preference given to the pension system and increase fiscal revenue. It would also likely be progressive, since participants in pension plans tend to be relatively high-income individuals and income tax systems tend to be progressive.

Improving Transparency

Better publication of pension systems' financial statements and actuarial reviews would improve transparency. Most actuarial reviews in the region are either unpublished or could be strengthened in their analysis. Publishing more detailed data on the finances and actuarial imbalances of pension systems would increase public awareness of the systems' difficulties, which should both build support for reforms and better inform public debate on possible solutions.[19]

Collecting and publishing information on the distributional incidence of government subsidies to pension systems may also prompt reform, since existing evidence indicates that participants in public pension systems in Latin America tend to be relatively high-income individuals, implying that general government subsidies to these systems are regressive (Lindert, Skoufias, and Shapiro, 2006). Such subsidies exhaust public resources that could be used for more pro-poor spending in such areas as primary education or health care.

Conclusions

Despite the implementation of reforms in some countries and reform attempts in others, further reforms are necessary. The pension systems in Central America remain either unsustainable or face high transition costs and potentially large contingent liabilities.

While all of the defined-benefit systems are currently running moderate cash flow surpluses (except Panama) and have built up reserves, the systems are in long-run imbalance. In the future, spending will grow more rapidly than revenue as the ratio of working age persons to the elderly falls from an average of about eight today to less than three in 2050. Internal-rate-of-return calculations corroborate the unsustainability of the systems, given that most have real rates of return close to 10 percent, which is substantially higher than

[18]These are equivalent in present value if cash flows are discounted by the rate of return earned on contributions and the income tax rate is the same at the time of contributions and withdrawals.

[19]Governments could also enhance fiscal transparency by adopting the accounting methodologies in the *Government Finance Statistics Manual* (IMF, 2001).

the real growth rate of the wage bill and the growth performance of the economies over recent decades.

Pension reforms in Central America need to be tailored to specific circumstances—there is no one-size-fits-all solution. However, some important recommendations are applicable across many countries. First and foremost, any reform should focus on sustainability. Depending on the country's circumstances, this might call for an increase in contribution rates or retirement ages, a reduction in benefits, or some combination of reforms. Reforms of defined-benefit systems should also aim to strengthen the link between contributions and benefits by lengthening wage-averaging periods. Links could also be improved by moving more toward notional defined-contribution or regular defined-contribution systems. However, the latter may expose participants to more financial market risk. Privatizing pension systems and switching to defined-contribution systems without addressing the systems' underlying shortcomings can also have adverse effects by converting implicit unfunded government liabilities (which typically have no legal guarantee and therefore can be altered) into explicit ones.

Countries that have moved to a defined-contribution system still need to implement further parametric reforms of their old defined-benefit system to reduce transition costs. In those countries, there is substantial scope for such reforms, given that the old systems offer relatively high replacement rates and low retirement ages.

Recent experience also highlights the difficulties involved with mobilizing public support for pension reform. In some countries this has caused reforms to be abandoned while in others it has led to a substantial weakening of the parametric components of the reforms. Therefore, to increase the likelihood of success, policymakers might want to:

- *Provide stakeholders with multiple options.* This approach was successfully followed in countries such as Barbados, where the authorities held broad consultations with stakeholders before adopting an extensive parametric reform. The consultations stressed that some combination of parametric reform was unavoidable, but that the distribution of adjustments across contribution rates, retirement ages, and benefits could be weighted in many different ways. Such broad consultations have also recently facilitated parametric reform in Costa Rica and Panama.
- *Publish actuarial reviews and other information that highlight the magnitude of the problem, the costs of inaction, and the relative trade-offs between different options.*
- *Study and publish the distributional effects of the current system and proposed reforms.* Such studies may prompt reform, since they are likely to show that the beneficiaries of subsidized pension schemes are mainly higher-income individuals. Similarly, governments may wish to express the opportunity costs of pension subsidies in concrete measures, such as the loss of x number of medicines or primary school textbooks. The redistribution of income from future to current generations implicit in most pay-as-you-go systems could also be quantified and highlighted to foster reforms that reduce the generosity of benefits for current pensioners.

As in other countries of the world, the real choice in Central America is not between reform or no reform, but between gradual and moderate reforms now or sudden and drastic reforms later. The later reform measures are adopted, the harsher they will have to be to address imbalances that will continue to accumulate under the current systems. Moreover, political resistance to pension reform may increase as pensioners become an increasing share of voters. Undertaking pension reform soon should therefore be a key priority for policymakers.

Appendix 3.1. Country-by-Country Descriptions of Recent Reforms

Costa Rica

Costa Rica started the process of reforming its old age pension system in 1990, with a view to enhancing financial sustainability. In 1990, retirement ages for the defined-benefit pension system under Costa Rica's social security administration (*Caja Costarricense de Seguro Social*–CCSS) were raised from 57 years to 61 years and 11 months for men, and from 55 years to 59 years and 11 months for women. In 1992, a general pension law was enacted whereby 19 different pension regimes were unified and consolidated under a single defined-benefit system, which was charged to the central government's budget, and incentives were given for affiliates to transfer to the CCSS regime.[20] Finally, the Worker Protection Act of 2000 transformed the national pension system into a four-pillar system by adding a mandatory defined-contribution pillar based on individual accounts and a voluntary defined-contribution pillar to the existing defined-benefit first pillar and the noncontributory, means-tested poverty alleviation pillar. The 2000 reform also transferred to the first pillar 15 percent of the profits of some public enterprises, with the amounts to be negotiated each year.

In April 2005, after a broad and extended consultation process, changes were introduced to the defined-benefit pillar that have improved its financial

[20]However, the National Teachers Union, the Finance Ministry, and the judiciary maintained separate regimes. For a summary of these reforms, see Acuña Ulate (2006).

sustainability. The reform raised workers' contributions by 0.5 percentage points every five years between 2010 and 2035, which will add 3 percentage points to the current 2.5 percent contribution rate. Replacement rates were also subjected to a progressive scale that effectively increased the rate for lower-income brackets and reduced it for higher-income brackets; as a result, average replacement rates were reduced by about 1.5 percentage points.[21] In addition, benefits are now based on average real earnings over the last 20 years of contributions, compared to average nominal earnings over the last four years of contributions before the reform. This reduces the scope for distortions, abuses, and inequity. The changes will be phased in gradually: for those aged 55 and over by the time of the reform, the old regime applies; for individuals between ages 44 and 55, the incidence of the changes varies inversely with age; for people under 44 years old, the reform applies in full. Finally, the minimum number of monthly contributions for those retiring at 65 was raised from 240 to 300. Overall, the reform is estimated to extend the financial sustainability of the regime by three decades.[22]

However, the reform was insufficient, and important challenges remain. In particular, the coverage of the pension system, though high relative to the region, is still unsatisfactory; evasion (lack of insurance or underreporting of salaries) and payment arrears are widespread; and administrative efficiency in terms of collection, investment performance, and benefit allocation could be improved. The special pension regimes in the government budget include privileges relative to the social security first pillar and are not subject to the same parameters as those introduced in the 2005 reform. And though the reform gave substantial breathing space to the social security administration's defined-benefit regime, further parametric revisions will be required to extend the life of the system beyond 2054. Finally, the design and structure of the mandatory and voluntary defined-contribution pillars may need rethinking, especially regarding the high administrative costs.

The new administration of President Oscar Arias has pledged to deepen pension system reform, in particular with respect to the noncontributory pillar, whose coverage and benefits it intends to improve.

[21]For instance, with 360 monthly contributions, the replacement rate for individuals earning less than twice the minimum wage was raised from 60.9 percent before the reform to 62.5 percent, while the replacement rate for individuals earning over eight times the minimum wage was reduced from 60.9 to 53 percent (Acuña Ulate, 2006).

[22]Thus, while the regime's reserves were projected to be depleted by 2024–28 before the reform, they are now estimated to last until 2054 (Acuña Ulate, 2006).

Dominican Republic

The Dominican Republic embarked on an ambitious reform of its pension system (old age, disability, and survivor insurance) in August 2001. The reform is scheduled to be phased in over a 10-year period and involves moving from a pay-as-you-go, defined-benefit system to privately-managed individual accounts. To integrate different groups within the same legal and institutional framework, three regimes were envisaged:

- A contributory regime designed for both private and public employees, under which participation is mandatory, except for workers above the age of 45 who could receive benefits under the old system;
- A subsidized regime designed to ensure that the elderly poor receive a minimum pension financed out of general revenue; and
- A subsidized-contributory regime designed to cover self-employed workers with earnings above the minimum wage, whose contributions would be supplemented by government subsidies that would vary inversely with a worker's income.

The reform of the pension system is being implemented gradually, though delays have arisen owing largely to the economic crisis of 2003–04. The key steps involving each of the regimes are detailed below.

The contributory regime was formally created in 2003. It requires employers and employees to contribute a combined 7 percent of the employee's earnings (increasing to 10 percent by 2008) to the employee's choice of one of eight pension funds. By end-2005, pension fund assets reached 2½ percent of GDP. The superintendency of pensions is evaluating measures to diversify investment opportunities (including real estate) and reduce the administrative costs of pension fund management companies.

The subsidized regime was launched in August 2004, although social assistance to the elderly is to be expanded gradually. The first stage envisioned providing minimum pensions to 150,000 poor households by the end of 2005.

The financial viability of some elements of the pension reform is being reconsidered in light of the fiscal constraints resulting from the banking crisis. The government is considering reducing the generosity and slowing down the expansion of the social assistance components of the reform, recognizing the need to bring public debt down from the current 50 percent of GDP to more comfortable levels.

El Salvador

The pay-as-you-go, defined-benefit system was replaced in 1998 by a system of privately-managed individual accounts. Participation in the new system was mandatory for workers under 36 years old and new entrants to the labor force, while women 50 and over and men 55 and over had to remain in the old system. Persons in the 36 to 50/55 age group had the option to remain in the old system or move to the new system. About 85 percent of these participants chose to move to the new system, as this was the default option. Recognition bonds, calculated at the time of transfer, were issued for each worker who switched. These bonds mature at the time of the participants' retirement.

The move to the new system created substantial transition costs because most of the contributors shifted to the private pension funds, while pension payments for older workers under the old system continue to require public funding.

The transition costs were significantly exacerbated by a decree in 2003 that offered a government guarantee to those who chose to switch to the new system. The decree guaranteed that those who chose to switch would receive a pension under the new system that is at least as large as the pension they would have received under the old system. This guarantee will require the government to top-up pensions at retirement for the vast majority of individuals in this cohort, since the returns on their individual accounts will almost certainly be less than the very high internal rates of return that they would have received under the old system. Consequently, this decree significantly increased the transition costs, which are projected to total 2 to 3 percent of GDP per year for the next several decades.

The Salvadorian government is exploring options to reduce the transition costs, including parametric reform of the old system that would reduce these costs while preserving the defined-contribution system with individual pension accounts.

In the second half of 2006, the obligations of the old pay-as-you-go system were transferred to a newly created fiduciary fund. Given the legal set-up of the fund, this change reduced the size of the measured nonfinancial public sector deficit. However, this (essentially accounting) change did not significantly affect the fiscal burden.

Guatemala

The Guatemalan authorities are in the process of devising a reform program to put the public pension system on a more sustainable path, but have not yet announced a specific plan. The authorities intend to address issues raised in the latest Financial Sector Assessment Program (FSAP) report, which suggests that, in the short term, Guatemala should:

- Conduct actuarial studies of the pension schemes for the private sector and civil servants and develop an actuarial capacity within the government and the social security administration;
- Complement actuarial modeling with comprehensive studies on possible reform options to address deficiencies;
- Develop principles for external audits and actuarial valuations of complementary pension funds and use moral suasion to encourage plan sponsors to follow them; and
- Review the fiscal framework of retirement products offered by financial institutions.

Furthermore, in the medium term, the FSAP suggests that Guatemala should:

- Prepare a reform agenda for the public pension schemes for the private sector and civil servants;
- Strengthen the overall governance and accountability framework of the public pension schemes; and
- Develop a proper regulatory and supervisory framework for complementary pension funds.

However, the prospect for social security reform during the tenure of the current administration is likely to diminish as the country enters the next presidential election campaign, scheduled for September 2007.

Honduras

In 2005, the Honduran government drafted a pension reform plan whose main features include parametric reforms of the existing defined-benefit first pillar; the gradual switching of government employees to the universal first pillar and the phasing-out of their current special regimes; and the introduction of a defined-contribution second pillar. The reform includes several positive elements that aim to correct some of the problems with the current system. However, the reform does not appear to fully put the pension system on a sustainable footing.

Since a new government was elected in November 2005, prospects for the previous administration's plan are unclear, since the new administration may develop a reform plan of its own.

Nicaragua

Nicaragua operates a pay-as-you-go, defined-benefit system. The system was originally put in place in 1955, the current law was enacted in 1982, and many of the parameters of the current system have been established by decree. While the system offers very generous benefits relative to contributions, it has historically remained in balance due to a young and growing population and the erosion of real pensions through inflation. Indeed, the system's cash flow is not projected to deteriorate significantly over the next decade. However, as the macroeconomic situation stabilizes and the population ages, the system will eventually require fundamental structural reform to be financially viable.

The authorities of the former government intended to prepare a reform strategy that would have put the public pension system on a sound financial footing, without relying on government subsidies. A previous reform in April 2000 aimed at transiting to a funded pension system, but this plan was dropped when a reassessment indicated that the transition costs would be prohibitively high. The national assembly approved a new social security law in May 2005 that increased benefits without raising contributions and weakened the system's governance structure. The president vetoed the law but was overridden by the assembly. Nonetheless, implementation of this law was deferred until after the November 2006 elections, and the next steps will be considered by the new government.

Panama

In Panama, the need for comprehensive pension reform became apparent by the early 2000s. During the 1990s, several assessments of Panama's pension system indicated a fundamental imbalance between contributions and benefits. By the early 2000s, financial reserves, which covered only a fraction of existing pension rights, started to decline and were projected to be exhausted by 2013.

Forging a political consensus on reform proved difficult. A national dialogue called by then-President Mireya Moscoso in 2001 failed to reach agreement on changes, as employers pressed for raising contribution rates and tightening eligibility and workers defended existing benefits. In 2004, the new government of President Martin Torrijos developed a parametric reform designed to tackle the system's actuarial imbalance, and the reform was passed by the assembly in June 2005. However, in response to strong popular opposition, the bill was not implemented, and President Torrijos launched a new national dialogue with civil society.

Following a five-month consultation process, the assembly approved a revised reform system in December 2005. It established a dual pension system in which individual pension accounts will coexist with a reformed defined-benefit scheme (after a transition period, the dual pension system will become fully effective in 2008). The reformed defined-benefit scheme will be similar to the partially-funded scheme in place before the reform, but with gradual parametric changes. Starting January 1, 2008, new members earning monthly wages of $500 or less will contribute solely to the defined-benefit system; workers earning more than $500 will contribute to the defined-benefit system on the portion of their salary up to $500, and to mandatory individual accounts managed by the social security administration on the portion exceeding $500, along with a "solidarity" contribution of 3.5 percent of their salary in excess of $500.

The new system will be phased in gradually. Under the transitional arrangements, new workers and workers age 35 or younger on January 1, 2006 will have the option to switch to the dual system by January 2008. Workers older than 35 will continue to contribute to the defined-benefit system based on their entire salary and will not have the option of contributing to individual accounts. It is estimated that about 70 percent of current and prospective affiliates are earning less than $500 a month and would therefore qualify solely for the defined-benefit system.

Increased financing for the defined-benefit system will come from the following main sources:

- Contribution rates (employee and employer combined) will be raised from 9.5 percent of wages to 11 percent in 2008, 12.5 percent in 2011, and 13.5 percent in 2013.
- The solidarity contribution (3.5 percent) levied on wages in excess of $500 will partially offset the loss of contributions channeled to individual savings accounts.
- The central government will provide substantial transfers to the defined-benefit scheme. In the long run, only the defined-contribution component, which is expected to be sustainable, will remain as the $500 per month limit shrinks in real terms.

Eligibility requirements will also be tightened. The minimum contribution period necessary to receive a full pension will be raised from 180 months at end-2007 to 216 months in 2008 and to 240 months in 2011. Arrangements will be introduced to mitigate the impact of the step-wise changes in eligibility requirements for pension benefits of workers within two years of the retirement age and having at least 180 monthly contributions. These workers will be entitled to a reduced pension. However, the retirement age will be unchanged unless mandatory annual actuarial reviews conclude that raising it is necessary to preserve the sustainability of the defined-benefit scheme.

The reform is expected to reduce the actuarial imbalance of the system by markedly increasing contribution rates, tightening eligibility requirements, and introducing safeguards that call for a revision of the main parameters if periodic actuarial assessments point to resurging imbalances. In this regard, increases in the retirement age may be required at some point in the future. Overall, the reform is an important step in the right direction, as it limits the contingent fiscal burden of the previous pension scheme and tightens the link between contributions and benefits.

References

Acuña Ulate, J.A., 2006, "Reformas recientes al régimen de invalidez, vejez y muerte," in *Los sistemas de pensiones: Presente y futuro,* ed. by G. López and C.E. Umaña (San José, Costa Rica: Academia de Centroamérica).

Cuevas, A., M. González, D. Lombardo, and A. López-Marmolejo, 2006, "Pension Privatization and Country

Risk" (unpublished; Washington: International Monetary Fund).

Holzmann, R., 1997, "Pension Reform, Financial Market Development, and Economic Growth: Preliminary Evidence From Chile," IMF *Staff Papers*, International Monetary Fund, Vol. 44, No. 2, pp. 149–78.

———, and E. Palmer, eds., 2006, *Pension Reform: Issues and Prospects for Nonfinancial Defined-Contribution Schemes* (Washington: World Bank).

International Monetary Fund, 2001, *Government Finance Statistics Manual 2001* (Washington: International Monetary Fund).

Lindert, K., E. Skoufias, and J. Shapiro, 2006, "Redistributing Income to the Poor *and* the Rich: Public Transfers in Latin America and the Caribbean" (unpublished; Washington: World Bank).

Organization for Economic Cooperation and Development, 2005, *Pensions at a Glance* (Paris: OECD).

Roldos, J., 2004, "Pension Reform, Investment Restrictions and Capital Markets," IMF Policy Discussion Paper No. 04/04 (Washington: International Monetary Fund).

Settergren, O. and B. Mikula, 2006, "The Rate of Return of Pay-As-You-Go Pensions Systems: A More Exact Consumption-Loan Model of Interest," in *Pension Reform: Issues and Prospects for Nonfinancial Defined-Contribution Schemes*, ed. by R. Holzmann and E. Palmer (Washington: World Bank).

Shoven, J., and S. Slavov, 2006, "Political Risk Versus Market Risk in Social Security," NBER Working Paper No. 12135 (Cambridge, Massachusetts: National Bureau of Economic Research).

Superintendencia de Pensiones, 2005, "Informe al Comite de Vigilancia del Regimen de Invalidez, Vejez, y Muerte" (San José, Costa Rica: Superintendencia de Pensiones).

Walker, E., and F. Lefort, 2002, "Pension Reform and Capital Markets: Are There Any (Hard) Links?" Social Protection Discussion Paper No. 0201 (Washington: World Bank).

World Bank, 2006, "Pension Reform and the Development of Pension Systems: An Evaluation of World Bank Assistance," Operations Evaluations Department Sector Study (Washington: World Bank).

IV Assessing Sovereign Debt Structures

André Faria and Guillermo Tolosa[1]

Since the Asian crises of the late 1990s, researchers and policymakers have put more emphasis on countries' balance sheets to identify sources of vulnerability. This has led several authors to advocate a "holistic" balance sheet approach as a complement to other surveillance practices to closely monitor these vulnerabilities and sectoral interlinkages.[2] A fragile balance sheet of a single sector of the economy might be enough to plunge a country into crisis due to the exposure of other sectors to that single sector. In Central America, assessing the vulnerabilities of the sovereign is of particular importance since the sovereign is the most important external debtor, with implications for the economy as a whole.[3] This chapter analyzes Central America's sovereign debt structures, considers how they evolved over time, and assesses the vulnerabilities implied by them.[4]

Analysis of Sovereign Debt Structure in the Context of a Balance Sheet Approach[5]

The balance sheet approach relies on the analysis of an economy's sectoral balance sheets to identify four types of risks that are typically at the origin of crises: currency, maturity, capital structure mismatches, and solvency risk.[6] Currency mismatches occur when assets and liabilities are denominated in different currencies; typically, a vulnerability may be present when assets are denominated in local currency, and liabilities are foreign-currency denominated. Likewise, maturity mismatches occur when assets and liabilities have different maturities: a vulnerability might be present when a sector has long-term assets and short-term liabilities. Capital structure mismatches are present when there is an excessive reliance on debt relative to equity. Solvency risk arises when the value of assets is lower than that of the liabilities. All these vulnerabilities tend to be inter-related.[7]

The public sector often plays a key role in the development of balance sheet vulnerabilities. Although the private sector was the root cause of several of the balance sheet crises in Asia—with the banking sector being the transmission mechanism for the rest of the economy[8]—the public sector is an important exter-

[1]We would like to thank Eduardo Borensztein, Marcos Chamon, Alfred Schipke, and Jeromin Zettelmeyer for helpful conversations and insightful comments to previous drafts. We also thank Luis Cubeddu, Mario Dehesa, Odd Hansen, Ivanna Vladkova Hollar, Koji Nakamura, and Jordi Prat for their help in gathering and cross-checking the data.

[2]Krugman (1999) was among the first economists to call attention to the importance of balance sheets in understanding the Asian crisis. For a review of the balance sheet approach, see Allen and others (2002) and Rosenberg and others (2005).

[3]For operational issues related to public debt management, see IMF and World Bank (2001).

[4]This chapter builds on previous work by the International Monetary Fund on sovereign structure and balance sheet vulnerabilities. The only Central American countries covered in this study are Costa Rica and Panama (Borensztein and others, 2004).

[5]The term "sovereign debt" is used to denominate the broadest possible category of public debt, including the central government (the sovereign) and subsovereign entities such as municipalities and nonfinancial sector public firms. Due to data limitations, coverage is not uniform across countries. Cowan and others (2006) and IDB (2006) collect data that are comparable across countries; however, in their dataset, composition of debt by currency or maturity is not available for several Central American countries.

[6]The sectors generally considered are the government, the financial sector (banks and other financial institutions), the nonfinancial private sector (corporations and households), and the rest of the world. This list follows the approach proposed by Allen and others (2002). They recognize, however, that there are several other risks or alternative categorizations. But the classification they adopt has "the advantage of highlighting the underlying mismatches that create sources of vulnerability from a debtor's perspective" (p. 15). As more data become available, a full balance sheet analysis for all Central American countries might be warranted.

[7]Rosenberg and others (2005) exemplify this approach by looking at countries that experienced balance sheet crises (Argentina, Turkey, and Uruguay) and at countries that avoided these crises (Brazil, Lebanon, and Peru). Lima and others (2006), in their study of sectoral balance sheet mismatches and macroeconomic vulnerabilities in Colombia, undertake probably the most complete country balance sheet analysis to date, especially focused on the private sector.

[8]For theoretical models on the vulnerabilities of private sector balance sheets as sources of currency crises, see Aghion, Bacchetta, and Banerjee (2000, 2001) and Krugman (1999). Burnside, Eichenbaum, and Rebelo (2001) and Schneider and Tornell (2004) develop models in which weak balance sheets of the private sector and banks subject to government bailout guarantees deliver "twin" currency and banking crises. Jeanne and Zettelmeyer (2002) survey this literature and study the role of international crisis lending in the context of models with currency and maturity mismatches that produce bank runs (for example, Burnside, Eichenbaum, and Rebelo, 2001), and in the context of models with currency (but no maturity) mismatches that result in credit crunches (Aghion, Bacchetta, and Banerjee, 2000 and 2001; Krugman, 1999; and Schneider and Tornell, 2004).

nal debtor in several emerging market and developing countries. In their comprehensive review of sovereign debt, Borensztein and others (2004) show that although sovereign debt stocks (as a percent of GDP) do not differ substantially between advanced economies and emerging market countries, the composition of public debt is strikingly dissimilar. Whereas government debt of advanced economies is typically placed domestically and denominated in local currency and at longer maturities, government debt of emerging market countries is placed internationally and denominated in foreign currency and at shorter maturities.[9]

A given debt structure is an endogenous outcome of political and institutional constraints and government behavior. For example, the currency composition of sovereign debt may be a reflection of the credibility of monetary policy (Bohn, 1990; Jeanne, 2003), and debt maturity may be a disciplining device to ensure that governments adopt good policies and are accountable to capital markets (Jeanne 2004; Tirole, 2002 and 2003).[10] That is, a given debt structure is the outcome of past and current economic policies and institutional circumstances, which in turn determine the level and quality of access to international capital.[11] Therefore, sound macroeconomic policies and better debt management, supported by a strengthened institutional framework, are likely to reduce the vulnerability of debt structures.[12]

Sovereign Debt Across Countries and Over Time

To assess potential vulnerabilities, this section analyzes sovereign debt structure in Central American countries over the past few years. It looks at the level and evolution of debt-to-GDP ratios, the jurisdiction of issue, creditor composition, currency denomination, and maturity structure.

The economies of Central America are very diverse. There are officially dollarized countries (El Salvador and Panama), nondollarized emerging market countries (Costa Rica, Guatemala, and the Dominican Republic), and countries that qualify for the Heavily Indebted Poor Countries (HIPC) Initiative (Honduras and Nicaragua). Keeping this in mind, this chapter highlights similarities and differences across the region.

Total Debt

Over the past few years, the non-HIPC countries have experienced, on average, an increase in sovereign debt as a proportion of GDP (Figure 4.1).[13] Guatemala has maintained a relatively low and stable debt-to-GDP ratio, while Panama's debt has been stable but at a higher level. By contrast, debt ratios have risen in El Salvador and especially in the Dominican Republic. From 2002 to 2003, the debt-to-GDP ratio in the Dominican Republic doubled from 27 percent to 56 percent. This abrupt increase in the level of debt is associated with a severe banking crisis, which resulted both in a bailout of a number of local banks and a sharp devaluation of the local currency.

As regards the HIPC countries, Honduras experienced a decline in the debt-to-GDP ratio during the period under consideration, while Nicaragua essentially had a similar debt-to-GDP ratio in 2000 and 2004. Both countries qualified for debt relief under the HIPC and Multilateral Debt Relief Initiatives from the IMF, the World Bank, and the Inter-American Development Bank, which are translating into significant debt reductions. In the case of Nicaragua, for example, public external debt levels are expected to fall from 120 percent of GDP in 2004 to about 45 percent of GDP in 2007.[14]

Creditor Composition

Creditor composition is strongly related to the overall economic performance of a country. In particular, access to international capital markets is an indication of strong economic performance. In addition, it has been found that the quality of policies is a fundamental variable to explain market access above and beyond the impact of those policies on growth (Gelos, Sahay, and Sandleris, 2004).

The creditor composition of the external debt of Central American countries highlights their heterogeneity (Figure 4.2). The two HIPC countries (Honduras and Nicaragua) have no access to international capital markets, whereas the non-HIPC countries (Costa Rica, El Salvador, Guatemala, Panama, and the Dominican Republic) have a profile similar to emerging market countries.

[9]This argument is developed extensively in IDB (2006) and Borensztein and others (2004).

[10]Other authors study the determinants of private sector debt composition and find that some of the factors that affect sovereign debt composition (credibility of monetary policy, risk of expropriation) also affect private sector debt composition (Arellano and Heathcote, 2004; Chamon, 2003; Jeanne, 2003; Tirole, 2002).

[11]Albuquerque (2003) and Tirole (2003) develop theoretical features that capture the financial, institutional, and political constraints that determine a country's access to international capital and the composition of its balance sheet. Faria and Mauro (2004) and Wei (2001) present evidence that good institutions tilt the balance sheet in favor of equity-like liabilities and increase the stock of foreign direct investment and portfolio equity (in percent of GDP).

[12]Sturzenegger and Zettelmeyer (2006) discuss institutional improvements that may make the debt structure less vulnerable.

[13]Comparisons are only indicative because the level of coverage varies across countries. This chapter only presents gross debt; net debt indicators could be significantly different. In addition, the level of implicit liabilities is also dramatically different given varying pension systems across the countries.

[14]This, however assumes full delivery of HIPC debt relief from non-Paris Club members and commercial creditors.

Figure 4.1. Composition of Sovereign Debt
(In percent of GDP)

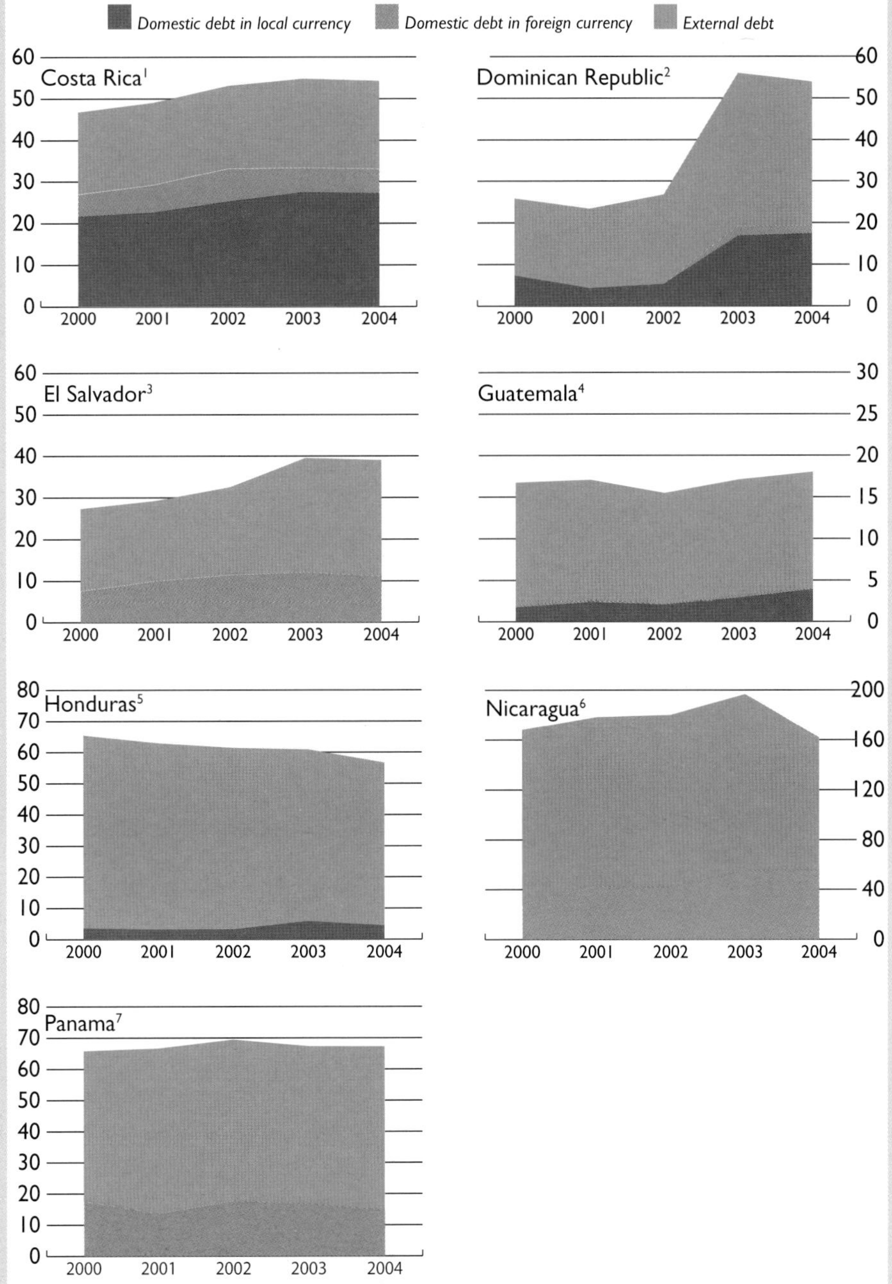

Sources: National authorities; and IMF staff calculations.
[1]Public sector.
[2]Nonfinancial public sector and central bank.
[3]Nonfinancial public sector.
[4]Central government.
[5]Nonfinancial public sector.
[6]Public sector and central bank.
[7]General government.

Figure 4.2. Structure of External Debt, 2001–05

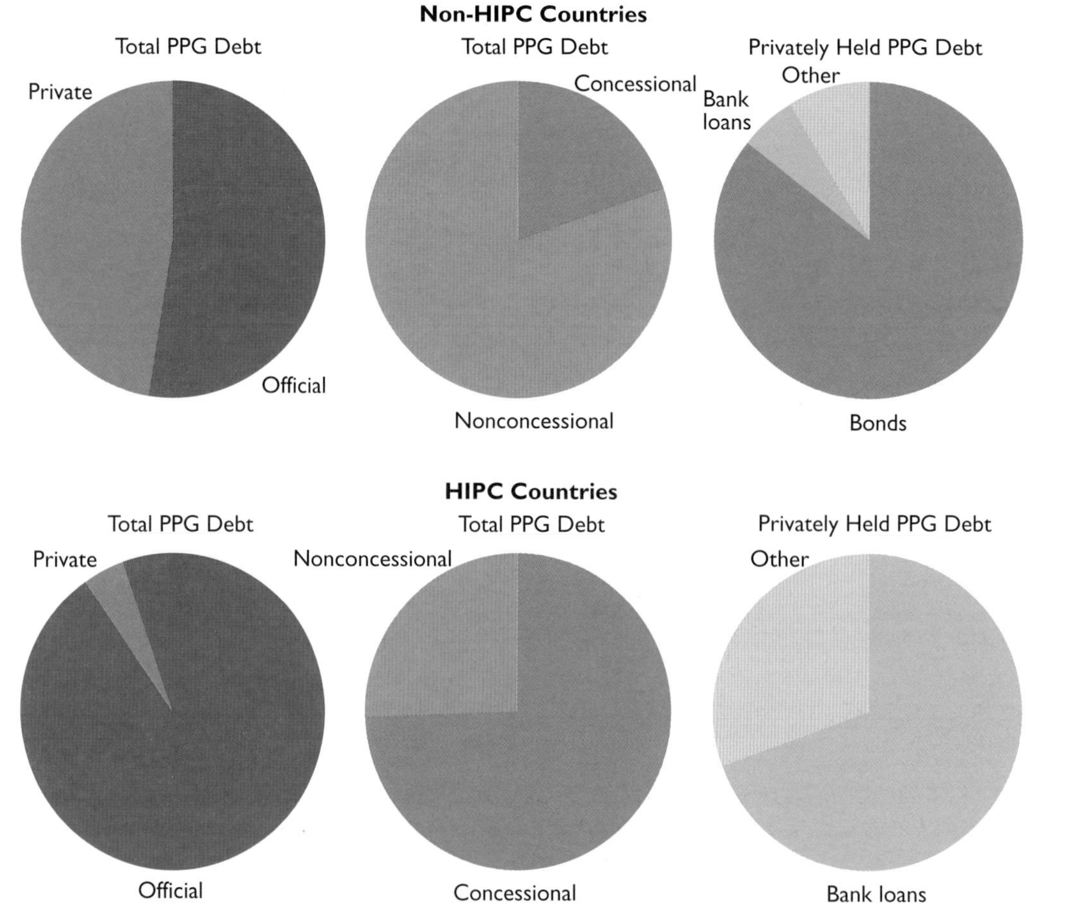

Sources: World Bank, *Global Development Finance* (2004); and IMF staff calculations.
Note: External debt is public and publicly guaranteed (PPG) debt. PPG debt is an external obligation of a public debtor (including the national government, a political subdivision, or an agency of either, and autonomous public bodies) or of a private debtor that is guaranteed for repayment by a public entity outstanding at year-end that has an original or extended maturity of more than one year. The non-HIPC group consists of Costa Rica, Dominican Republic, El Salvador, Guatemala, and Panama. The group of HIPC countries includes Honduras and Nicaragua.

The non-HIPC countries have roughly half of their debt held by the private sector,[15] 80 percent of total external debt is nonconcessional, and more than 85 percent of privately held financing takes the form of bonds. By contrast, HIPC countries are almost exclusively financed by the official sector, mostly through concessional loans, and 80 percent of privately held financing is done through the banking sector (and none takes the form of bonds).

Jurisdiction

The ability of the sovereign to place debt in local markets is a sign of economic strength. A larger share of domestic debt reflects a strong contractual environment. It allows the sovereign to reduce exposure to sometimes volatile international capital markets.[16]

[15]This average also disguises important heterogeneity among the group of emerging market countries. From 2001 to 2004, Panama was the only country whose creditors were mostly private (80 percent). Costa Rica and the Dominican Republic saw an increase in the percentage of debt held by private creditors toward the end of the period. In 2004, both countries had more than 50 percent of their debt held by private creditors.

[16]This chapter uses the terms domestic debt as debt issued in a domestic jurisdiction. Domestic debt is thus different from domestic currency debt.

Figure 4.3. Foreign Currency Debt
(In percent of total debt)

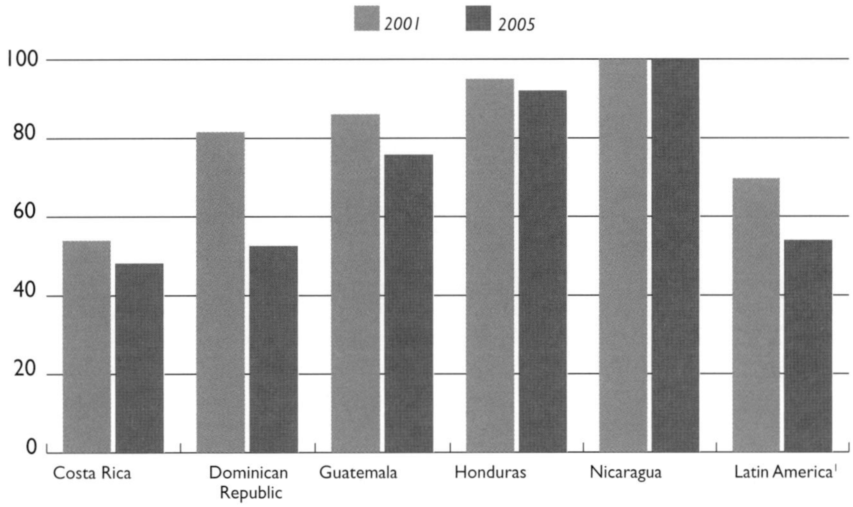

Sources: National authorities; and IMF staff calculations.
Note: Sovereign debt coverage differs across countries.
[1]Includes Argentina, Brazil, Chile, Colombia, Mexico, Peru, and Uruguay.

Developed countries have typically financed a large share of their total debt in their mature local markets. Developing countries in general, and Central America in particular, rely to a much larger extent on international markets. In Central America, on average, only 30 percent of sovereign debt is placed domestically. Costa Rica is the only country in Central America for which domestic debt represents more than 50 percent of sovereign debt.

However, in recent years, developing countries have been able to increase their share of debt financed in domestic markets (World Bank, 2005; IDB, 2006). Central America has been no exception to this trend, and every country in the region (with the exception of Panama) has increased the fraction of debt issued domestically. On average, this share increased by 5 percentage points. The country with the most dramatic change was the Dominican Republic. From 2002 to 2003, its share of domestic debt increased by more than 15 percent, reflecting in large part the need to engage in open market operations to offset the massive liquidity injection after the banking crisis.

Currency Denomination

It is now widely accepted that the currency denomination of debt has important macroeconomic consequences. In particular, it plays a critical role in macroeconomic adjustments to external shocks, and it has been a key factor in recent financial crises (Allen and others, 2002; Rosenberg and others, 2006). Currency mismatches not only increase the likelihood of a crisis, but also make it more costly to get out of one (Goldstein and Turner, 2004). Also, currency mismatches can severely constrain monetary and fiscal policies.

Central America has a higher share of foreign currency debt in total debt than other Latin American countries (Figure 4.3).[17,18] However, from 2001 to 2005, the region experienced some improvement, in particular in Guatemala and the Dominican Republic.[19] A reduction of currency mismatches was also experienced by other Latin America countries, and may be associated with benign worldwide conditions for emerging market countries.

[17]This basic indicator is used for comparability. See the section in this chapter on currency mismatch and Box 4.1 for a more complete discussion of measures of currency mismatches and their use in assessing sovereign debt vulnerabilities in Central America.

[18]We exclude from the analysis officially dollarized countries. While the real exchange rate could still move in these countries, they are unlikely to be subject to major shocks and, as emphasized by Mussa (1986), they are generally much less volatile under fixed exchange rate regimes (of which full dollarization is an extreme example) than under floating exchange rate regimes.

[19]Within Latin America, the ratio went up slightly for Mexico and Uruguay, and decreased significantly for Argentina and, especially, Brazil.

Box 4.1. Measures of Currency Mismatch Risk

A currency mismatch in the balance sheet of a sector exists when assets and liabilities are denominated in different currencies. Exchange variations are likely to affect assets and liabilities differently. Therefore, a meaningful measure of currency mismatch risk computes the impact a change in the (real) exchange rate has on the leverage ratio (ratio of liabilities to assets). This box presents the measure this chapter uses to assess currency mismatch risk—elasticity of the ratio of liabilities to assets to real exchange rate movements—and covers in a unified way the different measures proposed in the literature.

Standard Measure

A standard and widely used measure of currency mismatch looks at the ratio of foreign currency debt to total debt:

$$\sigma = \frac{eB^*}{B+eB^*},$$

where B and B^* are the sovereign debt in local and foreign currency, and e is the real exchange rate. This measure relates to the "original sin" index created by Eichengreen, Hausmann, and Panizza (2005). However, as it was discussed in detail by Goldstein and Turner (2004), it neglects the asset side of the sovereign (indeed, it implicitly assumes that all assets are in local currency—see below). Moreover, insofar as the tradable component of assets of the sovereign changes over time and across countries, this measure is not adequate for time series and/or cross-country comparisons.

Despite these shortcomings, this measure has been widely used, most of all because of its simplicity. For this same reason and for comparibility with the related literature, this chapter uses this measure for the analysis of the debt structure and its determinants. In the subsection dedicated to debt vulnerabilities, this is one of the three measures used to calculate the currency mismatch.

New Measure

In addition to the standard measure of currency mismatch, this chapter proposes a new measure of currency mismatch risk that looks at the composition of assets and liabilities. Assuming for now, for the sake of comparability with some standard measures, that GDP is a good proxy for the assets of the sovereign, an alternative currency mismatch measure is:

$$\gamma = \frac{\dfrac{eB^*}{B+eB^*}}{\dfrac{eY^*}{Y+eY^*}},$$

where Y and Y^* are the nontradable and tradable components of GDP, and B and B^* are the sovereign debt in local and foreign currency. If the ratio equals 1, the composition of liabilities and assets are perfectly matched. In the case in which the sovereign issues all its debt in foreign currency, the ratio is equal to the inverse of the share of tradables in the economy (therefore, larger than 1). If all sovereign debt is issued in local currency, γ is equal to zero. This ratio relates closely to the measure used throughout the chapter, ξ, which has a meaningful interpretation:

$$\xi = \frac{\partial \ln\left(\dfrac{B+eB^*}{Y+eY^*}\right)}{\partial \ln e} = \frac{eB^*}{B+eB^*} - \frac{eY^*}{Y+eY^*}.$$

In this case, ξ is a measure of currency mismatch risk: this elasticity gives the percentage change in the debt-to-GDP ratio as a consequence of a 1 percent increase in the real exchange rate. The standard measure, σ, equals ξ in the case in which the tradable component of GDP, Y^*, is zero. This assumption is obviously extreme, so σ is an upper bound to the effective change in the debt-to-GDP ratio as a result of a 1 percent increase.

To assume that the GDP is a proxy for the sovereign's assets is an extreme assumption, as the sovereign is not able to fully appropriate GDP without substantially reducing it (among other reasons, owing to incentive problems and the inalienability of human capital; see Hart and Moore, 1994). Government primary surpluses are a more reasonable proxy for the sovereign's assets; however, the division of the government accounts in

Maturity Structure

A high percentage of short-term debt can expose the sovereign to rollover risk. The sovereign's main assets are essentially illiquid and long term while its liabilities can be short term, leaving it exposed to a maturity mismatch that can potentially lead to a liquidity crisis.[20] In spite of the risks involved, it might still be optimal for governments to borrow short term under certain conditions, for instance because of investor risk aversion or of underlying fragilities that provide incentives to investors to avoid longer-term lending.[21]

The presence of short-term debt in market access countries in Central America is highest in Costa Rica and the Dominican Republic (Figure 4.4). Panama, Guatemala and El Salvador have minimal levels of short-term debt (indeed, Guatemala has no short-term

[20]Detragiache and Spilimbergo (2001) show that the share of short-term debt is important in explaining liquidity crisis.

[21]See Calvo (1988), Missale and Blanchard (1994), and Jeanne (2004) on moral hazard problems; see Broner, Lorenzoni, and Schmukler (2005) on investor risk aversion; and see Bussière, Fratzcher, and Koeniger (2004) on underlying fragilities.

tradable and nontradable components is nontrivial. An alternative measure that looks at the government's budget more seriously incorporates the net present value of government's expenditures on the liability side and the present value of government's revenues on the asset side. (Burnside, Eichenbaum, and Rebelo, 2006, show that for some countries the effect of currency devaluation in government accounts, or "implicit fiscal reforms," can be considerably large.)

This approach divides current government expenditures into two components: tradable and nontradable. Assuming the composition of government expenditures and the total share of government expenditure in GDP remain unchanged, it computes the net present value of local and foreign-currency-denominated government expenditures. These components are added to debt components and the totals are assumed to represent the totality of the sovereign's liabilities. For the asset side, the net present value of revenues is added to reserves to form total assets. The share of the tradable component of revenues is then assumed to be equal to the share of tradables in the economy (exports to GDP). Using this ratio, the net present value of the tradable component of revenues is computed. Foreign-currency-denominated assets are the net present value of the tradable component of revenues and reserves. The computation of the elasticity of the leverage ratio is then straightforward.

As discussed in the main text, elasticities alone may not provide meaningful information in terms of debt-sustainability analysis. Multiplying the elasticity by the initial debt-to-GDP ratio would allow the policymaker to fully realize the impact of changes of the real exchange rate on that ratio.

Other Measures

The new measure of currency mismatch proposed in this chapter, ξ, relates to other measures developed in the literature, namely those created by Goldstein and Turner (2004) and Calvo, Izquierdo, and Talvi (2003).

Rescaling γ by the ratio of (net) foreign currency debt to GDP delivers a sovereign debt equivalent of the aggregate effective currency mismatch measure proposed by Goldstein and Turner (2004).

The measure γ also relates to the one proposed by Calvo, Izquierdo, and Talvi (2003):

$$\tau = \frac{\frac{B}{eB^*}}{\frac{Y}{eY^*}}.$$

The scale of this measure is inverted when compared with γ: the closer to zero, the larger the currency mismatch risk; the larger the number, the smaller the currency mismatch. Its relation with γ is given by

$$\tau = \frac{Y + eY^*(1-\gamma)}{\gamma Y}.$$

When γ equals zero (no currency mismatch), τ is infinite; τ is zero when γ equals the inverse share of tradables in GDP, that is, when all sovereign debt is in foreign currency; when both economies are fully hedged both measures are equal to 1. The drawback of the measure proposed by Calvo, Izquierdo and Talvi (2004), τ, comes from the fact that it delivers the maximum currency mismatch risk when a country has no domestic debt, regardless of the openness of the economy.

To illustrate the difference between τ and γ, consider two economies, A and B, that borrow exclusively in foreign currency but which have different levels of openness: economy A has an ε share of its GDP in tradables, and economy B has an ε share of its GDP in nontradables, where ε is an arbitrarily small number different from zero. The measure proposed by Calvo, Izquierdo, and Talvi (2003) delivers the larger currency mismatch for both economies, $\tau=0$.

However, γ distinguishes clearly between both cases: for A, $\gamma=\frac{1}{\varepsilon}$, that is, very large (large currency mismatch) and for B, $\gamma=\frac{1}{1-\varepsilon}$, that is, very close to 1 (perfect hedging). The main advantage of τ is its invariance to the real exchange rate. In net terms, γ and especially ξ are more meaningful measures of currency mismatch risk.

debt at all). Overall, the region compares relatively well with other Latin American countries.[22]

The average remaining maturity of emerging markets' sovereign debt has increased considerably in recent years (IMF, 2006), and, over 2001–05, the short-term exposure of Latin American countries was reduced, albeit moderately. These broad movements across emerging markets reflect a cyclical reduction in the risk aversion of investors, a global decrease in long-term rates, and improved creditworthiness because of stronger economic conditions. In Central America, El Salvador reduced its short-term exposure while Panama's and Costa Rica's exposure remained broadly unchanged. In contrast, that of the Dominican Republic increased significantly.

Determinants of Debt Structure

Analyses of the determinants of debt structures have long been hampered by the paucity of data. Partly as a result, no consensus has yet emerged on optimal policies to make debt structures safer. Lately, new important data sets have been developed that have pro-

[22]The classification of short-term debt throughout the chapter is on the basis of original maturity.

Figure 4.4. Short-Term Debt
(In percent of total debt)

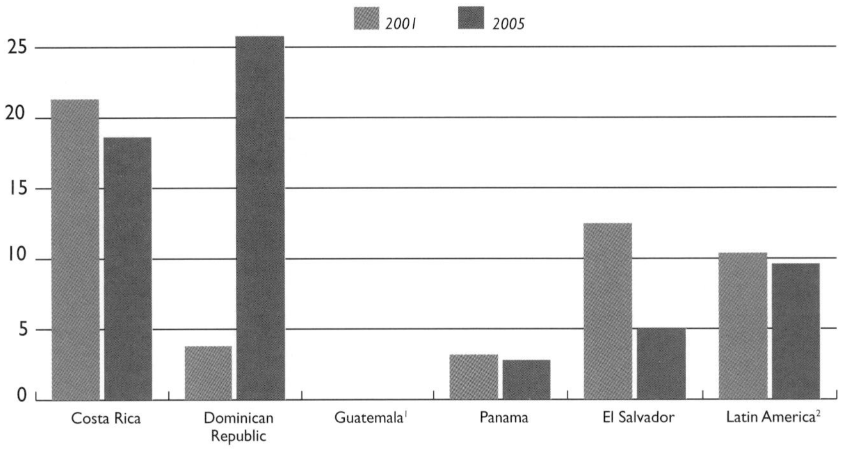

Sources: National authorities; and IMF staff calculations.
Note: Sovereign debt coverage differs across countries.
[1]Guatemala reported no short-term debt for either 2001 or 2005.
[2]Includes Argentina, Brazil, Chile, Colombia, Mexico, Peru, Uruguay, and Venezuela.

vided important insights.[23] This section aims to confirm some of the results obtained in the literature by using a sample of 27 market access countries to gain some additional perspective on the relative situation of the Central American countries.[24]

Domestic Debt

The literature finds that reliance on debt issued domestically depends importantly on contract enforcement, market size, and investor base. These results were confirmed in our sample by running a cross-country regression using as proxies, respectively, the rule of law indicator (obtained from Kaufmann, Kraay, and Mastruzzi, 2005), total GDP, and M2/GDP. These variables are all statistically significant at standard levels.[25] Countries with weaker contract enforcement give less protection to investors against confiscation risk and the severity of loss in case of default, creating more incentives for them to rely on debt issued in foreign jurisdictions. While foreign jurisdictions have not delivered much in terms of recovery of assets, they have been effective in excluding countries from debt markets, and thus create a credible threat that indirectly provides greater protection to investors.[26]

Differences in domestic issuance across non-HIPC Central American countries can largely be explained by these factors as well. Figure 4.5 and Table 4.1 show that they can account for the fact that Costa Rica relies more heavily on the domestic market than economies with smaller size and weaker performance on the rule of law indicator. Other less conventional factors, such as the exchange rate regime, could explain the remaining differences. The full dollarization of Panama may explain why it relies so little on the domestic market, as the perfect substitutability of local and foreign currencies may make it more attractive to place debt in international markets.

The determinants of debt jurisdiction in HIPC countries (Honduras and Nicaragua) are significantly different. Given that most external debt is official, which typically does not entail rollover risks, and is granted at concessional rates, this type of debt is generally a more attractive option from a vulnerability perspective.

[23]See Jeanne and Guscina (2006), Cowan and others (2006), and Jaimovich and Panizza (2006). See IDB (2006) for a comparative analysis.

[24]The data correspond to 2004. The main advantage of the data set collected from IMF country desks is that it provides data on currency denomination and maturity structure for a large set of countries. The main disadvantage is the inconsistency of debt definitions across countries, making an outright cross-country comparison vulnerable to criticisms.

[25]Variables are significant at the 95 percent level. Other variables, including GDP per capita were not significant. These results are consistent overall with other research on the determinants of domestic debt share. Claessens, Klingebiel, and Schmukler (2003) find poor enforcement of creditor rights and a narrow local investor base to be important. Also, Cowan and others (2006) find market size (measured by GDP) and level of development to be important.

[26]See Sturzenegger and Zettelmeyer (2006). The usual caveat applies in that it is also possible that the rule of law is correlated with other variables not included in the analysis.

Figure 4.5. Domestic Debt: Predicted and Actual
(Based on regression with financial development, total GDP, and rule of law as independent variables)

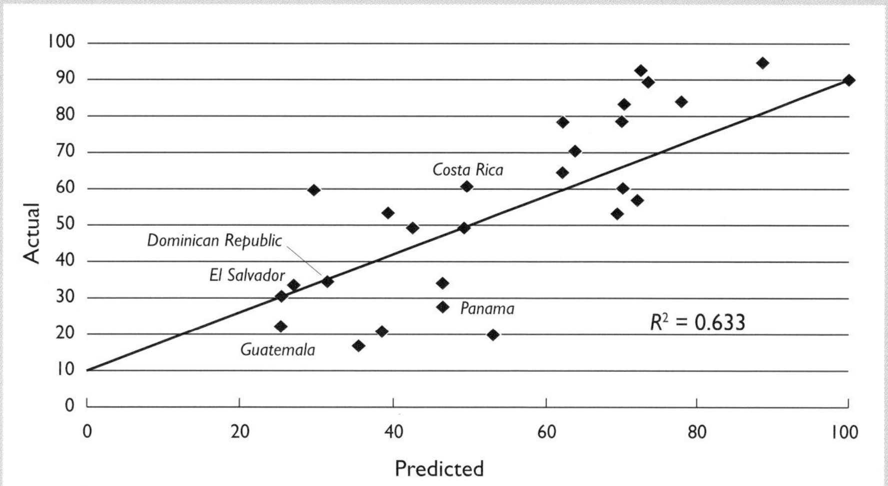

Table 4.1. Domestic Debt Share Determinants

	Rule of Law	GDP	M2/GDP
Costa Rica	0.57	18.53	37.62
Dominican Rep.	–0.54	18.44	38.17
Panama	–0.04	14.20	74.65
Guatemala	–0.96	25.96	30.53
El Salvador	–0.34	15.82	4.74
Sample average	–0.11	4.74	50.11

Sources: Kaufmann, Kraay, and Mastruzzi (2005); and IMF, *International Financial Statistics.*

The share of external debt in total debt is thus mainly constrained by the availability of official financing.

Foreign Currency Debt

For non-HIPC countries, the ability to issue debt domestically is critical to be able to issue debt in domestic currency (Figure 4.6a). Relying on a foreign jurisdiction for contracting debt with private creditors almost inevitably implies reliance on foreign currency debt.[27] In Central America, Costa Rica has been the most successful in issuing a high share of debt in domestic currency, while Guatemala has been least successful given its more limited ability to tap domestic markets. The Dominican Republic has stood in the middle of these two extreme cases.[28]

Countries may also be unable to issue domestic currency debt because of poor credibility of monetary policy.[29] Limited monetary policy credibility can in turn be related to a history of high inflation, which can potentially sharply reduce the ability of the sovereign to issue long-term debt in domestic currency (Figure 4.6b), or be associated with poor institutions or a weak policy framework (see Chapter VI).[30] While inflation has come down in Central America in line with other emerging markets, the fall in inflation does not immediately translate into improved debt structures, which tend to show significant persistence.

Foreign currency debt could also be a consequence of an unconstrained optimization of the debt portfolio, given the evolution of expected return and variance of portfolios. For example, it is the optimal hedging strategy when the volatility of inflation is considerably higher than the volatility of the real exchange rate.[31]

[27]For some hypothesis related to this fact, see Hausmann and Panizza (2003). For some notable country exceptions see IDB (2006, Chapter 2).

[28]Dollarized countries still face real exchange rate variations that can make debt service more burdensome in bad times, but they avoid the abrupt and sizable changes that typically come with currency crisis.

[29]This phenomenon has been dubbed as the domestic dimension of the "original sin."

[30]See Hausmann and Panizza (2003); Borensztein and others (2004); Mehl and Reynaud (2005); and Jeanne and Guscina (2006).

[31]See Ize and Levy-Yeyati (2003) for the theoretical argument; and IMF (2006) for an application for sovereign debt. We did not test this result on our sample given that restrictions referred to in the previous paragraphs are most likely be binding for many of the countries in the sample.

Figure 4.6a. Domestic Debt and Foreign Currency Debt Share

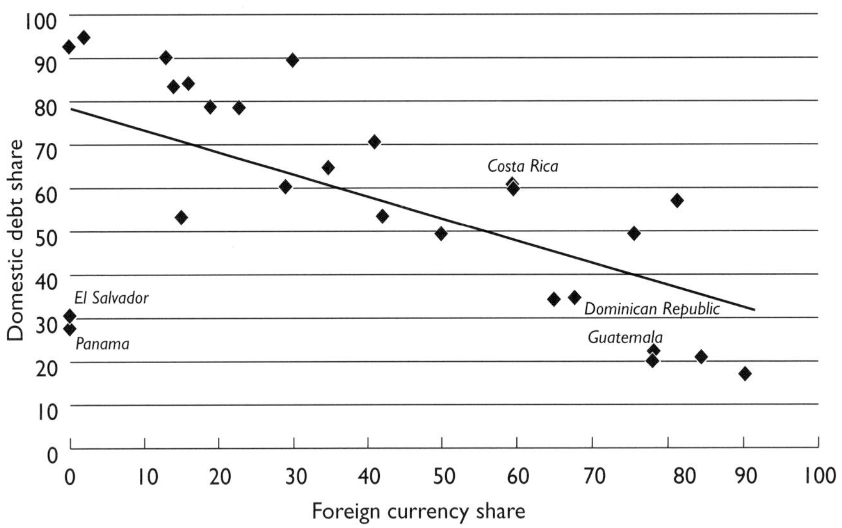

Another key dimension in the optimality of this type of debt is the correlation of the exchange rate with public revenue. A way to capture these elements is to consider the relative volatility of public revenue in terms of foreign currency, domestic currency, and indexed domestic currency. Ideally, debt should be denominated in those units in which public revenue exhibits the lowest volatility. Only Costa Rica seems to have a clear hedging argument to become indebted in dollars, which might be a possible reason why it seems to be issuing more foreign-currency-denominated debt than expected based on its capacity to issue domestically and its inflation history. In the case of Guatemala, there is no clear case for hedging, thus raising questions about the desirability of such a high share of foreign currency borrowing.

Short-Term Debt

The determinants of issuing debt at shorter maturities are less well understood, partly reflecting the limited empirical work in this area. Much of the literature deals with the common factors behind risky debt structures in general,[32] and while some authors do focus on the maturity profile of debt, they generally consider economy-wide debt as opposed to sovereign debt. However, one possible cause of this vulnerability is the presence of high total debt (Rodrik and Velasco, 1999; Missale, 1999). The higher the level of debt, the bigger the incentive to default could be, and thus the shorter the maturity at which investors are willing to lend.[33] Past defaults may also have important consequences on present investor willingness to lend longer term (Reinhart, Rogoff, and Savastano, 2003).

An empirical analysis based on our sample suggests that the level of total debt is the only significant variable to explain the share of short-term debt. The rule of law variable does not show a strong association in this case, and neither does M2/GDP, the size of the economy, or past inflation, casting doubt on the view of common underlying factors for both currency and maturity vulnerabilities. Nor did default history and income (proxied by GDP per capita), as indicators of institutional strength, turn up to be important determinants of the level of short-term debt in our small sample.[34] Finally, foreign currency debt was not significant either. Two contrasting channels may be at play here: the exogenous presence of foreign currency debt increases financial fragilities that translate into high short-term debt (Bussière, Fratzcher, and Koeniger, 2004);[35] and, in contrast, for a given level of institutional and policy weaknesses, short-term debt is an alternative risk-coping mechanism to foreign currency risk.

[32]See Hausmann and Panizza (2003); Reinhart, Rogoff, and Savastano (2003); and Mehl and Reynaud (2005).

[33]Total debt may be capturing the likelihood of future defaults. Our results thus suggest markets are forward-looking and have a short-term memory.

[34]Investor composition may also be an important factor as potential creditors aim to match duration of assets and liabilities.

[35]de la Torre and Schmukler (2004) explicitly make this argument, calling it, as suggested by Ricardo Caballero, the "conservation principle." Hausmann and Panizza (2003) and Mehl and Renaud (2005) implicitly assume that the determinants of maturity and currency denomination are the same by considering determinants of the amount of long-term debt in domestic currency, or what they call the liberation of "original sin."

Figure 4.6b. Inflation History and Foreign Currency Debt

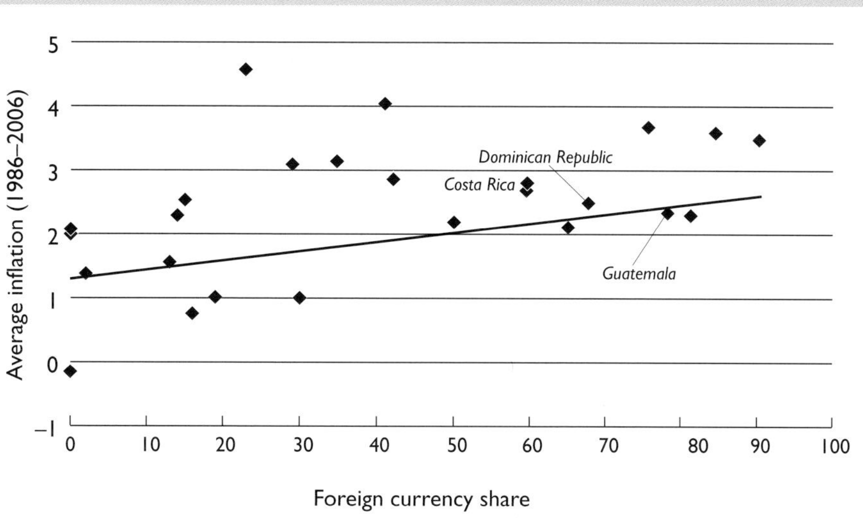

For Central American countries, the share of short-term debt can only be partially explained by the total level of debt, the only significant variable mentioned above. Costa Rica and the Dominican Republic show relatively more short-term debt than expected, Guatemala is near the predicted value, and Panama and El Salvador have considerably less short-term debt share than expected (Figure 4.7). These differences suggest that official dollarization might be playing a role in allowing countries to issue debt at longer maturities.

Closer Look at Vulnerabilities

Currency Mismatch

The first measure, shown in Table 4.2, computes for non-dollarized countries the elasticity of total debt to GDP with respect to the real exchange rate—the percentage change in the total-debt-to-GDP ratio following a 1 percent change in the real exchange rate. This measure assumes that the only effect of a real exchange rate change on GDP is a valuation effect.[36] This elasticity is computed by taking the difference between the share of foreign currency debt in total debt and the share of tradable goods (and services) in the economy. An elasticity of zero means that the economy is fully hedged, i.e., a change in the real exchange rate does not affect the debt-to-GDP ratio. An elasticity larger (smaller) than zero means that a devaluation worsens (improves) the debt-to-GDP ratio. Based on this measure, all Central American countries with the exception of Nicaragua reduced their currency mismatch between 2001 and 2004. Costa Rica even managed to fully hedge its position in 2004. In 2004, Nicaragua was the country with the largest currency mismatch.[37]

The elasticity of total debt to GDP with respect to the real exchange rate as a measure of currency mismatch is informative but, nevertheless, incomplete. This measure alone is unsuitable for a meaningful debt sustainability analysis because the initial ratios of debt are also important inputs. Rescaling such elasticity by the initial debt-to-GDP ratio would allow for a more meaningful stress test exercise.[38] In 2004, Guatemala had an elasticity larger than that of Costa Rica and the Dominican Republic. Despite this, Guatemala's debt-to-GDP ratio after a 30 percent devaluation would remain

[36]Despite the fact that this measure represents an improvement on traditional currency mismatch measures, it is not exempt from important caveats. It neglects three other effects besides the valuation effect: endogenous changes to the GDP structure (most notably, elasticity of exports); changes to GDP due to currency mismatches in the private sector—a currency mismatch on the private sector side might trigger a crisis with real effects (for example, a banking crisis), thus lowering GDP measured in local currency by more than the real exchange rate effect; and changes in debt due to currency mismatches in the private sector—the sovereign might be tempted to bail out the private sector, thus issuing more debt to finance it, further deteriorating the debt-to-GDP ratio.

[37]A transformation of this measure to include reserves on the sovereign's asset side does not change the elasticities significantly. For 2001, the largest change was a reduction in the elasticity of 1 percent in the case of Nicaragua; for 2004, the largest change was a reduction in the elasticity of 0.9 percent in the case of Honduras. Smallest changes were on the order of 0.1 percent for Panama (2001 and 2004) and the Dominican Republic (2004).

[38]A rescaling in this spirit was also proposed by Goldstein and Turner (2004).

Figure 4.7. Short-Term Share and Total Debt

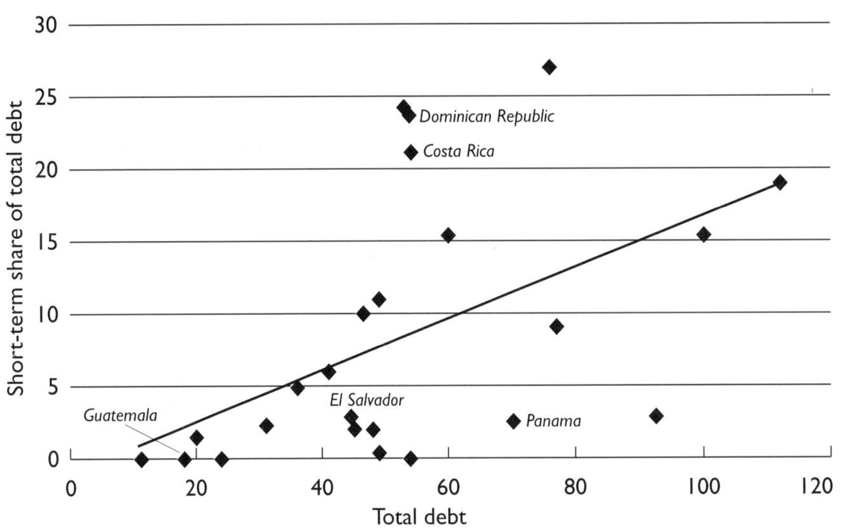

substantially lower than those of these other countries (Figure 4.8).[39]

As has been traditional in debt sustainability analyses and in the macroeconomic literature, the previous measures of currency mismatch risk for the sovereign assumed GDP as a proxy for the sovereign's assets. This is an extreme assumption, as the sovereign is not able to fully appropriate GDP. Government primary surpluses are likely to be a more reasonable proxy for the sovereign's assets. However, the division of the primary surplus in tradable and nontradable components is nontrivial. We develop a measure that looks at the government budget to compute the net present value of government revenue and expenditure. (See Box 4.1 for a more complete discussion of the methodology and related literature.)

The second alternative measure of currency mismatch, shown in Table 4.3, computes the elasticity of the sovereign's leverage ratio—total liabilities to total assets—with respect to the real exchange rate. This elasticity is simply the difference between the share of foreign currency liabilities in total liabilities and the share of foreign currency assets in total assets. As described above, this elasticity takes into account the composition of government expenditures and revenue by decomposing each of them in tradables and nontradables. Assuming the composition of government expenditure and the total share of government expenditure in GDP remain unchanged, it computes the net present value of local and foreign-currency-denominated government expenditure. These components are added to debt components and the totals are assumed to represent the totality of the sovereign's liabilities. For the asset side, the net present value of revenue is added to reserves to form total assets. The share of the tradable component of revenues is then assumed to be equal to the share of tradables in the economy (exports

Table 4.2. Elasticity of Ratio of Debt to GDP vis-à-vis the Real Exchange Rate

	2001	2004
Costa Rica	0.13	–0.01
Dominican Republic	0.43	0.16
Honduras	0.57	0.57
Nicaragua	0.76	0.78
Guatemala	0.67	0.61

Sources: National authorities; World Bank, *World Development Indicators* (2005); and IMF staff calculations.

Note: Foreign currency to total debt minus share of tradables in the economy. A value equal to zero implies perfect hedging. A value larger than zero worsens the debt-to-GDP ratio.

[39]In fact, such an exercise is biased against more open economies. As shown by Calvo, Izquierdo, and Talvi (2003), a more open economy is less likely to experience a devaluation. Therefore, for the same share of foreign currency debt in total debt, more open economies are less exposed to a crisis because the currency mismatch is smaller and the likelihood of devaluation is also lower.

Table 4.3. Elasticity of the Sovereign's Leverage Ratio vis-à-vis the Real Exchange Rate

	2001	2004
Costa Rica	–0.15	–0.20
Dominican Republic	–0.09	–0.21
Honduras	–0.05	–0.03
Nicaragua	0.30	0.24
Guatemala	0.07	0.07

Sources: National authorities; World Bank, *World Development Indicators* (2005); and IMF staff calculations.

Note: Foreign currency liabilities to total liabilities minus foreign currency assets to total assets. A value equal to zero implies perfect hedging. A value larger than zero worsens the leverage ratio.

to GDP). Using this ratio, the net present value of the tradable component of revenue is computed. Foreign-currency-denominated assets are the net present value of the tradable component of revenues and reserves. Given that a large fraction of government expenditure is nontradable, the currency mismatch measure is significantly lower than the previous one for all countries. As with the previous measures, in 2004, Nicaragua was the country with the largest currency mismatch.

Maturity Mismatch

The level of international reserves is an important indicator to assess the vulnerabilities associated with short-term debt.[40] As indicated earlier, the Dominican Republic and Costa Rica are the only countries with a significant short-term exposure. However, once reserves are considered, both countries exhibit a ratio of short-term debt to reserves larger than 1 (Table 4.4).[41]

Short-term debt is risky not only because of the rollover risk but also because it entails risk in terms of exposure to variation in interest rates. This interest rate risk also applies to debt of longer maturities issued at a variable interest rate. In Central America, variable interest rate debt is relatively common (Figure 4.9). El Salvador appears to be the most exposed to interest rate variations in this case. In this sense, El Salvador

[40]A longstanding rule of thumb, the "Guidotti-Greenspan rule," indicates that international reserves should be at least equal to short-term debt and amortization coming due.

[41]Rodrik and Velasco (1999) document that during the Asian crisis, Indonesia, the Philippines, South Korea, and Thailand all had a ratio larger than 1. Malaysia was the only country of the group surveyed that had a ratio smaller than 1. By the end of 1997, the ratio of Korea exceeded 3.

Figure 4.8. Sovereign Debt
(In percent of GDP)

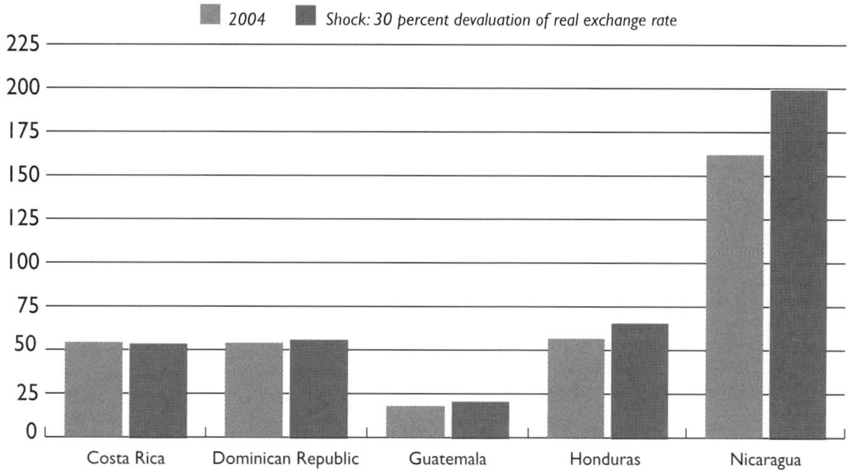

Sources: National authorities; and IMF staff calculations.
Note: Sovereign debt coverage differs across countries.

Table 4.4. Ratio of Short-Term Debt to Reserves

	2001	2005
Costa Rica	1.46	0.83
Dominican Republic	0.15	1.69

seems to be trading off the option of having higher short-term debt with having more debt at a variable interest rate. At the other extreme, Guatemala and Panama exhibit the lowest level of debt indexed to the interest rate, reflecting an overall safer profile of debt. Costa Rica and especially the Dominican Republic are more exposed. Given their high levels of short-term debt, their overall exposure to interest rate movements is considerably greater.

Capital Structure Mismatch

An often neglected risk concerns the typically noncontingent nature of debt, i.e., the fact that debt obligations are independent of the level of GDP or fiscal revenue.[42] This noncontingent nature could possibly be overcome if expenditure were flexible enough to adjust to the performance of revenue. However, this is seldom the case. Therefore, countries with a higher volatility of revenue tend to have higher financing needs at specific moments in time. Indeed, volatility of revenue has been proved to be an important determinant of "safe" thresholds of debt (IMF, 2003; Mendoza and Oviedo, 2004). This risk is likely to be exacerbated if countries have large maturity mismatches and/or high interest rate risk.

Nicaragua appears as the most risky country in Central America along this dimension (Figure 4.10), probably associated with a less diversified productive base. Revenue volatility also seems relatively high in the Dominican Republic, Panama and Guatemala. In contrast, public revenue in El Salvador and Costa Rica have been remarkable stable.

Conclusions

Central America has made important strides toward safer debt structures. Over the years, in line with broader developments in emerging markets, the Central American countries have reduced their reliance on riskier types of debt. In particular, the region has been able to increase its share of debt financed in domestic markets (with the exception of Panama) and has reduced its reliance on foreign currency, albeit modestly

Nevertheless, the main vulnerability in Central America remains its relatively high level of foreign currency debt. The region, with the exception of Costa Rica, has a high share of foreign currency debt in total debt when compared with the rest of the Latin American countries. This exposure may be partially hedged in some countries (especially in the Dominican Republic, Panama, and Honduras), given their high degree of openness to trade and a higher bias in government spending than in revenue stream toward nontradable sectors.

Beyond this, other relevant vulnerabilities tend to differ across countries of the region. A key issue for Honduras and Nicaragua seems to be the limited diversification of the creditor base. In Panama and Guatemala, high volatility of revenue is a particular concern. Costa Rica and the Dominican Republic exhibit relatively high levels of short-term debt. El Salvador is particularly exposed to movements in interest rates given its high share of variable interest rate.

The key to improving debt structures is sound monetary and fiscal policies and strengthened institutions.

Figure 4.9. Debt with Variable Interest Rate, 2005
(In percent of total debt)

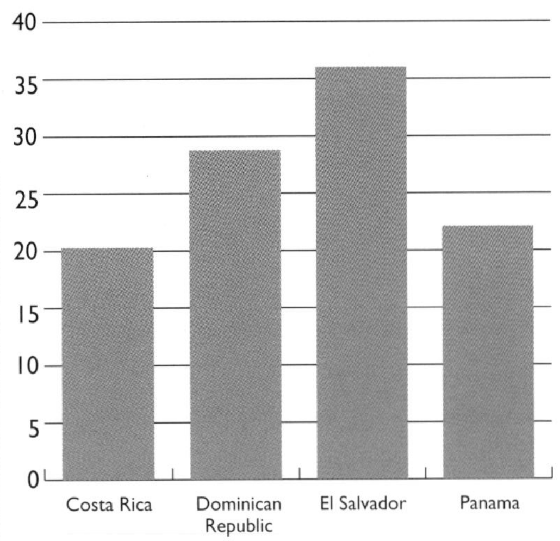

Sources: National authorities; and IMF staff calculations.
Note: Sovereign debt coverage differs across countries.

[42]Rogoff (1999) called attention to this fact and highlighted the benefits of the creation of equity-like instruments. Borensztein and Mauro (2004) went on to propose the creation of GDP-indexed bonds.

Figure 4.10. Volatility of Revenue Growth, 1990–2005
(In percent)

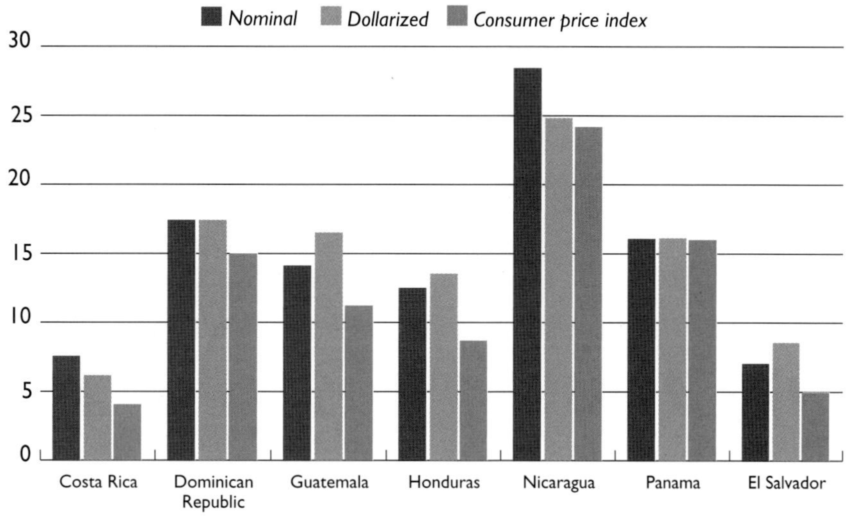

Sources: IMF, *International Financial Statistics* and *World Economic Outlook*; and authors' calculations.

Sound fiscal policy has an obvious direct impact on debt. Strong fiscal and monetary policies also have other important beneficial effects for debt structures, as they limit volatility, enhance resilience to shocks, and strengthen confidence in the domestic currency. Credible monetary policy, for example, is likely to have a positive impact on the currency composition of sovereign debt. A stronger institutional framework makes it easier for the government to issue debt in its own jurisdiction and currency. In this respect, the rule of law and strong contract enforcement play a particularly important role by reducing confiscation risk and the severity of loss in the case of default. The development of a domestic investor base, for which pension funds can be a catalyst (see Chapter III), can also bring important results. The more financially developed a country is, the lower the shares of foreign currency and short-term to total debt.

References

Aghion, Philippe, Philippe Bacchetta, and Abhijit Banerjee, 2000, "A Simple Model of Monetary Policy and Currency Crises," *European Economic Review*, Vol. 44, No. 4–6, pp. 728–38.

———, 2001, "Currency Crises and Monetary Policy in an Economy with Credit Constraints," *European Economic Review*, Vol. 45, No. 7, pp. 1121–50.

Albuquerque, Rui, 2003, "The Composition of International Capital Flows: Risk Sharing Through Foreign Direct Investment," *Journal of International Economics*, Vol. 1, No. 2, pp. 353–83.

Allen, Mark, Christoph B. Rosenberg, Christian Keller, Brad Setser, and Nouriel Roubini, 2002, "A Balance Sheet Approach to Financial Crisis," IMF Working Paper No. 02/210 (Washington: International Monetary Fund).

Arellano, Cristina, and Jonathan Heathcote, 2004, "Dollarization and Financial Integration," Society For Economic Dynamics 2004 Meeting Papers.

Bohn, Henning, 1990, "A Positive Theory of Foreign Currency Debt," *Journal of International Economics*, Vol. 29, No. 3–4, pp. 273–92.

Borensztein, Eduardo, and Paolo Mauro, 2004, "The Case for GDP-Indexed Bonds," *Economic Policy*, Vol. 38 (April), pp. 165–216.

Borensztein, Eduardo, Marcos Chamon, Olivier Jeanne, Paolo Mauro, and Jeromin Zettelmeyer, 2004, *Sovereign Debt Structure for Crisis Prevention,* IMF Occasional Paper No. 237 (Washington: International Monetary Fund).

Broner, Fernando A., Guido Lorenzoni, and Sergio L. Schmukler, 2005, "Why Do Emerging Economies Borrow Short Term?" (unpublished; CREI and Universitat Pompeu Fabra, MIT, and World Bank).

Burnside, Craig, Martin Eichenbaum, and Sergio Rebelo, 2001, "Hedging and Financial Fragility in Fixed Exchange Rate Regimes," *European Economic Review*, Vol. 45, No. 7, pp. 1151–93.

———, 2006, "Government Finance in the Wake of Currency Crises," *Journal of Monetary Economics,* Vol. 53, No. 3, pp. 401–40,

Bussière, Matthieu, Marcel Fratzcher, and Winfried Koeniger, 2004, "Currency Mismatch, Uncertainty, and Debt Maturity Structure," ECB Working Paper No. 409 (Frankfurt: European Central Bank).

Calvo, Guillermo A., 1988, "Servicing the Public Debt: The Role of Expectations," *American Economic Review*, Vol. 78, No. 4, pp. 647–61.

———, Alejandro Izquierdo, and Ernesto Talvi, 2003, "Sudden Stops, the Real Exchange Rate, and Fiscal Sustainability: Argentina's Lessons," NBER Working Paper No. 9828 (Cambridge, Massachusetts: National Bureau of Economic Research).

Chamon, Marcos, 2003, "Why Can't Developing Countries Borrow from Abroad in Their Own Currency?" Social Science Research Network Electronic Library Working Paper.

Claessens, Stijn, Daniela Klingebiel, and Sergio Schmukler, 2003, "Government Bonds in Domestic and Foreign Currency: The Role of Macroeconomic and Institutional Factors," CEPR Discussion Paper No. 3789 (London: Centre for Economic Policy Research).

Cowan, Kevin, Eduardo Levy-Yeyati, Ugo Panizza, and Federico Sturzenegger, 2006, "Sovereign Debt in the Americas: New Data and Stylized Facts," IDB Research Department Working Paper 577 (Washington: Inter-American Development Bank).

de la Torre, Augusto, and Sergio Schmukler, 2004, "Coping with Risks through Mismatches: Domestic and International Financial Contracts for Emerging Economies," *International Finance*, Vol. 7, No. 3, pp. 349–90.

Detragiache, Enrica, and Antonio Spilimbergo, 2001, "Crisis and Liquidity—Evidence and Interpretation," IMF Working Paper 03/222 (Washington: International Monetary Fund).

Eichengreen, Barry, Ricardo Hausmann, and Ugo Panizza, 2005, "The Pain of Original Sin" in *Other People's Money: Debt Denomination and Financial Instability in Emerging Market Economies*, ed. by Barry Eichengreen and Ricardo Hausmann (Chicago: University of Chicago Press).

Faria, André, and Paolo Mauro, 2004, "Institutions and the External Capital Structure of Countries," IMF Working Paper 04/236 (Washington: International Monetary Fund).

Gelos, R. Gaston, Ratna Sahay, and Guido Sandleris, 2004, "Sovereign Borrowing by Developing Countries: What Determines Market Access?" IMF Working Paper 04/221 (Washington: International Monetary Fund).

Goldstein, Morris, and Philip Turner, 2004, *Controlling Currency Mismatches in Emerging Markets* (Washington: Institute for International Economics).

Hart, Oliver, and John Moore, 1994, "A Theory of Debt Based on the Inalienability of Human Capital," *Quarterly Journal of Economics*, Vol. 109, No. 4, pp. 841–79.

Hausmann, Ricardo, and Ugo Panizza, 2003, "On the Determinants of Original Sin: An Empirical Investigation," *Journal of International Money and Finance*, Vol. 22, Issue 6, pp. 957–90.

Inter-American Development Bank (IDB), 2006, *Living with Debt: How to Limit the Risks of Sovereign Finance* (Washington: Inter-American Development Bank).

International Monetary Fund (IMF), 2003, "Public Debt in Emerging Markets: Is It Too High?" *World Economic Outlook* (Washington: International Monetary Fund).

———, 2006, *Global Financial Stability Report* (Washington: International Monetary Fund).

———, and World Bank, 2001, *Guidelines for Public Debt Management* (Washington: International Monetary Fund and World Bank).

Ize, Alain, and Eduardo Levy-Yeyati, 2003, "Financial Dollarization," *Journal of International Economics*, Vol. 59, No. 2, pp. 323–47.

Jaimovich, Dany, and Ugo Panizza, 2006, "Public Debt Around the World: A New Data Set of Central Government Debt," IDB Research Department Working Paper 561 (Washington: Inter-American Development Bank).

Jeanne, Olivier, 2003, "Why Do Emerging Market Economies Borrow in Foreign Currency?" IMF Working Paper 03/177 (Washington: International Monetary Fund).

———, 2004, "Debt Maturity and the International Financial Architecture," IMF Working Paper 04/137 (Washington: International Monetary Fund).

———, and Anastasia Guscina, 2006, "Government Debt in Emerging Market Countries: A New Data Set," IMF Working Paper 06/98 (Washington: International Monetary Fund).

———, and Jeromin Zettelmeyer, 2002, "'Original Sin,' Balance Sheet Crises, and the Roles of International Lending," IMF Working Paper 02/234 (Washington: International Monetary Fund).

Kaufmann, Daniel, Aart Kraay, and Massimo Mastruzzi, 2005, "Governance Matters IV: Governance Indicators for 1996–2004," World Bank Policy Research Working Paper No. 3630 (Washington: World Bank).

Krugman, Paul, 1999, "Balance Sheets, the Transfer Problem, and Financial Crises," in *International Finance and Financial Crises: Essays in Honor of Robert P. Flood, Jr.*, ed. by Peter Isard, Assaf Razin, and Andrew K. Rose (Boston: Kluwer Academic; Washington: International Monetary Fund).

Lima, Juan Manuel, Enrique Montes, Carlos Varela, and Johannes Wiegand, 2006, "Sectoral Balance Sheet Mismatches and Macroeconomic Vulnerabilities in Colombia, 1996–2003," IMF Working Paper 06/5 (Washington: International Monetary Fund).

Mehl, Arnaud, and Julien Reynaud, 2005, "The Determinants of 'Domestic' Original Sin in Emerging Market Economies," ECB Working Paper No. 560 (Frankfurt: European Central Bank).

Mendoza, Enrique G., and P. Marcelo Oviedo, 2004, "Fiscal Solvency and Macroeconomic Uncertainty in Emerging Markets: The Tale of the Tormented Insurer" (unpublished; University of Maryland and Iowa State University).

Missale, Alessandro, 1999, *Public Debt Management* (Oxford: Oxford University Press).

———, and Olivier J. Blanchard, 1994, "The Debt Burden and Debt Maturity," *American Economic Review*, Vol. 84, No. 1, pp. 309–19.

Mussa, Michael, 1986, "Nominal Exchange Rate Regimes and the Behavior of Real Exchange Rates: Evidence and Implications," *Carnegie-Rochester Conference Series on Public Policy*, Vol. 25, pp. 117-214.

Reinhart, Carmen M., Kenneth S. Rogoff, and Miguel A. Savastano, 2003, "Debt Intolerance," *Brookings Papers in Economic Activity*, No. 1, ed. by William Brainard and George Perry, pp. 1–74.

Rodrik, Dani, and Andrés Velasco, 1999, "Short-Term Capital Flows," in *Annual World Bank Conference on Development Economics* (Washington: World Bank).

Rogoff, Kenneth, 1999, "Institutions for Reducing Global Financial Instability," *Journal of Economic Perspectives*, Vol. 13, No. 4, pp. 21–42.

Rosenberg, Christoph, Ioannis Halikias, Brett House, Christian Keller, Jens Nystedt, Alex Pitt, and Brad Setser, 2005, *Debt-Related Vulnerabilities and Financial Crises—An Application of the Balance Sheet Approach to Emerging Market Countries,* IMF Occasional Paper 240 (Washington: International Monetary Fund).

Schneider, Martin, and Aaron Tornell, 2004, "Balance Sheet Effects, Bailout Guarantees, and Financial Crises," *Review of Economic Studies*, Vol. 71, No. 3, pp. 819–913.

Sturzenegger, Federico, and Jeromin Zettelmeyer, 2006, "A Primer on Sovereign Debt Crises: History, Economics, and Law" (Cambridge, Massachusetts: The MIT Press).

Tirole, Jean, 2002, *Financial Crises, Liquidity Provision, and the International Monetary System* (Princeton, New Jersey: Princeton University Press).

———, 2003, "Inefficient Foreign Borrowing: A Dual- and Common-Agency Perspective," *American Economic Review*, Vol. 93, No. 5, pp. 1678–702.

Wei, Shang-Jin, 2001, "Domestic Crony Capitalism and International Fickle Capital: Is There a Connection?" *International Finance*, Vol. 4, No. 1, pp. 15–45.

World Bank, 2005, *Global Development Finance 2005* (Washington: World Bank).

V Financial Sector Development: Public Debt Markets

Hemant Shah[1]

The development of public debt markets in Central America is critically important to the overall development of capital markets. As with many emerging markets, the Central American capital markets are somewhat underdeveloped. Problems in public debt management and underdevelopment of capital markets are related. The underdevelopment of capital markets, particularly institutional investors, limits the amount and maturity of funding available to the government locally, and can substantially increase the rollover and currency risks in managing public debt. At the same time, weak debt management practices, which result in fragmented issuance and a lack of a liquid benchmark yield curve, make it difficult for all borrowers (including corporate and home loan borrowers) to obtain long-term funding, and for institutional investors to undertake appropriate risk management. The broader development of capital markets is a complex and multifaceted problem that also needs to be addressed, but given the dominance of public debt in capital markets in the Central American countries, improving the public debt market is their logical first priority.

Even for the relatively small Central American economies, developing local public debt markets is important. Sovereign issuers in smaller economies suffer from many problems in terms of a limited local investor base, higher transaction costs, limited trading, and economies of scale. El Salvador and Panama are dollarized and several other countries have a significant amount of de facto dollarization. A high degree of domestic dollarization may force issuers—including sovereign ones—to rely on foreign currency funding for a significant part of their financing requirement, and create some preference for doing so from the more developed external markets and investors. A country with current account deficits may also need to rely on external capital flows to close the balance of payments. However, external debt financing in foreign currency cannot be obtained without incurring some risks of currency mismatch and sudden capital outflows. Recognizing this, virtually all sovereigns in the region have already undertaken domestic issuance programs, and from a sovereign debt management perspective, it would be appropriate to strengthen rather than abandon them, even if external debt issuance has to continue.

Development of a more integrated regional capital market, including that in public debt, entails complex benefits and difficulties that require further study. Given the small size of the Central American economies, a more integrated financial market may seem to offer substantial benefits to investors and issuers alike. For investors, it might mean more efficient capital allocation and risk diversification. For issuers, it might imply greater and more liquid access to regional savings. However, despite the relative openness of regional capital accounts and the substantial presence of regional financial groups,[2] sovereign debt markets (and, more generally, capital markets) remain divided in important respects by currency, creditworthiness, regulation, restrictions on domestic institutional investors, and the absence of a regional exchange. To advance toward a regional

[1]The underlying country studies were prepared by Andy Jobst, Laura Valderrama, and Ivan Guerra. The drafts of this study were presented to the technical staff of the central banks and ministries of finance at a conference in Guatemala in June 2006, and then to senior policymakers at another conference in the Dominican Republic in June 2006. Their comments have been incorporated. Generally, the chapter reflects data and public debt market conditions in Central America as of end-2005. In addition to the large number of public and private sector officials in the seven countries studied who generously provided information to the team, we would like to thank Alfredo Blanco, Jorge Barboza, Catiana García Kilroy (Central American Monetary Council), Elizabeth Curry (World Bank), Eliot Kalter, Ceyla Pazarbasioglu, Guy Meredith, Dominique Desruelle, Alfred Schipke, Humberto Arbulu-Neira, Ousmene Mandeng, Hunter Monroe, Erik Offerdal, Anthony Pellechio, and Parmeshwar Ramlogan for extensive assistance. For their comments on the chapter, we would like to thank Alfred Schipke, Humberto Arbulu-Neira, Francesc Balcells, Alona Cebotari, Ana Lucia Coronel, Luis Cubeddu, Rodrigo Cubero, Vikram Haksar, Geoffrey Heenan, Luis Jácome, Gabriel Lopetegui, Carla Macio, Rodolfo Maino, Rogelio Morales, Marina Moretti, Christian Mulder, Marco Rodriguez, Neil Saker, and Wendell Samuel.

[2]A 2006 IMF study, *Central America: Structural Foundations of Regional Financial Integration,* prepared by a staff team led by Patricia Brenner, discusses regional integration issues relating to consolidated supervision, the insurance sector, and payment and securities settlement systems.

sovereign debt market requires significant convergence and cooperation in terms of economic policies and regulation of financial markets, and potentially the creation of regional exchange or at least regional trading platforms. A full examination of such issues is worthwhile, but beyond the scope of this study, which focuses on the more pressing task of improving individual sovereign debt markets. Of course, several aspects of development of national debt markets discussed here, and in particular standardization of issues, will facilitate a more active regional debt market.

While developing an integrated regional market remains a longer-term goal, substantial progress is being made under a project to harmonize public debt market standards. As part of a project of the Central American Monetary Council, supported by the Inter-American Bank, the authorities of the seven countries signed a resolution to advance adoption of common standards in public debt issuance across the region in November 2003.[3] The effort involves promotion of common standards and good practices in such areas as organizing the primary market, public debt management, money markets and monetary policy operations, wholesale secondary market in public debt, payment and settlement systems, conventions in calculations relating to public debt, regulation of collective investments and secondary markets in public debt, and developing a regional wholesale/over-the-counter market in public debt. The program has led to important advancements in establishing common market conventions and calculation standards, adopting standardized securities in new issuance, building consensus toward analytical approaches and solutions to common problems, and offering training to debt managers. Further progress in implementing the 2003 resolution would depend on substantial additional technical and political support.

This chapter examines the strategic context of public debt management and the functioning of primary and secondary markets for domestic public debt. It proposes measures to improve the functioning of these markets and promote a more efficient regional market in public debt.[4]

[3]See Consejo Monetario Centroamericano, Secretaría Ejecutiva, Resolución CMCA/CMH-RE-02/11/03, "Aprobación de los Estándares para la Armonización de los Mercados de Deuda Pública," November 2003, and progress reports. Available via the Internet: http://www.secmca.org/Proyectos_DeudaPublica.htm.

[4]A more in-depth examination of both institutional and market-related issues concerning debt management can be found in World Bank reports on Guatemala, Costa Rica, and Nicaragua. Related work by the Central American Monetary Council and the Inter-American Development Bank promotes harmonization of technical standards of public debt issuance, and provides diagnostic analyses and technical assistance, much of which has benefited this chapter.

Financial Sector in Central America

The financial sector in Central America is dominated by banks, which are the largest financial intermediaries throughout the region (Table 5.1). The Dominican Republic and Guatemala have somewhat low levels of financial penetration in terms of a bank-assets-to-GDP ratio of around 35 to 40 percent. The numbers for Costa Rica, El Salvador, Honduras, and Nicaragua range from 50 to 90 percent and compare well with other emerging or developing markets. Panama, with a dollarized and open economy, has very high levels of financial penetration (250 percent), reflecting its offshore activities. Deposit levels in the region are typically about 60 to 80 percent of total assets, except in Costa Rica, where they are only a third of total assets. Private credit generally accounts for about half of the assets.

By contrast, capital markets are underdeveloped throughout the region. Except for Panama, the number of equity and corporate bond listings are generally in the single digits, and market-capitalization-to-GDP ratios are quite low. While complete data are unavailable, institutional investors (pension funds, mutual funds, and insurance companies) also are underdeveloped. In some countries, the enabling laws and regulation for important sectors such as pension and mutual funds need to be significantly upgraded, or remain to be implemented altogether. In all cases, these institutions intermediate a relatively small share of national savings. Thus, the principal investors in government securities are commercial banks and public sector entities such as pension funds.

Issuance of corporate securities is stymied by a variety of factors. Leading Central American businesses are often family-owned, and their reluctance to share even minority control or to comply with extensive transparency and disclosure requirements seems to be the principal hurdle. Anecdotal evidence suggests that the large majority of local businesses needing financing of under $10 million find it cheaper to seek bank financing, while the larger companies seeking from $25 million to $50 million source it overseas. Thus, domestic bond markets are approached for a relatively narrow range of financing needs. Bank loans are preferred because they have fewer information disclosure requirements, and those requirements are private rather than public. At times, this situation has been compounded by cyclical excess liquidity in the banking system that lowers bank lending rates. In some cases, brokerage and exchange fees and procedural requirements of the exchange are also deterrents to corporate debt or equity issuance. Mortgage- or asset-backed securities have yet to emerge in these markets. While the private financial sector has issued some bonds, this activity is also limited in light of the

Table 5.1. Structure of Financial System

Country	Costa Rica	Dom. Rep.	El Salvador	Guatemala	Honduras	Nicaragua	Panama
Financial Institutions							
				(Number)			
Banks							
Official	3	2	2	1	2	1	2
Domestic-majority owned	12	9	9	26	9	6	17
Foreign-majority owned	0	3	3	1	7	1	22
Branches of foreign banks	0	n.a.	2	n.a.	2	n.a.	31
Insurance companies	1	n.a.	17	18	10	5	18
Collective investment institutions	31	7	5	35	6	n.a.	18
Financial holding corporations	22	n.a.	9	16	9	n.a.	n.a.
Financial System Indicators							
				(In millions of U.S. dollars)			
Bank assets	13,037	10,009	10,709	11,653	6,990	2,601	36,225
Total deposits of banking system	4,167	8,144	6,612	8,830	4,285	2,026	25,118
Deposits (in percent of assets)	32.0	81.4	61.7	75.8	61.3	76.9	69.3
Private credit	6,784	4,393	7,027	6,344	3,405	1,107*	1,918
Insurance sector assets	n.a.	n.a.	353	410	272	93	107*
Mutual funds AUM	1,400*	n.a.	n.a.	n.a.	n.a.	n.a.	527
Pension funds AUM	1,076*	880	2,600	n.a.	n.a.	n.a.	72
Trading volume	34,585	7	7,511	24,518	2,039	153	1,681
Primary issuance	5,229	6	665	8,150	0	11	1,227
Secondary market	29,356	1	6,846	16,368	2,034	142	454
Volume of repo transactions	19,528	0	5,227	16,109	0	34	23
				(In percent of GDP)			
Banks assets	66.7	34.1	63.1	36.3	83.6	50.9	234.2
Private credit	34.7	15.0	41.4	19.8	40.7	21.7	141.7
Insurance companies	n.a.*	n.a.	2.1	1.3	3.2	1.8	0.7
Mutual funds AUM	7.2*	n.a.	n.a.	n.a.	n.a.	n.a.	3.4
Pension funds AUM	5.5*	3.0	15.3	n.a.	n.a.	n.a.	0.5
Trading volume	176.8	0.1	44.2	76.3	24.4	3.0	10.9
Volume of repo transactions	99.8	0.0	30.8	50.2	0.0	0.7	0.2
Memorandum items							
GDP (millions of U.S. dollars)	19,559	29,333	16,974	32,119	8,365	5,105	15,467
Exchange rate (local currency in U.S. dollars)	497.71	34.70	1.00	7.63	18.90	17.15	1.00

Source: IMF estimates based on official sources.
Note: Data are from December 2005, except for data with an asterisk, which indicates December 2004. AUM = assets under management.

relatively liquid condition of many regional banking systems.

Thus, public debt issues dominate Central American capital markets. The capital markets of Costa Rica, the Dominican Republic, El Salvador, Guatemala, Honduras, and Nicaragua consist almost entirely of public debt instruments, and public debt also dominates capital markets in Panama (see Chapter IV). Despite this, problems of fragmented domestic debt issuance and the large stock of nontradable public debt mean that there is insufficient trading and liquidity in domestic public debt markets.

Organization of Public Debt Management

None of the countries in the region has yet developed a clear debt management strategy that articulates the long-term role of domestic markets, domestic currency, and resident investors in funding public debt. Many countries depend heavily on external sources of funding or on foreign currency funding, and lack clarity regarding the strategic role of local currency and resident investors in funding public debt, goals regarding the amount of domestic currency issuance, and the preferred tenor up to which the sovereign desires building a yield curve. In the absence of a well-developed strategy, domestic debt issuance decisions are taken in a somewhat ad hoc fashion. There is little systematic dialog between issuers and investors concerning the medium-term goals of the former or the problems facing the latter.

The capacity of the Central American countries' debt management units needs to be substantially strengthened. Most units have grown out of traditional back-office operations. They typically have a weak front office and lack a clearly identifiable middle office charged with risk management. They generally do not have a regular investor relations program that involves meetings with key investors and institutions to incorporate market views or resolve problems relating to public debt issuance. That said, debt management unit staff are aware of the need to standardize debt issuance, facilitate secondary market trading, and extend yield curve. They also meet regularly at the regional level to discuss these issues as part of the Central American Monetary Council's harmonization program.

By and large, debt management does not adequately aim to manage the stock of existing debt. Except for Panama and, to some extent, Costa Rica, debt managers focus primarily on securing current funding needs, and secondarily on standardizing future issuance or extending the maturity of the yield curve. Most debt management units have limited capacity to undertake the more complex management of the overall stock of existing domestic debt. This is particularly important given the high debt-to-GDP ratio in many countries and the sizable nonstandard and nontradable domestic debt that requires restructuring.

Coordinating debt issuance of the sovereign and the central bank is an important challenge. In many ways, the debt management problems of the smaller Central American economies are more complex than those of the larger emerging markets. One problem is the sizable debt issuance by the central banks that requires considerable coordination with the ministry of finance. While some coordination is the norm, it is typically confined to operational issues such as the issuance calendar, standardization of instruments, and auction logistics.

In several countries there are some problems in the structure of authority and responsibility between the legislature and administration. First, debt managers sometimes have only limited clarity or authority to conduct debt management operations. In the Dominican Republic, Honduras, and, to a lesser extent, Nicaragua, issuance is authorized under somewhat restrictive laws that define the operational terms but can clash with current market conditions, leaving debt managers with limited discretion.[5] Second, in most countries debt managers lack the authority to conduct overall liability management operations that go beyond the financing of current cash flow needs. Third, as much of the nonstandard debt has been issued under provisions of specific laws, restructuring of that debt is likely to require more than general authority to finance the government or conduct liability management operations. Finally, the transfer of central bank losses to the sovereign is not routine and involves significant intervention by the legislature.

These problems are reflected in the differences between domestic and external market access. Several countries have access to external bond markets, and thus to advice from international underwriters and advisors. Their successes in the external markets often stand in sharp contrast to their efforts in domestic markets. For example, Panama has possibly the best developed domestic financial sector in the region, with considerable success in issuing eurobonds globally and in arranging a $980 million global bond swap in January 2006, issuing a 30-year bond in the process. At the same time, Panama is actually curtailing its domestic medium-term issuance program. Similarly, the Dominican Republic successfully issued a 20-year $300 million eurobond in March 2006, attracting the lowest coupon in the country's history and an oversubscription of 3.3 times. However, the Dominican Republic has not made a single "regular" debt issue in the domestic market.

Dual Sovereign Issuers: Government and the Central Bank

Public debt issuance is complicated by the simultaneous and often competing presence of the sovereign and the central bank as issuers of public debt. Ideally, public debt should be issued by the sovereign alone, with the central bank using a stock of sovereign public debt instruments to conduct open-market operations for monetary policy purposes. With the exception of Panama, the central banks in all five countries (Costa Rica, the Dominican Republic, El Salvador, Honduras, and Nicaragua) have sizable accumulated deficits arising from previous financial crises, financial system bailouts, and even just from normal central bank operations. This makes the central bank a frequent issuer

[5]In Honduras, the parliament required issuance of bonds by a public electricity company specifying low (below-market) interest rates, resulting in failure of the issue. In the Dominican Republic, individual debt contracts need to be authorized by the Congress.

Figure 5.1. Domestic Central Bank Debt/Domestic Government Debt, 2005
(In percent)

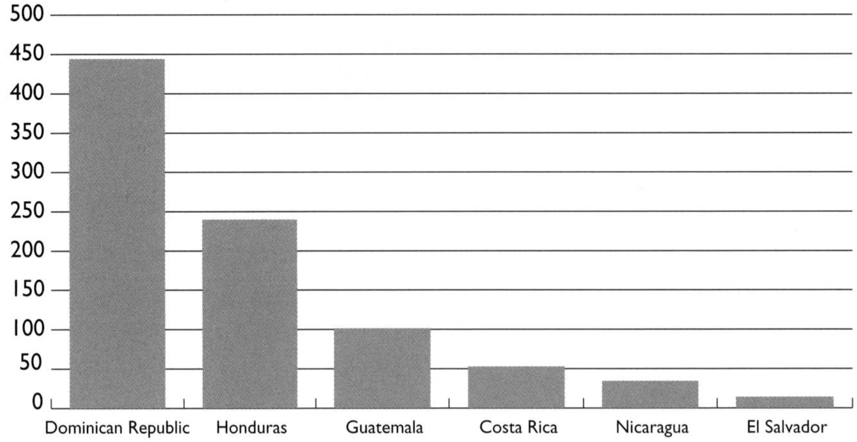

of debt in its own name. For example, in the Dominican Republic, the stock of central bank domestic debt is about 5½ times as large as that of the government (Figure 5.1). Moreover, as the bulk of government debt is not issued in the form of securities, the outstanding stock of central bank securities is about 17 times as large as the stock of government securities. In both Honduras and Nicaragua, the central bank is a far larger issuer, while in El Salvador and Costa Rica, central bank issuance is between a quarter and half that of the sovereign. Such large issuances by central banks, coupled with the frequency of issuance and a concentration in short-term tenors by both issuers, creates a number of problems.

First and foremost, debt issuance by a central bank to finance its own operations compromises monetary policy operations. The continuous need for the central bank to issue debt to finance its own operations or to roll over maturing debt may cause doubts in the markets about the bank's ability to conduct monetary policy consistent with the objectives of price stability and the proper choice of instruments and interest rate paths.[6] While this chapter does not focus on such monetary policy issues, this is perhaps the most important reason to recapitalize the central bank to a point that it can have a stock of suitable public debt instruments with which to conduct open market operations.

The substantial and simultaneous issuance by central banks also creates a significant burden in terms of coordinating the issuance of public debt. While the concerned authorities in the countries of the region seem to have the will to cooperate effectively, the need for extensive coordination on a calendar of issues, demarcation of maturities, issuance terms, eligible issuers, issuance/trading platforms, and the manner in which auctions are conducted adds many layers of complexity compared to a situation in which the sovereign is the sole issuer and the central bank at best a fiscal agent. In many countries, there are gaps in technical sophistication, familiarity with market conventions, and in some cases pay scales between central bank and finance ministry staff that deal with debt issuance, with the latter usually lagging behind. Often there are differences in the issuance practices of the two issuers, and the sensible need to harmonize them, even when addressed, nonetheless slows the adoption of desirable innovations. For example, in Guatemala, while the ministry of finance can issue standard instruments (carrying a common coupon), such issuance has been delayed until the somewhat greater legal difficulties in issuance of similar standard instruments by the central bank can be resolved.

The sizable issuance of central bank debt creates a potentially large rollover risk and a short-term orientation toward public debt in the market. For monetary operations, central banks have a preference for issuing short-term debt. This bias tends to be carried over in financing central banks' quasi-fiscal deficits that are not quickly or fully compensated for by the sovereign (which is the root cause of central bank debt issuance in Central America). Such decapitalized central banks are generally resource-constrained and loath to issue lon-

[6]Note that the rollover of debt to finance accumulated losses is more problematic than, say, debt issuance to mop up excess liquidity and build up reserves, in which case the rollover risk is mitigated by the presence of reserves.

ger-term debt that, all else being equal, entails higher interest rates and thus larger deficits. The sovereign authorities also are generally wary of issuance by the central banks at longer maturities, as they themselves intend to tap these maturities and prefer not to have competing paper from the central bank.

Resolution of a central bank's accumulated losses is typically delayed and inefficient. In many countries, the authorities do recognize the need to recapitalize the central bank, and, in turn, transfer the central bank losses to the fiscal accounts. However, this is not an easy process given the politics involved, the level of public deficits, and legislative complexities. Thus, such transfers—if they occur at all—are delayed. In some cases, they are still ad hoc—in the Dominican Republic, for example, the first such issuance of the recapitalization bond was authorized for 2005.[7] Even in countries where transfers are now more routine (e.g., Costa Rica, Guatemala, and Honduras) and losses are supposed to be transferred annually, the accounting and legislative process of determining the actual central bank losses and authorizing the issuance of government bonds nonetheless takes one to two years. As recapitalization entails a considerable legislative effort, a partial recapitalization that does not eliminate future operational losses allows a difficult problem to persist.

When it does occur, recapitalization of central banks is more often apparent than real. Typically, recapitalization bonds have unusually long tenors on the order of 25 to 100 years, with zero or below-market interest rates. In present value terms, this results in an effective recapitalization well short of the face value of the bond. For instance, in Guatemala, a recapitalization bond issued in 2005 to cover losses incurred in 2003 had a 30-year maturity and a 3.87 percent coupon rate, well below the 9.6 percent rate on the 10-year bonds issued during the same period. Another bond expected to cover central bank losses for 1982–2002 is expected to have even more off-market terms: a maturity of 100 years and a zero interest rate, resulting in a bond with a present value of approximately 1 percent of the face value. In Honduras, central bank losses in 2003 were covered with a 50-year bond with zero interest rate, while 2004 losses were covered with a 25-year bond, paying a market interest rate only on one-tenth of the bond issued.

Partial recapitalization with deep discount bonds may actually inflate the *nominal* level of public debt, while creating weak incentives to check future public deficits. Positive capitalization of a central bank is desirable to ensure full recognition of its losses by the sovereign and to preserve the central bank's independence.[8] The current practice of recapitalizing central banks with zero coupon or deep discount bonds not only fails to adequately reduce future central bank losses, but also overstates the widely followed nominal debt-to-GDP ratios than would have been the case with bonds paying current market interest rates.[9] The resulting reduction in future interest bills also probably weakens fiscal discipline.

The issuance of deep discount debt to the central bank has created a sizable stock of nonstandard and nontradable debt that reduces the liquidity of public bonds. Such debt is rarely traded due to its unusually long maturity, absence of liquid yield benchmarks at such maturities, and, above all, the central bank's incentives to not recognize the large capital losses if it were to sell such debt.

The division of sovereign debt issuance between the two issuers hinders development of larger benchmark issues and lowers liquidity. Central American sovereign debt markets are small, and the market for longer tenors has yet to develop adequately. Liquidity of most bonds is related to the size of individual tradable issues and aggregate tradable stock. The division of issuance between the two sovereigns and the nontradable nature of debt issued to the central banks prevents most issues from reaching volumes needed to become liquid benchmarks and reduces liquidity. These factors are also generally detrimental to development of a long-term yield curve and widening the investor base, particularly to foreign investors in local issues.

Primary Issuance of Public Debt

The primary debt issuance process throughout Central America suffers from several problems. Despite progress made under the harmonization project, many problems remain in the form of poor issuance mechanisms, issuance of nonstandard debt, fragmentation of issuance, and weak auction practices.

Issuance Mechanisms

Several countries use multiple issuance mechanisms, thus draining volume, liquidity, and competi-

[7]In 2006, the authorities in the Dominican Republic prepared a comprehensive plan to recapitalize the central bank, which is scheduled to be submitted to Congress in 2007.

[8]However, this may often be a higher standard of capitalization than needed solely to eliminate future central bank losses. As central banks do not always pay market interest rates on all their liabilities (due to reserve requirements), the level of recapitalization needed to eliminate future deficits may be lower than that implied by full transfer of their accumulated losses.

[9]While the true value of the net public debt of the central bank and the government remains unchanged, such an increase in the nominal debt-to-GDP ratio may add to a lack of transparency about public debt, and possibly to the cost of public debt and problems of access.

tiveness from auctions. In addition to regular auctions, several issuers (Costa Rica, the Dominican Republic, Guatemala) also rely on post-auction windows (Table 5.2) offered by the central bank or the ministry of finance.[10] The presence of such windows, for extended periods of time, drains liquidity from auctions themselves, and complicates the bidding and acceptance strategies for investors and issuers, respectively. In the Dominican Republic, the window creates a further segmentation of the market, as the fixed interest rates offered in the window are only loosely guided by the preceding auction or current secondary prices, the window is open only to retail investors, and longer tenor maturities are offered through the window than are auctioned. Securities issued through these windows are typically nonstandard and nontradable. Interestingly, in Costa Rica, the finance ministry takes advantage of the statutory restrictions on nonfinancial public sector entities by issuing public debt outside the competitive auction process at "negotiated" below-market yields and tenors, creating an additional source of nonstandard debt.

There are no primary dealer systems in Central America, although issuers often rely on brokers and exchanges to conduct primary auctions. None of the countries employ a true primary dealer system with clear market-making obligations. Nor are brokers or dealers capable of many of the functions performed by the primary dealers in larger government securities markets. However, reflecting the traditional dominance of exchange brokers (the largest of whom are typically affiliated with major banks), many countries employ a somewhat unusual process for public debt issuance by relying on brokers and exchanges to conduct the auction. These arrangements vary widely. In Panama, all auctions must be conducted through exchange brokers. In Costa Rica, banks can participate directly in an auction, while other investors must submit their bids through brokers and pay related commissions. In El Salvador, ministry of finance auctions are open not only to brokers but to other approved investors, including domestic and foreign banks, whereas central bank auctions are only open to brokers. As a general rule, it is difficult to make the case for value added by brokers during the primary auction process, particularly for institutional investors. As the banks typically have in-house brokers, as a group they tend to be neutral about the exclusive rights of the brokers and the fees charged by them, with the pension funds objecting most to such a monopoly.

[10]Often such windows are used for noncompetitive bids, although the point here pertains to their separation from the regular auction rather than the noncompetitiveness of the bids.

Issuance on Nonstandard Debt

The issuance of "nonstandard" debt without suitable characteristics that facilitate trading has been diminished, but not eliminated. In addition to issuance in irregular transactions (such as compensation for properties taken over by the state, arrears to suppliers, and issuance to central banks at off-market terms), several countries issue debt carrying amounts and interest rates specific to each holder (such as bank term deposits) rather than through standardized debt instruments, or they issue debt in physical (not dematerialized) form. The last two problems are directly addressed by the Central American Monetary Council's harmonization project. While all countries have agreed to start issuing standardized securities, the Dominican Republic, Costa Rica, El Salvador, Guatemala, and Nicaragua continue as of this writing to regularly issue some nonstandard securities. In addition, all recapitalization bonds issued or planned for issuance by the sovereign to the central banks in the Dominican Republic, Costa Rica, Guatemala, Honduras, and Nicaragua remain nonstandard.

Fragmentation of Public Debt Issuance

Despite the relatively small volume of domestic issuance, public debt is issued in an extremely fragmented fashion across Central America for a variety of reasons (Table 5.3). First, as discussed earlier, debt issuance is undertaken by the sovereign and the central bank in five countries. Second, there is a high frequency of issuance—all countries schedule auctions on a weekly or biweekly basis, except for Panama, which conducts auctions monthly (Figures 5.2 and 5.3). While many issues are re-opened and consolidated, their eventual total size is unclear. Third, Central American public issuers attempt to issue a large number of maturities relative to their total domestic issuance. Fourth, some of the nondollarized issuers (e.g., Nicaragua) are unable to issue all of their financing requirements in local currency, and while attempting to develop a local currency market have to divide their local issuance in different currencies. Finally, issuance of nonstandard debt with different interest rates to winning bidders (rather than different prices) obviously creates extreme fragmentation.

Conduct of Auctions

Investors throughout the region complain of gaps in information regarding primary auctions. As part of the harmonization initiative, in all countries there is now a pre-announced calendar of issues from both issuers. However, the overall annual calendar announcement is rather generic, and the amount offered is typically announced only about a week before the actual auction. There are considerable uncertainties about the actual issuance volume, as in some countries (e.g., Costa Rica and Honduras) the government and central bank often

Table 5.2. Securities Issued by the Ministry of Finance and Central Bank

	Auction Frequency	Types of Securities Offered at Each Auction	Scheduled Number of Auctions	Actual Number of Auctions	Average Auction Issuance Amount (US$)	Median Auction Issuance Amount (US$)
Costa Rica						
Government/Ministry of Finance						
Property securities (TP), zero coupon	Biweekly	1	26	7	37.6	18.8
Property securities (TP), fixed rate	Biweekly	1	26	21	28.7	22.5
Central Bank						
Monetary stabilization bonds (BEM), fixed rate	Biweekly	1	26	9	93.2	84.8
Monetary stabilization bonds (BEM), zero coupon	Biweekly	1	26	18	38.9	24.7
Dominican Republic						
Central Bank	Weekly	2	52	52	35.1	32.9
El Salvador						
Government/Ministry of Finance						
Treasury bills (LETES)	Biweekly	3	24	31	2.0	0.9
Government bonds	Monthly	2	24	1	35.5	35.5
Central Bank						
Negotiable liquidity certificates (CENELI)	Weekly	5	52	22	3.4	1.7
Guatemala						
Government/Ministry of Finance						
Certificates representative of treasury bonds	Biweekly	3	26	24	24.0	17.1
Central Bank						
Term deposit certificates	3–5/week	3	156–260	155	6.3	5.7
Term deposit certificates	Daily	3	260	247	0.1	0.1
Honduras						
Government/Ministry of Finance	Biweekly	4	26	17	3.0	3.0
Central Bank	Weekly	5	52	37	16.0	14.4
Nicaragua						
Government/Ministry of Finance						
Bonds	Biweekly	1	26	3	3.5	1.0
Central Bank						
Bills	Weekly	3	52	49	2.2	1.9
Panama						
Government/Ministry of Finance						
Notes	Monthly	1	12	12	32.0	25.0
Bills	Monthly	1	12	9	17.0	19.0

Sources: Central Banks, Ministries of Finance.

Table 5.3. Auction Mechanisms for Public Debt Securities

		Auction Mechanisms			Issued Securities			
		Competitive auction?	Non-competitive bids allowed?	Post-auction window?	Standardized security?	Dematerialized security?	Directly placed with creditor?	Exchange-based primary issuance?
Costa Rica								
MOF	Treasury bills	N	-	N	N	N	Y	N
MOF	Property securities, zero coupon (TPCER)	Y	Y	N	Y	Y	N	Y
MOF	Property securities, fixed interest, colones (TPC)	Y	Y	N	Y	Y	N	Y
MOF	Property securities, fixed interest, dollars (TPS)	N	-	N	Y	Y	N	Y
MOF	Property securities, variable interest, dollars	Y	N	N	N	Y	N	N
MOF	Basic rate securities, variable interest, colones	Y	N	N	N	Y	N	N
MOF	Property securities in development institutions (TUDES)	N	-	N	N	N	Y	N
CB	Short-term certificates (short-term investments)	N	-	Y	N	N	Y	N
CB	Monetary stabilization bonds (BEM)[1]	Y/N	-	Y	Y/N	Y/N	Y/N	Y/N
CB	Deposit certificates, term, dollars	Y	N	N	Y	Y	Y	Y
Dominican Republic								
CB	Investment certificates	N	-	Y	Y	Y	Y	N
CB	Zero coupon certificates	Y	Y	N	N	N	N	N
CB	Term certificates	Y	Y	N	Y	Y	Y	N
CB	Fixed-rate notes	Y	N	N	N	N	N	N
CB	Long-term certificates	Y	N	N	Y	Y	N	N
El Salvador								
MOF	Treasury bills (LETES)	Y	N	N	Y	Y	N	Y
MOF	Government bonds	Y	N	N	Y	Y	N	Y
CB	Negotiable liquidity certificates (CENELI)	Y	N	N	N	Y	N	Y
Guatemala								
MOF	Certificates representative of treasury bonds	Y	Y	Y	N	N	N	Y
CB	Term deposit certificates	Y	N	Y	N	N	N	Y
Honduras								
MOF	Government debt securities	Y	Y	N	Y	Y	N	Y
MOF	Budgetary bonds	Y	Y	N	Y	Y	N	N
CB	Monetary absorption certificates (CAMs)	Y	Y	Y	Y	Y	N	Y
CB	Monetary absorption certificates denominated in US$ (CADDs)	Y	Y	Y	Y	Y	N	Y
Nicaragua								
MOF	BPI[2]	D	N	N	N (Y)	N	Y	N
MOF	T-bills	Y	N	N	Y	Y	N	N
MOF	Bonds	Y	N	N	Y	Y	N	N
CB	Bills	Y	N	N	Y	Y	N	N
CB	Bonds	Y	N	N	Y	Y	N	N
CB	Bank bonds	D	N	N	N	N	Y	N
CB	TEI	D	N	N	N	N	Y	N
Panama								
MOF	Treasury bills	Y	Y	Y	Y	Y	Y	Y
MOF	Treasury notes	Y	Y	Y	Y	Y	Y	Y

Sources: Central Banks, Ministries of Finance.

[1]The auction of BEMs in Costa Rica is competitive for zero coupon and fixed-rate BEMs denominated in local currency, and noncompetitive for variable rate BEMs denominated in U.S. dollars.

[2]BPIs in Nicaragua are partially standardized.

Figure 5.2. Potential Debt Auctions Per Year
(Number)

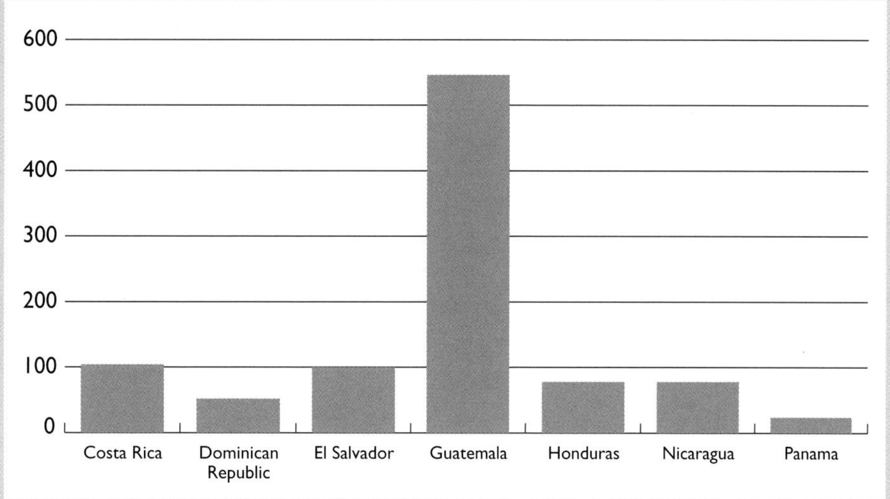

issue the same paper jointly. Allocation rules are not always fully formalized, and at times are perceived as murky by both investors and issuers. Investors are not always assured which issuer's securities will be awarded to them, which is a nontrivial problem in markets where the prices differ, or of the eventual size of a particular bond issue.

Fragmented and frequent issuance of a small quantity of debt appears to be partly driven by the desire of issuers to systematically capture the most aggressive bids or beat down the yields. Issuers routinely complain that the market is not sufficiently competitive, and that domestic investors, particularly those in the private sector, "overcharge" the government. There is thus a widespread reluctance on the part of the issuers to offer larger auction volumes, or commit to issue the announced volume when auctions are fully subscribed. Some of the most aggressive bids often come from banks that temporarily are very liquid, or from pension funds that, for regulatory reasons, must heavily invest in government paper. From time to time, this results in bids that other market participants regard as unrepresentative for the full spectrum of investors. Debt managers with weak authority and lacking a clear strategy to develop domestic markets and an investor base find it easier to defend small issuances or large rejections than a higher interest rate.

While there may be some validity to these concerns, they ignore the fact that investors will eventually factor in such defensive behavior of the issuers and adjust their bids accordingly. Smaller volumes can be placed at seemingly lower yields from time to time. But unless the overall volume of sovereign and domestic issuance is reduced, smaller issuance in individual auctions itself cannot reduce the interest rate in the long run. Moreover, as smaller issues are less liquid, the market is likely to charge a premium for such issues. As the domestic rates in both primary auctions and secondary markets are generally higher than the yields for comparable eurobonds, where they exist, small and fragmented local issues ultimately appear to carry a higher cost.

This widespread lack of agreement on "market clearing prices" between issuers and investors results in frequent auction failures or rejections. Auctions are often undersubscribed and at times are "deserted" (especially in Nicaragua)—that is, they receive no bids at all. Neither is it uncommon for the issuers to reject many bids in a fully or oversubscribed auction, while not filling the entire amount offered (e.g., in Panama). Apart from the uncertainties they imply in public financing, such auction failures or rejections signal market-wide disequilibria that should best be avoided.

There are also concerns about the role of dominant public sector investors. There is some consensus that public sector investors should be excluded from competitive bidding, as they could be influenced by the issuers and may result in an unrepresentative market-clearing interest rate or at least the perception thereof. However, the Central American experience indicates that there may not be a simple solution to this situation. In Panama, public sector bidders are allowed to participate only through noncompetitive bids, whereas elsewhere they are allowed to participate with competitive bids as well (e.g., in Costa Rica). Frequent and sizable participation of public sector investors through noncompetitive bids is likely to influence the issuer's acceptance of competitive bids, and, in

Figure 5.3. Actual Debt Auctions Per Year
(Number)

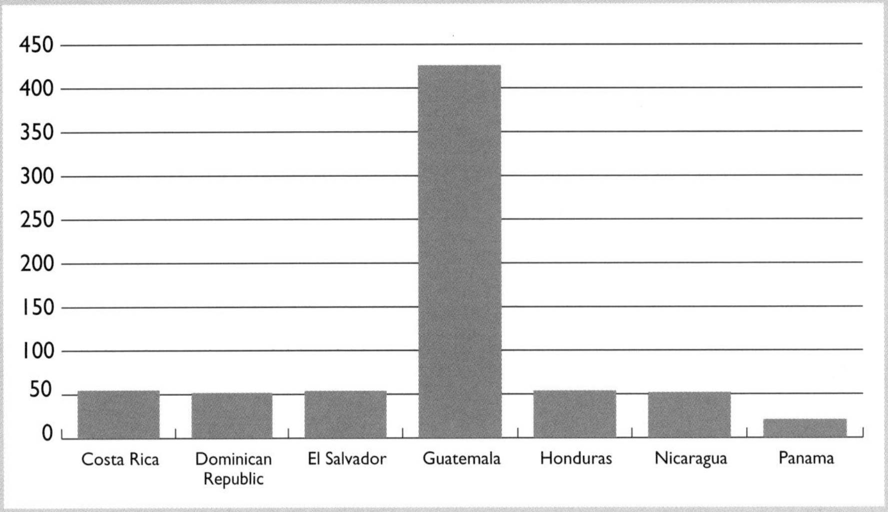

turn, the competitive bids by the private bidders. There thus may be a need to frankly discuss the role of the public sector vis-à-vis the private sector, provide public sector investors enough regulatory leeway and operational autonomy to bid as much on an arms-length basis as possible, and encourage the largest possible participation in competitive bids.

Secondary Markets

Public debt securities account for the lion's share of secondary market trading throughout Central America. Given the relative underdevelopment of corporate securities markets, trading in public securities dominates overall trading in regional exchanges (Table 5.4).

However, the bulk of domestic issuance in Central America is in short-term paper, and most of the domestic trading is in repo transactions, resulting in a lack of liquid, long-term secondary market yield curve. Few of the issuers (barring Panama and Guatemala) have managed to issue domestic debt for longer than a few years. This failure contrasts with the issuance of up to 30 years in the eurobond markets by Costa Rica, the Dominican Republic, El Salvador, Guatemala, and Panama. Moreover, the bulk of the trading is in repo transactions of a few days. Thus, despite accounting for 90 percent or more of local exchange trading, government securities do not provide a meaningful benchmark yield curve, and even for the short durations involved, secondary prices and yields are not sufficiently current.

Transaction costs in the smaller local securities exchanges—including brokerage and exchange fees involved in trading public bonds—as a rule are extremely high. On an annualized basis, they amount to 1 to 3 percentage points in the Dominican Republic, 1 to 2.5 percent in Nicaragua for an outright transaction and 1.25 percent for a repo transaction, and 0.1 to 1 percent in Guatemala.[11] Transaction costs are somewhat lower in Costa Rica, Guatemala, and Panama. High brokerage and bolsa fees may be justified by the low trading volumes and the small size of many issues, but they create a chicken-and-egg problem. More importantly, low liquidity eventually must raise the market-clearing interest rates demanded by investors.

Central American brokerages and exchanges face an uncertain future given their limited viability and difficulties in terms of consolidation. It should be kept in mind, of course, that brokers and exchanges may have played an important role historically in raising the transparency of government securities trading and, to a limited extent, popularizing investment in public securities by retail investors. In an environment of extremely limited private sector security issuance, exchanges may not have developed without some support from public issuers. Nonetheless, continued support of Central American exchanges and brokerages through higher charges and fees on public debt issuance and trading may have questionable value, especially considering the ownership of many brokerages by banks. The low trading income, the opposition of institutional investors to paying fees,

[11]By comparison, the bid-ask spreads for government securities in the larger, well-developed emerging markets are on the order of 5 to 10 basis points.

Table 5.4. Secondary Trading of Fixed-Income Domestic Securities
(In millions of U.S. dollars, 2005)

	Public Debt		Private			
	Outright	Repo	Debt	Equity	Others	Total
Costa Rica						
Trading volume	4,881	19,528	-	28	4,919	29,356
In percent of GDP	*25.0*	*99.8*	-	*0.1*	*25.2*	
Dominican Republic						
Trading volume	-	-	0.8	-	-	0.8
In percent of GDP	-	-	*0.0*	-	-	
El Salvador						
Trading volume	407	5,227	408	80	724	6,846
In percent of GDP	*2.4*	*30.9*	*2.4*	*0.5*	-	
Guatemala						
Trading volume	259	16,109	-	-	-	16,368
In percent of GDP	*0.9*	*58.9*	-	-	-	
Honduras						
Trading volume	2,034	-	-	-	-	2,034
In percent of GDP	*25.5*	-	-	-	-	
Nicaragua						
Trading volume	108	34	-	-	-	142
In percent of GDP	*2.1*	*0.7*	-	-	-	*2.8*
Panama						
Trading volume	120	23	74	203	34	454
In percent of GDP	*0.8*	*0.2*	*0.5*	*1.3*	*0.2*	*2.9*

Source: National stock exchanges.

and the growing reluctance of public issuers to pay issuance fees may make consolidation both necessary and desirable. There is a need to examine the consolidation of the brokerage industry within the region and encourage well-capitalized foreign brokerage houses, cross-listings across countries, and, eventually, consolidation of the trading platforms themselves. Consolidation of domestic exchanges is also worth considering in Guatemala, where there are two competing exchanges within a small market. However, cross-border consolidation entails many important challenges in countries without a common currency or regulatory bodies. While these issues need to be examined in detail, the global impetus toward consolidation of smaller bourses needs to be recognized and harmonization of listing and trading practices within the region needs to be speeded up.

Investor Universe and Regulation of Investments in Public Debt

A preliminary examination of the regulation of principal institutional investors in public debt markets finds three broad problems: inadequacies in the regulatory framework for the securities markets themselves, limitations on the institutional investors, and limitations on those investors' investment portfolios.

The enabling framework for securities issuances, markets, and regulation of markets is either lacking or in need of upgrading in many countries. In Nicaragua, a draft securities market law pending congressional approval for some years would allow the dematerialization of securities and the issuance of asset-backed instruments, thereby widening the set of available securities and facilitating development of a liquid secondary market. In Guatemala, weak institutions (e.g., a securities registry) act as a temporary substitute for a proper securities regulator.[12] The absence of a superintendency of securities has also seriously hindered the creation of a central depository of securities.

Throughout the region there are also gaps in the legal and regulatory framework for institutional investors. In turn, these gaps affect development of local government securities markets. In particular, the regulation of private pension funds and mutual funds is inadequately developed in most countries. In Nicaragua, design of a law to regulate the creation of private pension funds

[12]A securities law was passed in 2006.

was abandoned in 2003 following a vigorous debate in congress. In the Dominican Republic, pension funds are not permitted to invest in government or central bank securities, mainly because of opposition from other investors who fear losing a lucrative investment opportunity. In the absence of well-developed mutual funds, brokers in many countries are offering less well-regulated variations such as participations in so-called "investment portfolios." Investors are not always aware of the liquidity and pricing of such investments, and at times bank deposit clients are drawn into such investments (e.g., in Costa Rica) without fully realizing the possibility of capital losses or the illiquidity of such products. The introduction of well-developed mutual fund laws, together with sound governance, pricing, and mark-to-market practices, would help develop the investor base for government securities in the long run.

The Challenge of Creating a Regional Market

Despite trade and political links, Central America's regional public debt markets and capital markets more generally are not well integrated. There are many benefits of greater regional integration of financial markets, but getting there involves addressing several important challenges and complex issues. The paragraphs that follow sketch some of the issues involved in the context of sovereign debt.

Smaller economies such as those in Central America appear to have much to gain from regional financial integration. Small financial markets suffer from high transaction costs, small volumes, a small investor base, and a small universe of investment products and instruments. For issuers of securities, including the sovereign, small domestic markets may limit the size and tenor of issues, competitive pricing, or the speed of execution. For investors as well as financial intermediaries, the limited investment universe may result in suboptimal diversification and risk concentration. Brokers and markets, particularly security exchanges, may find it difficult to survive or grow without a critical mass of trading. Smaller economies can partly offset these well-known problems by integrating within a common financial space. Within Central America, these benefits are relatively easy to obtain given the geographical proximity, shared language, common time zones, relatively free trade and capital movements, presence of several regional financial groups, and political will to promote regional ties.

But in the absence of further economic and regulatory convergence, significant problems hamper further integration of regional capital markets in general and the sovereign debt markets in particular. Central America remains divided by currencies. Macroeconomic policies, debt burdens, sovereign ratings, and debt sustainability are materially different across countries. Thus, sovereign debt issued by different countries remains as securities with very different risk characteristics. Eurobonds issued by the regional sovereigns can be easily invested in and traded by regional investors. But underwriting and over-the-counter trading of such issues will remain located largely in global financial centers, given the advantages of the large global investor universe, speed of execution, competitiveness, and low cost they offer. Thus, it is more meaningful to think of regional integration within sovereign debt markets in terms of a common market and investor base for sovereign debt issued in regional currencies. As the situation currently stands, further integration of the regional currency debt is likely to be hampered by two important factors: the separation of regional security exchanges, and the restrictions on institutional investors such as banks, insurers, and pension funds.

First, tradable domestic debt of each issuer is typically listed only in local bourses and often in local currencies. In the absence of any centralized links between regional exchanges themselves, and the absence of regional brokerage firms, nonresident transactions in such locally listed securities typically entail working through a local broker. Such transactions generally are less efficient than the purchase of eurobonds through a broker based in Miami or New York. The listing of government securities across regional exchanges is often cumbersome, as the exchanges do not have completely common listing standards. While some bilateral arrangements to overcome these problems have been undertaken,[13] they fall short of a regional securities exchange, coupled with a regional custodian and clearing and settlement systems. The latter is a major initiative that would require substantial effort, study, and cooperation by the private sector participants.

Second, institutional investors face substantial restrictions on the purchase of regional foreign government securities that cannot be readily harmonized. Pension funds, and sometimes banks, are subject to prohibitions or tight limits on the purchase of foreign government securities. In all cases, banks face higher capital adequacy requirements on foreign than on domestic government securities, which carry zero risk weighting. In Nicaragua, the 1995 regulatory framework on the investment portfolio of commercial banks requires the prior authorization of the bank regulator to acquire sovereign securities (with the exception of Nicaraguan and U.S. instruments). Similarly, the 2005 bill regulating the investment portfolio of insurance and reinsurance companies requires the prior authorization of the regulator for the acquisition of all foreign sovereign securities. In a nutshell, prudential restrictions on

[13]Various bilateral agreements have been undertaken to facilitate the cross-listing of securities, as in the case of El Salvador, Costa Rica, and Panama.

foreign government securities are tight. Capital adequacy standards cannot be readily harmonized given the substantial differences in sovereign credit ratings, as well as implications for currency risk. As for pension fund investments, most countries would have to carefully balance the cost and benefits of foreign investments and consider the interests of the fund beneficiaries rather than sovereign debt issuers. While eurobond issues may be readily sold to a global investor base, local currency issues cannot be so seamlessly sold to the regional investor base.

Key Problems and Recommendations

Central American countries face many important challenges in developing local public debt markets. Establishing ready sovereign access to domestic funding and a liquid and efficient domestic secondary market are at best medium-term goals. This section highlights the key problems in public debt management and the steps needed to resolve them.[14] While the problems are not unknown to regional officials, significant political, legal, and fiscal constraints have prevented more effective resolution to date. Thus, it is worth emphasizing at the outset that successful implementation of the recommended measures would require strong macroeconomic performance, political stability, a clear political consensus for the desired reforms between the legislative and executive branches, and substantial technical capacity or technical assistance.[15] The measures recommended below are grouped thematically, and while certain key actions are singled out as particularly important, further detailed work must be done to identify more precise country-specific action plans and timing for implementation. While substantial progress in implementing these measures can be made in two to three years, it is important to establish a clear, ambitious, and unambiguous goal leading to restoration of ready sovereign access to domestic markets at a reasonable cost, and efficient functioning of the secondary markets.

The most critical and strategic steps for improving public debt management in virtually all the countries in the region involve (1) developing a medium-term debt management strategy and formally defining and building capacity for debt management units; (2) eliminating the central bank's quasi-sovereign deficit; (3) converting a large stock of nontradable and nonstandard domestic debt through liability management operations; and (4) eliminating future issuance of nonstandard debt. These four steps need to be undertaken as an integral and well-coordinated package that can be labeled "strategic debt management." A variety of other measures are also needed to simplify and improve primary market issuance, make price discovery more efficient, and improve secondary market trading. But without the four strategic debt management measures, additional measures would only make a marginal contribution to solving the larger problems at hand.

Strategic Debt Management

It is important for all countries to develop a formal, medium-term debt management strategy, as advocated by the IMF as part of a debt sustainability framework. Several Central American countries have large debt problems relative to their economic aggregates. Moreover, their debt problems are exceedingly complex. The present approach of managing these problems through routine issuance decisions with inadequate debt management units does not fully recognize the gravity of the problem. The inability of virtually all countries to place in local markets, say, issues on the order of $100 million for five years with a reasonable assurance of full subscription, is a strategic limitation. It also stands in sharp contrast to improvements in domestic market access by some other highly-indebted countries (e.g., Jamaica and Uruguay) and to the considerable successes of Panama, Guatemala, El Salvador, and the Dominican Republic themselves in accessing eurobond markets. Again, while highly desirable and feasible, the task of developing an adequate medium-term strategy cannot be underestimated. It would need substantial country-specific technical assistance, with an important role again for the international financial institutions.

The overall capacity for debt management needs to be significantly strengthened in all Central American countries. While this chapter has not focused much on institutional aspects, it is generally clear that the regional debt management units within the ministries of finance have significant weaknesses in terms of mandate, skills, staff size, and resources. Strengthening these entities requires adequate formal recognition of them as debt management units, definition of their mandate and accountability requirements, and adequate staffing and budget support. Such units need not require large staff; most offices may not need more than five employees. But staffing with the right personnel is critical.

The five countries with significant accumulated central bank debt or continuing central bank deficits—Costa Rica, the Dominican Republic, El Salvador,

[14]While this regional study naturally focuses on the more common problems of the region, and the authorities have a strong interest in regional solutions, a full program of local sovereign debt market development would address individual country situations.

[15]The authorities have accepted most of the recommendations of this study and formally requested further technical assistance to improve the region's debt management capacity and debt structure. In early 2007, there was an agreement in principle between the IMF and the regional authorities on a multi-year technical assistance program with potential participation of the World Bank as well.

Honduras, and Nicaragua—need to consider full recapitalization of central banks at market terms so as to eliminate or substantially reduce central bank debt issuance in a phased manner.[16] While the sustainability of overall public finances is an important macroeconomic challenge beyond the scope of this chapter, recognition of central bank debt is more of a political, legal, and technical problem. While such problems ought not to be minimized, recapitalization of the central bank should be addressed as part of a comprehensive strategy to eliminate future central bank losses and integrate the fragmented sovereign debt market. Most countries have already taken important first steps in recognizing such losses and establishing precedents for recapitalization. It is now desirable to speed up this process, issuing marketable bonds in future recapitalizations, and replacing existing recapitalization bonds with marketable instruments. Both new issuance at market terms and conversion may need to be suitably phased in to accommodate certain fiscal and legal constraints. But the goal should be to clearly restore the central bank's solvency and future profitability, and eliminate the perpetual problem of dual sovereign issuers in the medium term. Designing appropriate options, assessing the related evolution of central bank profit and capital and of sovereign debt, and reconciling the latter with the current program targets of international financial institutions may require substantial technical assistance. Institutions such as the IMF can play an important role in supporting this effort.

Where needed, central banks could be provided tradable government securities for open market operations. In some cases, recapitalization of the central bank (i.e., transfer of losses) may not leave it with a sufficient stock of public debt with which to carry out monetary policy operations effectively. In these circumstances, consideration could also be given to issuing a stock of "sequestered" government securities to the central bank for such purposes, in lieu of an additional capital injection or issuance of central bank securities. Important details—including the appropriate treatment for fiscal accounting, public debt statistics, and debt issuance authority—would need to be customized and fleshed out for individual country situations. But the broad outline of such an operation would entail issuance of standard government securities to the central bank, with the bank maintaining "contra" accounts in its books. The latter would reflect both the acquisition of government securities as assets as well as a corresponding liability to repay the government with identical interest and amortization terms. The transactions between the central bank and the government would thus not entail any net cash flow. The central bank could then use these special government securities, which would be identical to other public debt, for open market operations or repos.[17]

Conversion of existing nonstandard debt issued to the central bank and other creditors is another highly promising but technically challenging effort that warrants high priority. In addition to the nonstandard debt issued to the central bank, virtually all countries have a substantial stock of nonstandard and nontradable debt issued to private holders in lieu of arrears, confiscation of property, and other measures. In the rare instances that such debt trades, it carries huge discounts. Trading benefits primarily the few market intermediaries, typically at the expense of the often unsophisticated holders of such debt. While conversion of such debt into marketable debt is not easy, several recent examples of complex domestic debt transformations by Brazil, Colombia, and Mexico, and of external debt by the Dominican Republic and Panama, suggest the fundamental feasibility of such transactions. Conversion of current nonmarketable debt also holds major benefits for the sovereign. First, most conversion has the potential for significant reduction in the nominal value of public debt, thus reducing the well-published level of debt. Second, conversions could be particularly useful to introduce new longer-term maturities in the domestic market and extend the current yield curve gradually.[18] Fleshing out such internal debt restructuring may also require substantial country-specific technical assistance for designing appropriate options and implementing the same.

Issuance Process and Auction Mechanisms

In countries that continue to issue securities under a discriminatory price auction, the practice of issuing *nonstandard* securities with different rates of interest (rather than at different prices) should be stopped forthwith. Technically, this change is easily accommodated in the existing auction arrangements, and market participants would be able to adapt to it easily. Internal procedural rules or laws could be modified—with interim decrees, where needed—to expedite the transition.

Concurrent issuance of government and central bank paper in a single series and auction should be phased out. While central bank issuance in its own name should

[16]While this chapter does not deal with central bank autonomy issues, such recapitalization should be part of an overall plan to ensure adequate independence of the central banks.

[17]In fact, such securities of an appropriate tenor may be issued to the central bank at market-clearing prices determined in the relevant standard competitive auctions.

[18]For instance, suppose it is difficult to introduce a 10-year maturity local bond because the domestic market is illiquid and the sovereign, to date, has issued bonds only up to 5-year maturity to investors. Conversion of, say, a 30-year bond issued to the central bank into 7-year and 10-year bonds with reasonable extrapolation of current yield curve could start some trading up to 10-year maturity, allowing the "market rates" for 7-year and 10-year maturities to be gradually discovered.

be eliminated altogether, if it does have to be continued, the two issuers should not seek to force a single auction upon investors. Such commingled auctions, such as those in Costa Rica, are more likely to raise the cost of funding for both issuers and cannot prevent secondary market prices from diverging. That said, in several countries, at present, the sovereign faces considerably more difficult access to the market than the central bank, and this transition would take time (perhaps a few years) to improve market access. However, there needs to be a recognition that improved sovereign access to the market must come about from fundamental improvements in debt sustainability, developing a strict culture of honoring debt-service payments, and more generally all sovereign payment obligations, rather than "association" with the central bank in a joint auction.

Throughout the region, the issuers should slowly develop a commitment to accepting market discipline. Regional sovereign issuers should naturally retain the legal right to reject bids they consider inconsistent with the market rate. There are also concerns in many markets that the bidders, both from public and private sectors, could exercise oligopolistic power and raise interest rates payable by the sovereign. However, the issuers' behavior at auctions must also be guided by a long-term commitment to open and transparent auctions as the principal mechanism to raise funding domestically. Most sovereigns also have a compelling financing need that requires them to re-enter the auction market in a matter of days after undersubscribed or even deserted auctions. Thus, all things considered, there seems to be a stronger case for issuers to phase in greater acceptance of market bids, developing a long-term and steady investor base, and developing a convergence about the appropriate level of interest rates. In particular, once an auction amount is announced and is covered (i.e., bids cover the amount offered), rejection of competitive bids short of the offered volume (minus any noncompetitive bids) should be an exception rather than the rule. To avoid excessive uncertainty and costs for competitive market participants[19] and the resulting long-term loss of investor interest, convergence of interest rate expectations of issuers and investors should be encouraged through several measures. These include developing a more liquid secondary market that would provide continuous quotations on current interest rates, holding a regular dialog with market participants, especially concerning new maturities, widening the investor pool by developing domestic institutional investors, and attracting regional and foreign investors. Where rejections are considered necessary, an effort should be made to explain the issuers' stance and provide guidance to the market for future auctions. Again, while such a commitment to market discipline would be an appropriate medium-term goal for most countries, the pace of transition would need to be carefully analyzed and implemented in a country-specific manner.

Multiple avenues of noncompetitive bids should be closed, while all noncompetitive bidders should be encouraged to participate in the announced auctions. As a rule, the reliance on separate post-auction windows should be stopped. At times, issuers justify such windows on the grounds that auctions are insufficiently competitive, and such specialized windows (say, to retail investors or public sector investors) enable issuers to fulfill financing needs at more reasonable interest rates.[20] However, when it is a routine practice, the use of such windows eventually drains interest and competitiveness from the "mainstream" auctions, reduces the volume of securities issued in large, competitive, and publicly announced auctions, and signals the unwillingness of issuers to accept market rates in competitive auctions. While noncompetitive bids per se can be allowed, noncompetitive bidders should be encouraged to participate in the *same* auction. This should also apply to the forced placement of government paper with public sector enterprises, as in Costa Rica.

Consideration should also be given to allowing competitive bids by public sector borrowers. The standard advice to keep public sector investors out of competitive bids, and thus prevent them from influencing market clearing prices, has validity in certain situations. However, in the specific context of the region, and Panama in particular, it appears not to serve a useful purpose, as the participation of such bidders is large and indirectly affects the cutoffs set at competitive auction as well. Accordingly, it appears preferable to allow all public sector investors—including banks and pension funds—to participate in competitive bids, but with enough operational autonomy for them to set their own bids without "guidance" from the government.

Countries that use discriminatory price auctions—Costa Rica, El Salvador, Honduras, and Panama—could consider adopting uniform price auctions. While there is enough precedent for both auctions globally, there is a stronger theoretical justification on balance to adopt uniform price auctions. While discriminatory

[19]Market participants complain of the need to maintain very short-term liquidity ahead of auctions and the opportunity cost thereof in case of rejection of their bids.

[20]Some issuers justify the use of windows on the grounds that they use the immediately preceding cut-off or average interest rates in the preceding auctions as reference rates. In active trading environments, the rate determined in an auction a week or two earlier would not necessarily constitute the current "market" rate. More importantly, the existence of post-auction windows either provides incentives to eligible private participants in the window to drop out of auctions, thus compounding the loss of competitiveness in auctions, or creates mechanisms to give public sector investors access to below-market interest rates. In some cases, windows are used to offer securities not generally available in regular auctions, as is the case of the retail window for longer-term central bank paper offered by the Dominican Republic.

price auctions need not involve nonstandard issuance, adoption of uniform price auctions would allow a faster transition away from nonstandard issuance. Again, it is important to recognize the variation in convergence on market rates across the region, take measures to educate and consult with market participants, and phase in the adoption of such changes at a pace appropriate to specific country circumstances.

Several steps are needed to eliminate fragmentation of current securities issuance and extend yield curves. As discussed, an important step would be the recapitalization of central banks with the issuance of longer-term, standardized, and tradable bonds, and the elimination of short-term central bank issuance for its own financing purposes. Second, conversion of the large stock of existing nontradable securities would enable most governments to jumpstart the creation of medium- to long-term securities of up to 10 years, which would start generating secondary market quotes and a benchmark yield curve. Subsequent medium-to-long-term placements could be considered through the re-opening of these issues. Issuance calendars could be consolidated, particularly for longer-term securities. As sovereigns become the principal issuers of long-term debt, they need to commit to issuance in minimum volumes, which is one of the key goals of the Central American Monetary Council's harmonization project. For the region, a minimum domestic issuance size of $100 million equivalent would seem an appropriate target.

Secondary Market Trading

Brokerage fees need to be reduced in most countries. The simultaneous solution to the chicken-and-egg problem of low trading volume and high transaction costs requires a multipronged approach that includes (1) reduction of exchange and brokerage fees; (2) equal access to all institutional investors in primary auctions with uniform participation rules for government and central bank auctions; and (3) other measures outlined above for extension of the yield curve and conversion of nonstandard government debt into more standardized and tradable instruments. Using stock exchanges and brokers for primary auctions of sovereign or central bank debt is of somewhat dubious value. While the still-limited stage of development of local securities exchanges must be kept in mind, it would be preferable to shift attention to promoting secondary market trading through the measures discussed above.

Certain institutional problems in specific markets need to be resolved expediently, perhaps with some gentle public encouragement. There may be merit in encouraging the various parties involved in Guatemala to consider uniting the two exchanges. Authorities in the Dominican Republic need to facilitate a solution to the dispute between the two competing custodial agencies. Issuance of dematerialized securities needs to become the norm in countries that do not yet issue them in this manner.

Other Measures

There is a need to expedite the passage of broader securities market legislation in several countries. Across the region, there are bills to improve the regulatory framework for the securities market, replace ad hoc presidential decrees, create interbank trading platforms, dematerialize securities, introduce asset-backed securities, and facilitate the formation and regulation of institutional investors. These measures would have profound beneficial effects on the depth and efficiency of public debt markets.

Conclusions

The countries of Central America face substantial challenges in managing their public debt burden and ensuring debt sustainability. Development of domestic public debt markets is of crucial importance for developing capital markets. While macroeconomic and fiscal discipline are of fundamental importance, regional public debt managers also address several important technical problems to achieve reliable access to domestic financing and create wider and more liquid public debt markets. The most important responses include developing and implementing a medium-term debt management strategy, building the technical capacity of debt management units, transferring the quasi-fiscal debt of central banks to the government, restructuring nonstandard and nontradable debt, and taking a series of steps to promote capital markets generally and pension and mutual funds in particular. While such a comprehensive reform must be implemented carefully, over the medium term, and at a pace consistent with the particularities of individual markets, a clear vision and political commitment at the highest levels are needed in most countries. Taking action on the measures that have been proposed may require substantial technical assistance to individual countries and sustained political will. Developing an efficient regional public debt market that overcomes the limitations of size and scale is an important long-term goal. Development of a more solid domestic debt market would provide the foundation on which such an integrated regional market could be built in the future.

VI Characterizing Monetary Policy

Luis I. Jácome H. and Eric Parrado[1]

Compared with the rest of Latin America, Central America has a history of low inflation (Figure 6.1).[2] No country except Nicaragua has fallen into the clutches of hyperinflation, and during the 1990s and early 2000s, inflation dropped into single-digit rates. Nonetheless, price stability—defined in this chapter as the inflation in industrial countries—was never achieved, as inflation stalled above that in the rest of the Western Hemisphere. In addition, Central America appears vulnerable to a rebound of inflation—more than other countries in the region—as seen in the wake of the current oil price shock (Figure 6.2).

The downward trend in inflation across Central America has been accompanied by different patterns of monetary policy regimes. In particular, Panama and, more recently, El Salvador, adopted the U.S. dollar as legal tender; Costa Rica, Honduras, and Nicaragua have chosen an exchange rate-based policy regime; the Dominican Republic has in place a money targeting scheme; and Guatemala just shifted from money to inflation targeting. On these grounds, the fully dollarized economies have abdicated their right to conduct monetary policy, whereas those using the exchange rate as a nominal anchor maintained at best small room for maneuver. Only countries with a flexible exchange rate regime have been in a position to preserve the independent conduct of monetary policy—provided the exchange rate is effectively floating.

Today, the nondollarized Central American countries are revisiting how they conduct monetary policy, including in some cases a possible change of their policy regime. New developments are taking place, generally associated with growing regional integration with the U.S. economy. The Central American economies are increasingly open, dollarization is likely to continue at high levels, remittances from abroad are hitting record highs year after year, and, in general, countries in the region are expected to become more and more integrated into international capital markets. These trends inevitably pose challenges to the conduct of monetary policy, which explains the quest of central banks for the policy regime that better serves fulfilling their policy mandate under the new rules of the game.

This chapter discusses how monetary policies are conducted in Central America. Particular emphasis is given to the institutional underpinnings of monetary policy, the modalities of policy execution, and the factors underlying central bank reactions, mainly to inflation pressures.[3] Despite the importance of monetary policy in an environment of elusive price stability in Central America, the analysis of monetary policy has not been addressed recently in the literature.[4] Thus, the outcome of this chapter may offer information to practitioners and policymakers in these countries who are looking for the appropriate policy regime and its execution to achieve price stability.

Institutional Framework for Monetary Policy

During the last 15 years, all countries in the region have strengthened the institutional underpinnings for formulating and executing monetary policy. New central bank legislation was enacted, starting with Nicaragua in 1992 (and 1999) and followed by Costa Rica in 1995, Honduras in 1996 (and 2004), and Guatemala and the Dominican Republic in 2002.[5] The central bank reform focused monetary policy on efforts to achieve and preserve price stability. To fulfill this objective, central banks were granted enhanced autonomy, although comparatively less than in other Latin American countries that also reformed central bank legislation during the 1990s.[6] This section discusses

[1]Eric Parrado is affiliated with the Central Bank of Chile.

[2]"Central America" in this chapter refers to Costa Rica, Guatemala, Honduras, Nicaragua, and the Dominican Republic. References to El Salvador and Panama are occasionally made for comparative purposes.

[3]An analysis of exchange rate policies was already developed by Kim and Papi (2005) and Papaioannou (2003).

[4]See recent regional analyses such as Rennhack and Offerdal (2004) and Rodlauer and Schipke (2005), which focus on macroeconomic, structural reform, and integration issues, but do not address monetary policy.

[5]Even El Salvador reformed its central bank law in 1991, well before adopting the U.S. dollar as its legal tender in 2001.

[6]However, Central American central banks are by law more independent than central banks in the Caribbean, as reported in Jácome and Vázquez (2005).

Figure 6.1. Inflation in Central America and the Western Hemisphere
(In percent)

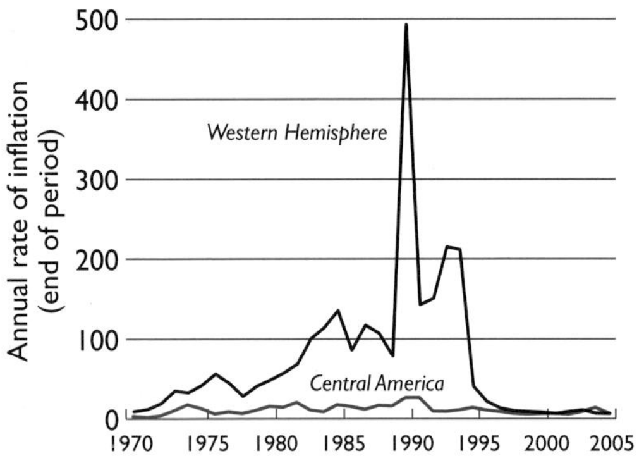

Source: IMF, *International Financial Statistics.*
Note: Central America excludes Nicaragua.

Figure 6.2. Inflation in Central America, the Western Hemisphere, and Industrialized Countries
(In percent)

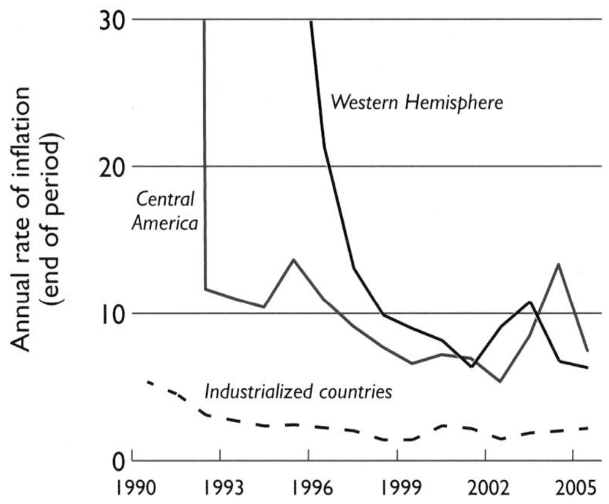

Source: IMF, *International Financial Statistics.*
Note: Central America includes Nicaragua.

the main features of central bank laws in relevant Central American countries, both across the region and compared with South American countries and Mexico. A stylized presentation of such legislation in each country is found in Table 6A.1.

Central Bank Reform

Following the reform of monetary legislation, central banks in the region no longer play the role of development banks with the aim of fostering growth. Today, they do not provide credit to specific sectors in the economy under preferential financial conditions, and they are not dependent on governments' economic policy guidelines. Rather, they concentrate on achieving stability conditions as a necessary—although not sufficient—condition for economic growth. To distill the main features of current central bank legislation, this chapter emphasizes five main criteria: policy mandate, political autonomy, economic independence, financial autonomy, and accountability and transparency.[7]

The policy mandate of central banks in Central America is focused on preserving price stability, although in some countries the banks also give attention to the competitiveness of tradable activities. Except for Guatemala, where the Monetary Board (the governing body of the Bank of Guatemala) is charged with "preserving the liquidity and solvency of the banking system, safeguarding the stability and strengthening of the national savings," the banks in the other four countries cite price stability as their policy objective.[8] Central banks in Costa Rica and Honduras also have as an objective to preserve the external value of the domestic currency, together with the responsibility to assure the normal functioning of the payment system, which is also posted as an objective in Nicaragua's central bank charter. The simultaneous focus on preserving the internal and external value of the domestic currency explains the pursuit of real exchange rate targeting in Costa Rica and Honduras. This duality in the central banks' policy mandate is also prone to policy conflicts, as when the banks respond to capital inflows to prevent a real appreciation trend despite the disinflation effects.

The governing structure of central banks in Central America is less uniform, with some countries more than others featuring some degree of political autonomy. Despite progress on this front with respect to their historical submission to government policies, most central banks in the region still have only limited

[7]"Autonomy" and "independence" are used interchangeably in this chapter, although they may have slightly different meanings. See Lybek (1998).

[8]The objective of the Monetary Board of the Bank of Guatemala is defined in the 1986 Constitution (Article 133). However, the 2002 Organic Law of the Bank of Guatemala establishes that its fundamental objective is "to contribute to create and preserve the most favorable conditions for an orderly development of the national economy and, to this end, it will favor the monetary, exchange rate, credit conditions that promote price stability." Given that the Monetary Board is by constitutional mandate in charge of determining monetary, exchange rate, and credit policies, its objective unambiguously prevails over that of the Bank of Guatemala.

political autonomy de jure. In all Central American countries, central bank governors are appointed by the president, as was the case prior to the monetary reform. In addition, in most countries the executive branch has substantial leeway to remove central bank governors and other members of the board of directors, which implicitly puts central bank authorities in a vulnerable position.[9] In turn, the term of the central bank governors coincides with that of the executive branch, and, notably, in the Dominican Republic it is only two years. As for the rest of the members of the board, their term varies from the two-year period in the Dominican Republic to an expanded term of 90 months in Costa Rica. On the other hand, it is remarkable that in the Dominican Republic and Guatemala, the private sector still has strong involvement in appointing the members of the Monetary Board, as is called the government body of the central bank in those countries—indirectly in the former country and directly in the latter (Table 6A.1).[10] Putting all these provisions together, it can be concluded that in theory the legal reform in Central America did not untie the horizon of monetary policy decisions from the political business cycle.

Economic independence of central banks is common across the region. In general, central banks feature "instrument independence," as they are empowered to freely execute monetary policy to attain their goals. In particular, central banks have the legal authority to use without interference monetary policy instruments to influence market interest rates, thereby potentially affecting inflation. They are legally restricted—and even prohibited, as in Guatemala—from extending credit to finance government spending, except for short-term advances to cope with seasonal liquidity shortages (Honduras and Nicaragua). Furthermore, in Costa Rica, Honduras, and Guatemala, the central bank serves as a legal filter to restrain pubic debt increases, as those banks have to provide a technical opinion about the appropriateness of new public debt issuance. What is not clear is whether central banks in Central America legally enjoy "target independence," given that the new legislation does not stipulate central banks' capacity for defining a policy target, such as inflation, independently from the government, although, in practice, governments in the region have proved to be quite supportive of de facto target independence.

However, economic autonomy is undermined in some countries by the lack of financial autonomy of central banks. On this front, there has been no major improvement following the reform of central bank legislation. This is particularly true in Costa Rica, Guatemala, and Honduras, where there is no legal provision to protect the integrity of central bank capital. Alternatively, in the Dominican Republic and Nicaragua, governments are compelled to make up for central bank losses if they cannot be compensated with statutory reserves. In practice, however, this legal mandate has not materialized, as both central banks feature a large negative capital, since they absorbed the bulk of the losses stemming from the banking crises that hit both countries during the early 2000s.[11] Weak financial autonomy raises market concerns about central banks' abilities to effectively conduct monetary policy, as persistent large losses may undermine the operating independence of central banks and eventually curtail the effectiveness of monetary policy actions. This is because the accumulation of central bank losses may limit either their capacity to mop up excess liquidity or their ability to raise interest rates when conducting open-market operations, as they become an undesirable source of monetization that will require subsequent sterilization and additional costs.

Accountability and transparency requirements are a key innovation in central bank legislation in Central America. Before the legal reform, central banks in the region were basically committed to developing and publishing an annual report that took stock of the major economic developments of the country in a given year and focused on central bank policies, but not to the extent to which those policies attained their goals. The annual reports hence became a source primarily of academic interest, and were neither an instrument to monitor monetary policy nor a source of timely information for market participants. With the current legal provisions, central banks have become more accountable with respect to the autonomy they enjoy. They must appear before congress and report on the status of their policy goals. In Guatemala, accountability goes farther, as the central bank is required to disclose an explanatory monetary report twice a year. Transparency by law has also improved in most countries, as all central banks are required to disclose their financial statements, in some cases certified by an external private auditor (the Dominican Republic and Guatemala). Transparency conditions are also more stringent from a legal perspective in Guatemala, where the Bank of Guatemala is legally required to publish policy decisions to level the information playing field.

In sum, monetary policy in Central America has received an injection of institutional strength as a result

[9]Moreover, in Guatemala, congress has the right to dismiss the governor of the central bank—with a qualified majority—if its annual report to congress is not found to be satisfactory.

[10]The same happens in Nicaragua, since the president appoints the members of the central bank board in consultation with the private sector.

[11]Financial weakness is exacerbated in Honduras because the central bank budget has to be approved by congress. Guatemala also faces a potential restriction to maintaining operational autonomy, as congress has to authorize the issuance of central bank stabilization bonds, which, however, are not currently used for open market operations.

of the reform of central bank legislation, though important flaws still remain. Progress is noticeable in focusing the mandate of central banks on combating inflation and preserving price stability and in granting banks operational autonomy. However, this progress is undermined in those countries where the central bank is also required to preserve the external value of the domestic currency because of the potential policy conflicts entailed vis-à-vis the objective of price stability. Also, political autonomy is still less than what is needed to assure the formulation of monetary policy, disregarding political business cycles. In addition, strengthening financial autonomy of central banks could enhance the effectiveness and credibility of monetary policy.[12] Finally, there is room to step up accountability and transparency procedures.

Measuring Central Bank Independence

As a result of legal reforms, central banks in Central America have enhanced their autonomy and institutional strength on all fronts. This improvement is captured through an index of legal central bank independence that, in essence, gives credit to central banks for their institutional capacity to arrest inflation and penalizes their role as government financers and active participants in political business cycles.

The index used in this chapter is based on the Cukierman (1992) index, which is the best known and most widely accepted metric to assess legal central bank independence. The index here incorporates the same four broad criteria included in the Cukierman index to capture key aspects of legal central bank independence, plus some additional features such as lender-of-last-resort and financial independence provisions. It also incorporates a fifth criterion, namely, accountability and transparency requirements.[13] After applying different weights for each criterion, the resulting value of the index gives a score that varies in the scale between zero and one. Specifically, the first criterion measures the political autonomy of central banks by assessing how central bank governors and their board of directors are appointed, the length of their tenure—relative to the term of the executive branch—and the legal provisions for their removal. Thus, legal provisions that untie monetary policy from the political business cycle are rewarded (20 percent weight). The second criterion refers to the nature of the central bank mandate, assigning the highest marks to those banks that primarily pursue the objective of preserving price stability (15 percent). The third criterion gives credit to autonomous central banks in the formulation of monetary policy (15 percent). The fourth criterion primarily rewards central bank restrictions in lending provisions to the government, but also penalizes provisions that entail excessive room for monetization when central banks act as a lender of last resort. In addition, it assigns high marks for the legal basis that requires the government to preserve central banks' financial integrity (40 percent). The fifth criterion positively evaluates central bank accountability and transparency requirements (10 percent).

Applying this index to central bank legislation—and the relevant aspects of national constitutions—it can be stated that central banks in Central America are today more independent than in their pre-reform period (Figure 6.3).[14] Yet they still lag behind most central banks in South America and Mexico (Figure 6.4). A cluster analysis reveals the aspects where Central American central banks are by law less independent than those in South America and Mexico. Decomposing the index into the five main criteria described above, major weaknesses relate to political autonomy and policy mandate criteria (Table 6.1). Political autonomy is greater in most other central banks in the region because the appointment of government bodies' and their dismissal generally requires legislative approval, and because their term exceed or overlaps electoral calendars, thereby reducing central banks' exposure to potential political interference. In turn, the policy mandate of other Latin American central banks is focused on preserving price stability, which is less prone to policy conflicts than in Central America, where central bank charters sometimes assign them conflicting objectives.

However, central banks in Central America perform better when it comes to measuring autonomy for policy formulation, since other countries in Latin America, such as Argentina, Mexico, and Venezuela, face de jure influences from the executive and legislative branches in the formulation of exchange rate policy.[15] Another factor underlying this result stems from the provision that gives powers to Central American central banks to restrict pubic debt expansion.

Both groups of countries rank nearly even in terms of lending restrictions to the government and accountability provisions. The latter mirrors the general consensus that exists relative to the inflationary effects of monetizing the fiscal deficit and the importance of holding central banks accountable as a key ingredient of their autonomy.

[12]To avoid extending a blank check from the government to the central bank, the latter should foster governance policies to make its operational expenses transparent, particularly the aggregate wage bill and other administrative outlays.

[13]A detailed specification of this index and its difference from the Cukierman index is found in Jácome and Vázquez (2005).

[14]The slight deterioration in the autonomy of the Central Bank of Honduras following the 2000 reform is because today, the executive branch has some more leeway than before to remove members of the central bank board of directors.

[15]In practice, this distortion is less of a problem when countries have in place a flexible exchange rate, as in Mexico, although the central bank still has no practical autonomy for maintaining a policy for the accumulation of international reserves.

Figure 6.3. Legal Central Bank Independence before and after Reform
(Index)

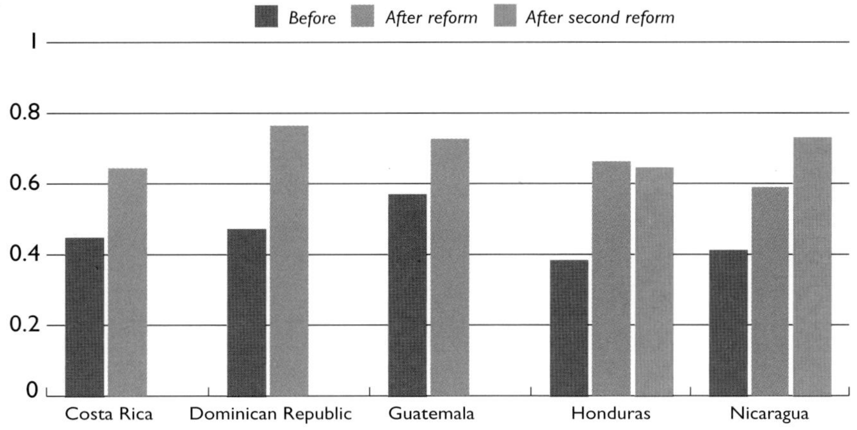

Note: There were two reforms in Honduras and Nicaragua.

Figure 6.4. Legal Central Bank Independence, All Latin America
(Index)

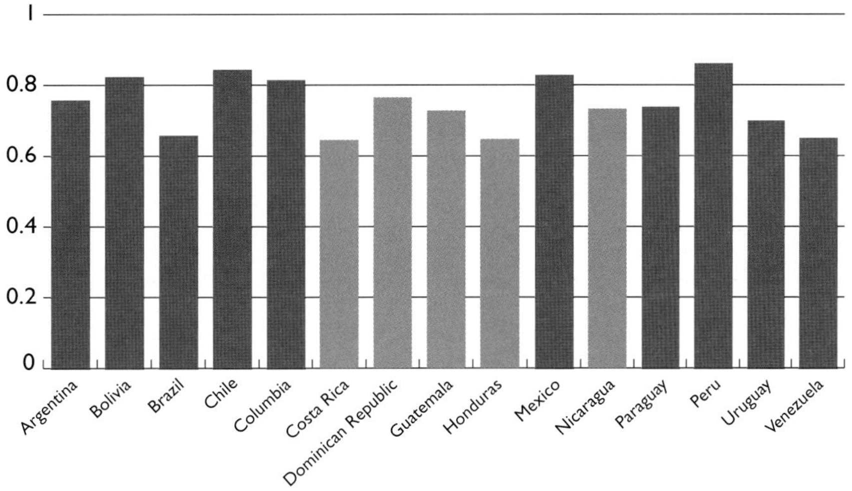

Central Bank Reform and Inflation

The years that followed the reform of central banks in Central America coincide in most countries with a period of lower inflation. The late reformers—the Dominican Republic and Guatemala—stand as exceptions. Inflation in the Dominican Republic soared in the aftermath of the full-fledged banking crisis in 2003, whereas in Guatemala it picked up due to the adverse effects of the oil shock in 2004–05. The other countries—including El Salvador in the 1990s—exhibit a decreasing inflation trend following the institutional reform of central banks, although in no country except for El Salvador did inflation converge to price stability, as measured by the rate of increase in prices in the industrial countries.

Table 6.1. Breakdown of Index of Legal Central Bank Independence: Central America versus South America and Mexico

	South America and Mexico	Central America
Total index as of 2005	0.769	0.704
Political autonomy	0.759	0.318
Central bank mandate	0.800	0.650
Monetary policy formulation	0.720	0.896
Central bank lending	0.753	0.820
Accountability	0.875	0.800

While the reform of central banks was not a triggering factor for reducing inflation in Central America, it served to lock in and preserve the momentum of an anti-inflation monetary policy. Indeed, there are no grounds to claim causality running from enhanced legal central bank independence to lower inflation in Central America because in almost all countries, inflation was already falling when the central bank legal reforms were adopted (Figure 6.5).[16]

[16]This outcome is consistent with the result obtained in the empirical analysis conducted by Jácome and Vázquez (2005) for Latin America and the Caribbean.

Figure 6.5. Central Bank Reform and Inflation in Central America
(In percent)

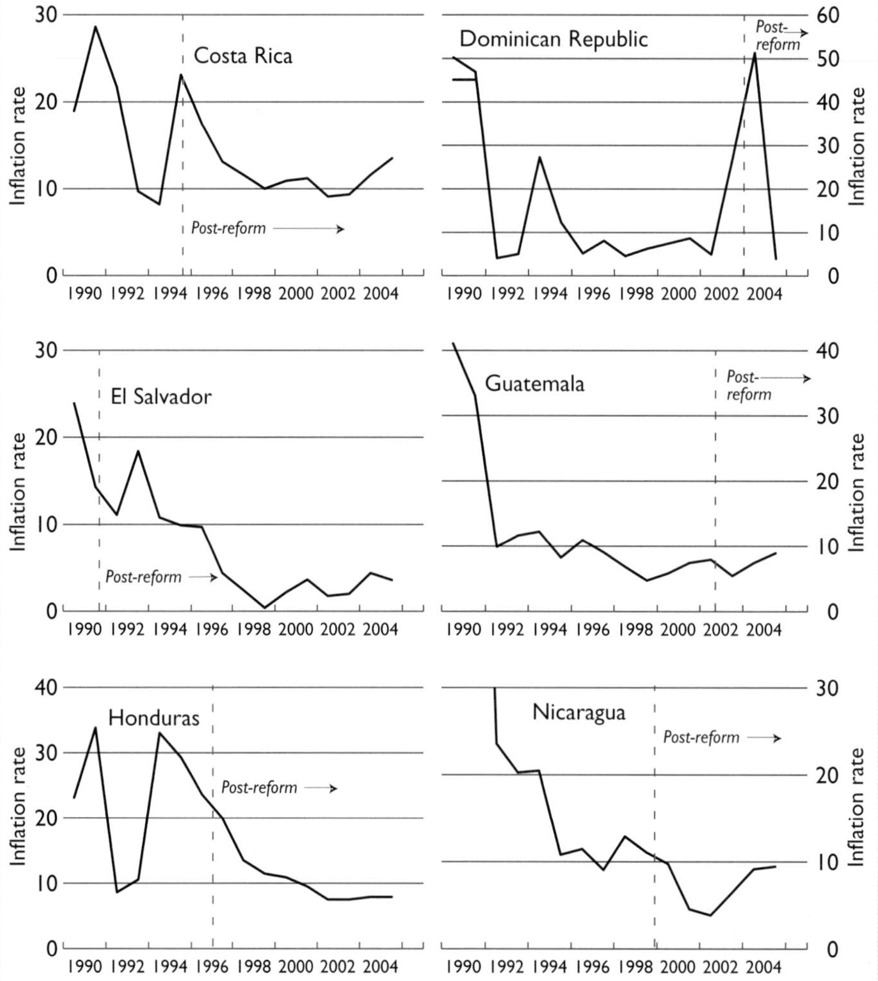

Sources: IMF, *World Economic Outlook*, various issues; and central bank legislation.

Figure 6.6. Inflation and Legal Central Bank Independence (CBI) in Latin America, 2000–03

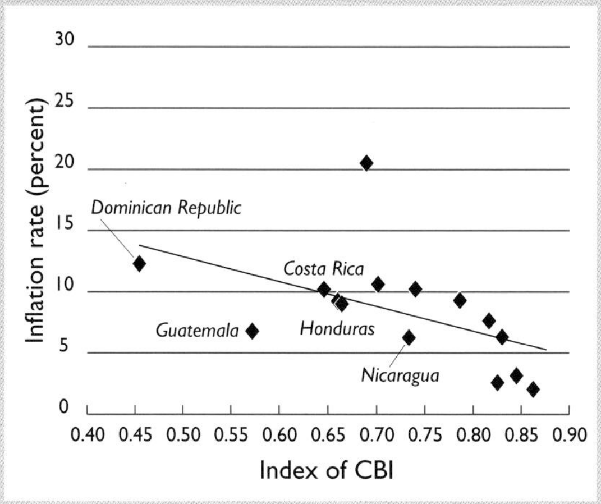

Figure 6.7. Inflation and Legal Central Bank Independence (CBI) in Latin America, 2004–05

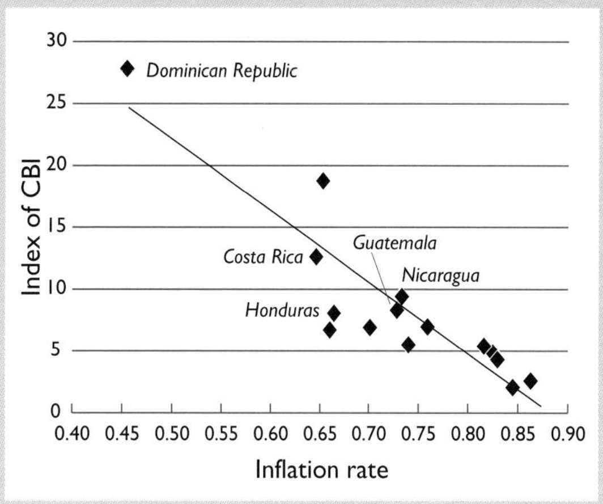

Despite the success of the Central American countries in reducing inflation, there is no room for complacency. On one hand, inflation never converged to price stability, as happened in other Latin American countries. On the other hand, inflation picked up again in all countries in the midst of the current oil shock more than in other countries in the region. This is evident when one compares average inflation in Latin America during 2000–03 and 2004–05, and notes that in the latest period, when world oil prices hit record highs, inflation picked up the most in the Central American countries—except for Venezuela.[17]

This seemingly greater vulnerability of the Central American economies to real external shocks may be attributed, at least partially, to their relatively lower legal central bank independence vis-à-vis most other countries in Latin America. As pictured in Figures 6.6 and 6.7, the inverse correlation between legal central bank independence and inflation in Latin America increased in 2004–05, which suggests that more independent central banks have been in a stronger position to weather the inflationary effects of the recent oil shock.[18]

The notion behind this statement is that the greater the independence of central banks, the higher is their credibility, and hence, their capacity to mitigate the impact on inflation stemming from the pass-through from increasing world oil prices to domestic oil prices.[19]

This outcome cannot be explained because the Central American economies are oil importers, and hence, they shifted the whole increase in oil prices into domestic fuel prices. In fact, many countries in Latin America applied the same policy rule and yet they have achieved a better inflation performance. For instance, while Chile, Colombia, and Peru—with the most independent central banks in the region—allowed even a higher pass-through from world oil prices to domestic fuel prices, this effect was not factored into the consumer price index as much as in the Central American countries.[20] Why? Because although all countries accommodated the first-round effects from the oil shock, central banks in the three South American countries better managed to mitigate the impact on inflation resulting from the second-round effect. The latter is associated with a more effective conduct of monetary policy against inflation and/or stronger policy credibility.

[17]In particular, the Central American countries rank above Chile, Peru, Colombia, Bolivia, and Mexico, with the Dominican Republic behaving as an outlier as a result of the effects of the 2003 systemic banking crisis.

[18]Besides the Central American countries, the figures include observations for all Latin American countries in South America (except for Ecuador) plus Mexico.

[19]The thrust of the argument prevails when we exclude the Dominican Republic from the figures, which is explained, in part, because central banks in countries like Colombia, Mexico, Chile in 2004, and Peru in 2005, continued making progress in abating inflation despite the adverse effects of the oil shock.

[20]According to the IMF (2006), the pass-through to domestic gasoline prices during 2003–05 in Chile, Colombia, and Peru was higher than in all the countries in our sample, except for the Dominican Republic.

Table 6.2. Taxonomy of Monetary Policy Strategies

	Monetary Targeting	Exchange Rate Targeting	Inflation Targeting
Final policy goal	Inflation	Competitiveness	Inflation
Secondary policy goal	Competitiveness	Inflation	Competitiveness
Intermediate target	Money supply	Real exchange rate	Forecasted inflation
Operational target	Money base	Rate of crawl	Overnight interest rate
Primary shock absorber	Nominal exchange rate	International reserves	Nominal exchange rate
Secondary shock absorber	Real interest rate	Real interest rate	Real interest rate

A Snapshot of Monetary Policy Formulation and Execution

Central America has a long tradition of exchange rate-based policy regimes. Besides Panama's century-old formal dollarization, El Salvador maintained a long period of a fixed exchange rate before adopting the dollar as its legal tender in 2001. Costa Rica, Honduras, and Nicaragua have followed an exchange rate targeting, with short interruptions in some of these countries during the early 1990s. This policy feature is not surprising given the structural economic characteristics of the Central American countries. They have widely open economies, closely integrated with the U.S. economy, and increasingly dollarized. Thus, the external sector is the main driver of economic activity, with most exports purchased by the U.S. market.[21] In this environment and with relatively high inflation, dollarization became a natural response from economic agents, in particular in those countries where the exchange rate was not allowed to fluctuate.[22] With the exchange rate playing a key role in affecting economic activity and price formation—and, in general, consumption and investment decisions—policymakers in Central America explicitly (due to a legal mandate) or implicitly have historically attached great importance to the external stability of domestic currencies.

While targeting the exchange rate favored anti-inflation efforts, it also imposed costs. In contrast with other Latin American countries, the use of the exchange rate to anchor inflation expectations in Central America—together with prudent fiscal policies—served well to reduce and maintain relatively low inflation. However, this also fostered dollarization among market participants without adopting appropriate hedging practices. In this environment, Central American central banks developed the "fear of floating" syndrome (Calvo and Reinhart, 2002) and entered into a vicious circle, where unhedged dollarization inhibited central banks from adjusting the exchange rate—to avoid damaging economic agents' balance sheets—and the lack of exchange rate flexibility encouraged further unhedged dollarization. In addition, targeting the real exchange rate may have introduced inertia to inflation, thereby hampering its convergence to price stability.

In what follows, this section briefly reviews the main features of monetary policy formulation and execution in the Central American countries and identifies recent developments. We use a taxonomy of monetary policy regimes as a guideline to distinguish between money, exchange rate, and inflation targeting. This taxonomy provides a comprehensive and consistent analytical framework to characterize the nature of policy regimes and their associated operational arrangements (Table 6.2).

The key notion behind this taxonomy is the identification not only of the final policy goal but also of the main shock absorber and the intermediate and operational targets consistent with each policy regime. Thus, money and inflation targeting allow the exchange rate to work as the main shock absorber in response to policy-induced or exogenous shocks, whereas exchange rate targeting relies on international reserves as its primary shock absorber. In addition, the practical experience shows that the real interest rate is a secondary shock absorber in all monetary policy strategies alike. On the other hand, money and inflation targeting share the same primary goal but differ as to which intermediate and operational targets they use to achieve their final policy goal. In turn, exchange rate targeting assigns priority to the competitiveness of tradable activities as a policy objective and relies on the real exchange rate and the rate of crawl as intermediate and operational targets, respectively.

Recent Trends in Policy Formulation

Formally, all Central American countries use financial programming as the cornerstone of monetary policy formulation, but they have adopted different monetary

[21]In particular, in Honduras and Nicaragua, the sum of exports and imports of goods—including net exports from *maquilas*—exceed 80 percent of GDP, with more than half of exports sold to the United States.

[22]Financial dollarization—defined as foreign currency deposits over total deposits, not including offshore institutions—is particularly noticeable in Nicaragua (close to 70 percent), Costa Rica (more than 55 percent, and 75 percent when the offshore is included), and Honduras (nearly 40 percent), as of end-2005.

regimes (Table 6A.2). Costa Rica, Honduras, and Nicaragua follow an exchange rate targeting rule. In particular, Nicaragua has in place a crawling peg regime; Costa Rica recently introduced a band that substitutes a crawling peg; and Honduras has been operating with a wider band, although effectively it was a crawling peg since the rate has been persistently evolving along the lower end of the exchange rate band.[23] In turn, the Dominican Republic and Guatemala allow the exchange rate to adjust, although, in practice, with limitations,[24] and are classified as money and inflation targeters, respectively (IMF, 2005). Thus, as small and very open economies, most countries in Central America rely on the exchange rate as the main factor guiding inflation expectations.

While in theory targeting the exchange rate leaves no room for policy maneuver, Central American central banks working under exchange rate targeting identify monetary aggregates as intermediate targets (see Table 6A.1). By definition, targeting the exchange rate makes monetary policy endogenous—provided there is perfect capital mobility. So, how can we explain this seemingly contradiction? From a practical standpoint, this is because Central American central banks are molded from the traditional financial programming framework, and hence, they target monetary aggregates and tend to adjust interest rates should deviations from targets occur. In any case, this can operate—in the short-run—because despite having open capital accounts, the Central American countries feature less than capital mobility.[25] As a result, the so-called "impossible trinity" may be less binding, and hence, central banks may have some scope to affect the money supply.[26]

In the absence of convergence of inflation to price stability, some countries in the region are starting to revisit their monetary policy regimes. In particular, Guatemala recently introduced an inflation targeting regime after having gradually abandoned its previous money targeting strategy. The reform of the organic law of the Bank of Guatemala in 2002 was a milestone to strengthen the bank's autonomy from the government. Based on this enhanced operational autonomy, the Bank of Guatemala has recently made progress in fostering its modeling and inflation forecasting capabilities, and in boosting the transparency of monetary policy formulation and execution, all of which are key building blocks for an inflation targeting regime.[27] Costa Rica seems to be moving in the same direction. However, its transition to inflation targeting will be more challenging as it also requires shifting to a flexible exchange rate regime after more than 20 years of maintaining a crawling peg. This transition has already started with the recent introduction of an exchange rate band that replaces the previous crawling peg regime.

How does this brief characterization of monetary policy regimes on the basis of banks' information in Central America reconcile with actual central bank data? The information in Table 6.3 provides preliminary answers to this question. It shows the volatilities of relevant macro-monetary variables during 2000–05 as a way of getting a flavor of the policy regime that is currently in place in the five Central American countries. We then compare the results with similar computations for other Latin American countries, including an exchange rate targeter such as Bolivia, and inflation targeters such as Chile, Colombia, Mexico, and Peru.

The results raise doubts about the true policy framework prevailing in some of the Central American countries. They only allow us to label Costa Rica and Nicaragua, and to a lesser extent Honduras—because of the low variability of international reserves—as exchange rate targeters. On the other hand, it appears more difficult to ascertain the policy regime embraced by the Dominican Republic and, in particular, Guatemala. These two countries feature more exchange rate flexibility than the former but far less flexibility than the inflation targeting countries in Latin America, which suggests that Guatemala and the Dominican Republic care systematically about exchange rate stability. On these grounds, Guatemala does not seem to be working yet as an inflation targeting but rather as a hybrid of inflation and exchange rate targeting, given the high variability of international reserves. The performance of real interest rates—with respect to contemporaneous inflation—does not exhibit major differences across countries, which suggests that they all use real interest rates as shock absorber.

Modernization of the Operational Framework

Today, all countries in Central America rely on indirect instruments to conduct monetary policy. Reserve requirements are used in all countries, but they are

[23]Recently, Honduras has been classified as featuring a fixed exchange regime because the lower end of the band became a horizontal line.

[24]During 2004 the exchange rate appreciation trend in Guatemala—associated with a surge in capital inflows—was coupled with a more than 20 percent increase in international reserves. The Bank of Guatemala's intervention in the foreign currency market explains a significant portion of this increase.

[25]For example, capital mobility is hindered in Honduras because of the restrictive effects imposed by the mandatory surrender requirement of foreign currency to the central bank, whereas in Costa Rica commercial banks are unable to increase their net foreign exchange position in excess of 0.5 percent per day.

[26]Moreover, a significant component of capital inflows to Central America stems from workers' remittances in the United States, which are inelastic to changes in the domestic interest rate.

[27]The disclosure of an inflation report and the publication of the minutes of the monetary policy committee meetings are two important landmarks that strengthen the transparency of monetary policy in Guatemala.

Table 6.3. Volatilities of Selected Macroeconomic Variables, 2000–05
(Standard deviations)

	Nominal Depreciation	Reserves (% change)	Real Interest Rates
	Central America and the Dominican Republic		
Costa Rica	0.13	7.54	2.19
Dominican Republic[1]	1.14	9.88	3.11
Guatemala[1]	0.71	6.69	1.74
Honduras	0.16	2.92	1.42
Nicaragua[1,2]	0.05	7.40	3.75
	Other Selected Countries in Latin America		
Bolivia	0.27	8.43	3.67
Chile	2.51	2.62	2.60
Colombia	2.23	2.41	1.36
Mexico	1.71	2.89	2.52
Peru	0.93	3.04	4.72

[1]The calculations cover the period 1996–2002 in the Dominican Republic and 2002 onward in Nicaragua in order to avoid capturing the effects on monetary variables of their systemic banking crises. In Guatemala, the period starts after late 2001, when a large sovereign large debt placement caused a once-and-for-all 50 percent increase in international reserves.

[2]For Nicaragua, given the lack of a consistent central bank interest rate series, the one-month deposit rate in the commercial banks is used as an imperfect substitute.

not envisaged as a dynamic tool of monetary control, except probably in Nicaragua, which tightens reserve requirements when the target of international reserves is challenged. In general, reserve requirements in most countries have remained over time almost invariably at about 15 percent (Table 6A.2). From another angle, reserve requirements are used as a buffer to cope with potential liquidity shortages in the banking system. In Honduras, they are also used as a buffer to cope with the limitations imposed by financial dollarization on the central bank's role as lender of last resort by establishing discriminatory rates against foreign currency deposits.

With the aim of shaping operational autonomy now established in the new central bank charters, most countries in Central America have created open market operation committees. The new institutional arrangement is intended to strengthen short-term policy responsiveness and separate the execution from the formulation of monetary policy—the latter typically a responsibility of central bank boards in these countries. This reform is particularly important in Central America, given the limited political independence of central banks, as was discussed earlier in this chapter. Yet, the institutional reform has not borne all its fruit, as the conduct of monetary policy exhibits important flaws.

In most countries in Central America, monetary policy lacks effectiveness. The main instrument of monetary policy is open market operations, which are used to steer monetary aggregates within the limits established in the financial programming of central banks. However, the effectiveness of open market operations is hindered because they are not executed under market premises.[28] In particular, interest rates are not allowed to adjust to reflect market preferences and expectations. Central banks use cut-off rates to restrain interest rate increases either because of potential political pressures that see such increases as undermining economic growth, or due to the limitations imposed by the already-weak financial position of most central banks.[29] Under these conditions, a meaningful yield curve is absent in all countries. This restricts central banks from extracting valuable information about markets' inflation expectations. In addition, central banks do not aim to manage short-term liquidity, and hence, interbank short-term interest rates in some countries

[28]There are also other practices that potentially hinder the effectiveness of monetary policy. For instance, in the Dominican Republic, the central bank focuses simultaneously on managing domestic debt, which at times is not consistent with the achievement of monetary policy goals. Another example is that of the Central Bank of Costa Rica, which conducts simultaneous auctions of government paper and its own securities (with equal maturities), and defines a single cut-off rate together with the treasury. If the central bank needs to tighten monetary policy a conflict of objectives emerges because the government generally prefers lower rather than higher interest rates to minimize the cost of servicing the current large sovereign debt.

[29]In Central America, central bank deficits are as high as more than 1 percent of GDP in most countries. As central banks' operating losses become an ongoing distortion, markets may have doubts about the long-term ability of the banks to preserve price stability.

tend to be volatile, a situation exacerbated by the relative shallowness of the money markets.

Recently, Costa Rica, the Dominican Republic, Guatemala, and Honduras established a policy rate, typically a short-term interest rate. However, it has had little effect on improving the transmission mechanism of monetary policy.[30] With this innovation, central banks seek to use an operational instrument as a way of boosting the effectiveness of monetary policy and signaling changes in the monetary policy stance. In practice, however, the policy rate is playing little or no role, as its changes are rarely followed by market interest rates. The lack of proper liquidity management by central banks helps to explain this disconnection, as the banks' policy rate does not reflect the underlying liquidity conditions. In Costa Rica and Honduras, the effectiveness of the policy rate is limited by the exchange rate regime, given that the rate of crawl is effectively the operational target and because this policy regime reduces the capabilities of central banks to manage systemic liquidity.

Another factor hindering the effectiveness of monetary policy during the last two years stems from persistent capital inflows. To cope with this situation, central banks have intervened in the foreign exchange market to head off appreciations of domestic currencies, thereby fueling a persistent increase of international reserves. At the same time, to prevent excessive monetization, central banks have stepped up sterilization through open market operations, and in many cases, via standing facilities—typically of short-term maturities—amid fears of exacerbating central bank losses and perpetuating capital inflows due to the premium paid in domestic interest rates vis-à-vis dollar interest rates. Eventually, liquidity surplus has prevailed in most countries, which tends to limit the effectiveness of monetary policy due to the reduced ability of central banks to influence commercial banks' short- and hence long-term interest rates.

Empirical Regularities Supporting the Characterization of Monetary Policy

This section examines monetary policy in the Central American countries by estimating the reaction functions of central banks. The purpose of this exercise is to assess, on a preliminary basis, how monetary policy has in practice reacted to recent shifts in underlying economic fundamentals, especially inflation, in each country. The main idea behind the proposed analysis is to ascertain whether central banks work under clear and predictable rules that would make them more likely to deliver lower inflation rates over time. This exercise also allows us to verify empirically the previous characterization of monetary policy spelled out from central banks' information.

Methodology

The analysis focuses on the standard reaction function based on the interest rate as the policy instrument, but also evaluates exchange rate crawl and money reaction functions. Expanding the analysis from the standard approach is warranted given the heterogeneity of monetary policy regimes observed in Central America, which include money, exchange rate, and inflation targeting.[31]

Against this backdrop, this chapter considers a mix of policy instruments to separately estimate several policy reaction functions along the general lines of Taylor (1993), Parrado (2004), and McCallum (1988), depending on the instrument considered:[32]

$$i_t = (1-\rho)\alpha+(1-\rho)\beta\pi_{t+n}+(1-\rho)\gamma x_{t+m}+\rho i_{t-1}+\varepsilon_t \qquad (1)$$

$$\Delta e_t = (1-\rho)\alpha+(1-\rho)\beta\pi_{t+n}+(1-\rho)\gamma x_{t+m}+\rho\Delta e_{t-1}+\varepsilon_t \qquad (2)$$

$$\Delta m_t = (1-\rho)\alpha+(1-\rho)\beta\pi_{t+n}+(1-\rho)\gamma x_{t+m}+\rho\Delta m_{t-1}+\varepsilon_t \qquad (3)$$

where i is a policy interest rate or a repo rate, π is the inflation rate, x is the output gap, m is a monetary aggregate defined as the intermediate target (typically the money base), and e is the exchange rate. The method of estimation is the generalized method of moments (GMM).

The methodological approach is one of "letting the numbers talk," and hence, we estimate all three equations for each country regardless of the a priori characterization of the current policy regime. Given the seeming inconsistency between Central American central banks' characterization of their policy regime—according to Appendix 6A.2—and how, in principle, their monetary policy really appears to operate (Table 6.3), we estimate all three reaction functions, although placing more emphasis on the first two equations, which better picture monetary policy management in most countries in Central America.

Equation (1) provides the critical analytical framework to assess the reaction functions of central banks. On the one hand, monetary-based policy regimes adjust interest rates to affect monetary aggregates and, indirectly, inflation. On the other hand, even central banks that have adopted exchange rate crawls may use interest rates as a policy instrument to defend the peg,

[30]Guatemala and Honduras chose the seven-day central bank interest rate, whereas Costa Rica initially selected the 30-day interest rate and later the overnight rate paid in the central bank deposit facility.

[31]Corbo (2002) finds that, in setting their policy rates, central banks consider not only inflation but also other objectives such as output and the exchange rate.

[32]See Appendix 6.1 for further details.

reduce inflation, or protect international reserves in times of financial turbulence. In turn, inflation targeting countries adjust the interest rate as a policy variable to guide expectations and steer actual inflation toward forecasted inflation.

Equation (2) usually provides valuable information about countries using an exchange rate crawl as a policy instrument, but it may also be relevant when it comes to floating exchange regimes. Typically, this equation assumes that the rate of crawl is regularly adjusted to compensate for differentials of inflation with respect to its "target." A clear example of this policy approach is found in Singapore, where the monetary authorities presume that small open economies cannot manage interest rates and only have control over the exchange rate.[33] In some countries, this policy rule may also serve to compensate for differentials of actual from potential output. Under this approach, this policy rule may not be as relevant in Central America. While targeting the exchange rate may give some signals about the long-term direction of exchange rate policy, in the short run this information has less of a foundation in Costa Rica and Nicaragua, as their central banks tend to favor a predictable path for the exchange rate, and hence do not use it as a policy instrument on a short-term basis. Honduras, in turn, can adjust the rate of crawl on a short-term basis, and hence, has the potential for using it as a policy instrument either to moderate inflation or to target a real exchange rate. On the other hand, equation (2) may also be relevant to gauge whether central banks using flexible exchange rate regimes in reality care about the competitiveness of the economies' tradable activities, which may materialize by means of interventions in the foreign exchange market.

The specification in equation (3) is tailored to capture the policy reaction of central banks that directly adjust monetary aggregates in response, for example, to inflation pressures. Thus, it is applicable to central banks that have in place a flexible exchange rate regime, which makes room for exogenous management of monetary aggregates. In particular, this equation addresses the question of whether the central bank adjusts the money base in response to inflation or other policy shocks. The experiment may also apply to exchange rate targeters like Honduras and Nicaragua, which have negotiated successive economic programs with the IMF during the period of analysis. The policy framework associated with these economic programs envisages that central banks should tighten monetary policy to cope with inflation pressures.

[33]In particular, the Monetary Authority of Singapore explicitly uses a trade-weighted index to conduct monetary policy and offset fluctuations both in inflation and output. See Parrado (2004).

As a baseline specification, we consider output and inflation as the standard targets of monetary policy in the reaction functions of central banks. Depending on the reaction function, we then include other objectives such as the exchange rate, the real exchange rate, and international reserves into the baseline specification and analyze the behavior of some key model parameters. In the baseline specification, we pay special attention to the parameters associated with inflation and, to a lesser extent, output. This is because, as discussed earlier, fighting inflation is a key feature of the mandate of Central American central banks, whereas output stability or fostering economic growth is no longer an objective in their charters.

Data

The analysis is based on monthly data for 1996–2005.[34] The selected period corresponds to the time span that follows the inception of the new institutional setting that granted most central banks enhanced operational autonomy. Choosing this period allows for isolating the analysis from the first half of the 1990s, when Central America experienced a steep decrease in inflation, which would probably distort the empirical analysis. To control for the adverse effects of systemic banking crises on monetary policy, we included dummy variables. In particular, the estimations control for the expansionary monetary stance associated with the central banks' involvement in the full-fledged banking crises that hit Nicaragua in 2001–02 and the Dominican Republic in 2003. In addition, to test whether the Bank of Guatemala has been lately formulating monetary policy as an inflation targeter, we break down the analysis for Guatemala into two periods.[35]

The data series' were obtained directly from each central bank. The quality of the data is rather good, except for the monthly series of economic activity, which is an imperfect substitute for a GDP series. On a country basis, a consistent series for central bank interest rates in Nicaragua is not available, and hence, we used the one-month deposit interest rate in commercial banks as an imperfect substitute. In addition, measures of output gap are not available, and hence, output is used directly. With these caveats in mind, we should be cautious in being too conclusive when interpreting the outcome of the empirical assessment

[34]The data for the Dominican Republic was collected on a quarterly basis because this country lacks a monthly measure of economic activity.

[35]While the Bank of Guatemala claims to have gradually started the transition to inflation targeting in 2000, we chose to artificially divide the two periods in connection with a large sovereign debt placement that took place in late 2001, and which produced a once-and-for-all 50 percent increase in international reserves, and hence a structural break in the series.

Table 6.4. Interest Rate Reaction Function of Central Banks, 1996–2005

	Lagged Instrument	Constant	Inflation	Output	Exchange Rate
Costa Rica	1.05*	–0.16	1.25*	–0.27	2.53*
	–90.03	–2.17	–3.21	–1.07	–3.98
Guatemala-1[1]	0.94*	–0.11	1.98*	1.11*	0.66*
	–155.98	–2.88	–5.32	–2.14	–5.68
Guatemala-2[2]	0.96*	–0.06	1.93*	–0.21	0.48*
	–476.23	–3.67	–9.17	–0.69	–4.98
Honduras	0.93*	–0.01	0.62*	0.62*	0.89*
	–72.89	–0.46	–1.72	–4.99	–3.38
Nicaragua[3]	0.96*	–0.06	0.71*	–0.02	0.73*
	–87.62	–1.83	–2.18	–0.17	–5.10
Dominican Republic[3,4]	0.40	–0.07	0.70*	2.19*	0.03
	–1.41	–0.77	–4.36	–2.05	–0.25

Note: *t*-statistics in parentheses. *Coefficients are statistically significant at the 5 percent level.

[1]Guatemala-1 is based on the period from 1996 to 2005.

[2]Guatemala-2 corresponds to late 2001 to 2005, when the Bank of Guatemala started to formulate and implement monetary policy as an inflation targeter.

[3]Dummy variables are used to control for banking crises periods.

[4]Estimations for the Dominican Republic are based on quarterly data.

of central bank reaction functions in Central America, particularly when it comes to analyzing the response of policy instruments to output behavior.

Estimations

The results stemming from this quantitative analysis shed some light on central banks' actual policy implementation. In particular, they show that, regardless of the monetary regime, all central banks respond by raising interest rates in light of inflation pressures, but the magnitude of the response differs across countries such that some central banks are thus more effective than others in coping with inflation pressures. The estimations also stress that some central banks simultaneously seek to preserve exchange rate stability—which can be a source of policy conflicts. The estimations also reveal the difficulties in trying to effectively target the real exchange rate. Finally, they suggest that most central banks tighten money to tackle inflation, regardless of whether they target money or the exchange rate.

Interest Rate Reaction Functions

Assuming a forward-looking horizon of zero months, the coefficients associated with expected inflation are positive and significant in all countries. They indicate that in response to a 1 percent change in inflation, the interest rate is modified in the range of 0.6 to nearly 2 percent depending on the country (Table 6.4). The coefficient associated with inflation is much higher than 1 in Costa Rica and, in particular, Guatemala—in both periods alike— which implies that the real interest rate moves in the same direction as the nominal rate. This means that the interest rate is temporarily altered to affect aggregate demand, and thus, inflation (the aggregate demand function is then negatively sloped with respect to the inflation rate). On the other hand, the value of the inflation coefficient in the Dominican Republic, Nicaragua, and Honduras suggests a partial accommodative reaction, as the increase in nominal interest rates in response to inflationary pressures is insufficient to prevent the real interest rate from falling. This outcome could be explained by the fact that the central banks in these two countries may also use other policy instruments to cope with inflation pressures.

The estimations also show that central banks, except for the Dominican Republic, react positively and significantly to exchange rate depreciations. This relationship has at least two possible readings, depending on the monetary policy regime in each country, that eventually point to a "fear of floating" scenario. In an environment of exchange rate targeting

(Costa Rica, Honduras, and Nicaragua), central banks may increase interest rates in response to exchange rate depreciations to preserve a covered interest parity condition. Rising interest rates may also be the case—in particular in Costa Rica because of the high value of the exchange rate coefficient—to defend the pre-announced exchange rate path, thereby preventing major disturbances in the foreign exchange market, which potentially could have a negative impact on market participants' balance sheets. Alternatively, when it comes to money and inflation targeting, this reaction may show that central banks also care about exchange rate stability.

The affection that central banks hold for preserving the external stability of their currencies could be justified on many possible fronts. One explanation is that central banks believe that exchange rate pass-through to prices is significant and hence they need to cap exchange rate swings. This is a plausible explanation in small and very open economies, like those of Central America, where exchange rate performance has a great impact on price formation. An alternative rationalization is that central banks in Central American economies assign a relatively higher weight to the exchange rate to maintain trade competitiveness and even financial stability. Regarding the latter, Calvo and Reinhart (2002) argue that the "fear of floating" found in a number of emerging markets is explained by the high risk premium they have to pay because of their low institutional and policy credibility. The resistance to floating the exchange rate may be predominantly high in countries with shallow markets, which are susceptible to herd behavior. Also, financial imperfections such as a large amount of external debt or debt indexed to the exchange rate, as in Nicaragua and Costa Rica, make the case for preventing exchange rate fluctuations. Eichengreen (2002) and Goldstein and Turner (2004) have recently highlighted the adverse consequences of exchange rate depreciations in countries with a high degree of dollarization. Sharp currency depreciations can cause widespread bankruptcies, as foreign exchange credit risk has an adverse effect on unhedged borrowers. This rather unconventional and contractionary impact of exchange rate depreciations makes it necessary for central banks to raise interest rates defensively against major exchange rate shocks.

Despite the caveats associated with measures of output in the Central American countries, it is worth cautiously mentioning the seemingly countercyclical role of some central banks. In particular, Guatemala, during the money targeting phase, Honduras, and especially the Dominican Republic seem to reduce interest rates to confront a slowdown in economic activity.

In addition, some central banks adjust inversely interest rates to changes in international reserves. In particular, the central banks in Nicaragua, the Dominican Republic, and especially Costa Rica appear to raise interest rates to safeguard the stability of international reserves (not reported). One can understand this behavior as an effort of central banks to underpin the stability of the exchange rate, which in countries with high capital mobility critically hinges on preserving an appropriate level of international reserves.

Exchange Rate Crawl Reaction Function

While the estimates of this reaction function have generally resulted in unstable and rather erratic coefficients, depending on the combination of endogenous variables, some interesting results are worth mentioning from our experiments.[36] We run a baseline scenario with a forward-looking horizon of zero months, except for the real exchange rate, which is lagged one period.[37] The estimates show that, among the exchange rate targeters, only Costa Rica designs its exchange rate policy with the aim of preserving the competitiveness of domestic activities, given that the coefficient associated with the inflation rate is positive and statistically significant (Table 6.5). Strikingly, the results also show that Guatemala features an accommodative exchange rate policy with respect to inflation, which points in the direction of a central bank that cares about tradable activities—as observed before—despite being in transition to inflation targeting. In this connection, an accommodative exchange rate policy in response to inflation may cast doubts on market participants about the true primary objective of the central banks. Seeking to simultaneously preserve the internal and external value of domestic currencies may become mutually incompatible, particularly when the country experiences exchange rate appreciation trends.

The results also show that maintaining a stable real exchange rate is a difficult endeavor. This may be due to the use of a backward-looking rule in announcing the future path of the peg in an environment of unstable inflation, which makes it more difficult to target a given real exchange rate. Strikingly, by managing the exchange rate more flexibly—although intervening in the exchange rate market—the Bank of Guatemala has preserved a real exchange rate parity, which signals its concern for an exchange rate that is either appreciated

[36]Even at a conceptual level, the impact of changes in the rate of crawl on inflation and output volatility is unclear and depends on the characteristics of the monetary transmission channels. Should the interest rate effect dominate the exchange rate effect, at least in the short run, a demand shock may need to be met by an *increase* in the rate of crawl (that allows for a rise in interest rates). A *reduction* in the rate of crawl would otherwise be appropriate.

[37]The real exchange rate is lagged in order to avoid collinearity with the nominal exchange rate. A one-month lag reflects the delay in the availability of this information in the Central American central banks.

Table 6.5. Exchange Rate Crawl Reaction Function, 1996–2005

	Lagged Instrument	Constant	Inflation	Output	Real Exchange Rate (*t*–1)[1]
Costa Rica	0.94*	0.02*	0.39*	0.55*	0.06
	–129.02	–1.41	–3.71	–8.66	–1.63
Guatemala-1[2]	0.65*	0.03	–0.18	0.92*	– 0.69*
	–9.18	–1.62	–0.74	–5.40	–9.08
Guatemala-2[3]	0.51*	– 0.03*	1.16*	– 1.21*	– 0.77*
	–11.60	–3.65	–13.44	–10.52	–17.26
Honduras	1.04*	0.12	–0.78	0.25	0.16
	–49.35	–1.12	–0.63	–1.47	–0.35
Nicaragua[4]	1.01*	0.10	–0.15	0.2	–0.35
	–187.74	–1.24	–0.18	–0.47	–1.49
Dominican Republic[4,5]	0.69*	0.54	–2.82	– 3.90*	2.33
	–2.76	–1.04	–1.07	–0.90	–1.34

Note: *t*-statistics in parentheses. *Coefficients are statistically significant at the 5 percent level.

[1]Guatemala-1 is based on the period from 1996 to 2005.

[2]Guatemala-2 corresponds to late 2001 to 2005, when the Bank of Guatemala started to formulate and implement monetary policy as an inflation targeter.

[3]A fall in the real exchange rate implies an appreciation and vice versa.

[4]Dummy variables are used to control for banking crises periods.

[5]Estimations for the Dominican Republic are based on quarterly data.

or depreciated in real terms. The failure of most central banks in Central America to maintain a given real exchange rate level is in accordance with the conventional wisdom that claims that real exchange rates are endogenous in the short run.

Money-Base Reaction Function

The results from the money reaction function are mixed for both money and exchange rate targeters. Among the former, only the Bank of Guatemala adjusts the money base to cope with inflation pressures, whereas the coefficient of inflation in the Dominican Republic has the expected sign but is not statistically significant. The value of the coefficients also suggests that the use of the money base to tackle inflation pressures has declined in Guatemala during the transition to inflation targeting. As for the exchange rate targeters, despite the limitations that targeting the exchange rate impose on the control of monetary variables, the central banks in Nicaragua and, in particular, Honduras, seem to have a strong capacity to tighten the money base in response to inflation (Table 6.6).

One possible explanation for this puzzling outcome is that the assumption of perfect capital mobility, in particular in Honduras, but also in Nicaragua, is less binding, which makes room for central banks to exercise some monetary control. This explanation is mostly relevant for Honduras because the surrender requirement of foreign currency to the central bank inhibits the creation of a foreign exchange market.[38] In addition, in both countries the money market is shallow, which makes interest rate adjustment sluggish. The use of monetary aggregates to cope with inflation pressures in Honduras and Nicaragua, despite being exchange rate targeters, may also be associated with IMF programs that have been in effect in these two countries during most of the period of analysis. As noted, standard IMF programs require central banks to observe quarterly monetary targets as performance criteria.

Conclusions

Most Central American countries have succeeded in reducing inflation to the single-digit range. This outcome is not only the result of a drop in inflation in the rest of the world; it also follows from the Central American nations having maintained sound macroeconomic policies and adopted far-reaching structural reforms

[38]Other than this, in both countries capital inflows are less responsive to changes in the interest rate as they are large net recipients of foreign exchange from workers' remittances and foreign aid.

Table 6.6. Central Banks' Money Reaction Function, 1996–2005

	Lagged Instrument	Constant	Inflation	Output	Exchange Rate
Costa Rica	0.90*	– 0.40*	2.25	0.65	3.34*
	–52.84	–2.74	–1.61	–0.78	–1.83
Guatemala-1[1]	0.87*	0.10	– 2.38*	7.95*	– 0.82*
	–22.24	–1.23	–2.73	–3.78	–2.22
Guatemala-2[2]	0.57*	0.19*	– 0.79*	– 1.16*	0.51*
	–12.90	–16.19	–6.02	–2.31	–4.98
Honduras	0.93*	0.67*	– 6.99*	– 3.26*	5.39*
	–43.85	–3.37	–2.75	–2.54	–2.84
Nicaragua[3]	0.54*	0.21*	– 1.20*	– 0.41*	1.26*
	–10.74	–5.77	–2.94	–3.13	–4.88
Dominican Republic[3,4]	0.38*	0.01	0.23	1.33	0.23
	–0.98	–0.05	–0.40	–0.64	–0.85

Note: *t*-statistics in parentheses. *Coefficients are statistically significant at the 5 percent level.
[1]Guatemala-1 is based on the period from 1996 to 2005.
[2]Guatemala-2 corresponds to late 2001 to 2005, when the Bank of Guatemala started to formulate and implement monetary policy as an inflation targeter.
[3]Dummy variables are used to control for banking crises periods.
[4]Estimations for the Dominican Republic are based on quarterly data.

over more than 10 years. A key component of this macroeconomic strategy has been to give central banks enhanced autonomy to formulate and execute monetary policy. Today, central banks in Central America, like their peers in the rest of the region, are no longer development banks. They focus their policies on fighting inflation, although in some countries this sometimes conflicts with the parallel objective of preserving the external value of domestic currencies.

Despite the progress achieved by the Central American central banks in reducing inflation, there is no room for complacency. Inflation in most countries is still high by regional and world standards. Moreover, central banks are still in the process of building their reputation and credibility, which is expected not only to help them further reduce and stabilize inflation, but also to better withstand exogenous events such as the recent oil shock that shifted inflation in some countries to low two-digit rates.

While all central banks in the region today enjoy more solid institutional strength, additional steps should be taken to underpin their credibility and achieve better inflation results. Progress is still necessary in four main areas: (1) clarify the mandate of central banks to eliminate the latent policy conflict that emerges when monetary policy simultaneously seeks the internal and external stability of the domestic currency; (2) strengthen political autonomy to untie potential links between monetary policy horizons and political cycles; (3) grant financial autonomy to reinforce the current de jure operational autonomy of central banks; and (4) set more rigorous accountability and transparency procedures for central banks to bolster the credibility of monetary policy.

Central banks in Central America have made important strides in modernizing monetary operations, but there is still room for improvement. While central banks established indirect instruments of monetary policy many years ago, open market operations do not allow for price discovery, as interest rates are generally determined exogenously by central banks. As a result, money markets are still shallow, whereas yield curves are rather artificial and convey meaningless information to both central banks and market participants. During recent years, central banks have not appeared to be proficient in managing liquidity surplus—stemming from an abundant international liquidity—and hence, changes in short-term central bank interest rates are not followed by similar changes in commercial bank rates.

Tracing the reaction functions of central banks in Central America allows for establishing a connection between their institutional setting and monetary policy implementation. The quantitative analysis developed in this chapter allows for verifying the main thrust of monetary policy in the sample countries, which suggests that central banks formulate and execute monetary policy in a way that is not fully consistent with the nature of the policy regime in place. In particular, it confirms that central banks, in general, behave by increasing interest rates to curtail inflationary pressures regardless of their policy regime. However, they react with different impetus, and hence, some central banks are raising interest rates less than what is required to tame inflation pressures.

A second empirical regularity is that some central banks also care about the stability of the exchange rate, which may blur their true policy objective vis-à-vis price stability. They react by adjusting interest rates upward either to prevent deviations from the targeted purchasing power parity, or to confront pressures on the exchange rate with the aim of mitigating pass-through effects of exchange rate depreciations on prices and because of the so-called "fear of floating." By the same token, these central banks also seem to systematically resist exchange rate appreciations, which would otherwise support disinflation. In addition, central banks in Costa Rica and Guatemala exhibit a policy of accommodating inflation trends into exchange rates performance with the aim of preserving the competitiveness of their tradable activities.

The potential policy conflicts featuring central banks in Central America are probably undermining markets' confidence in their commitment to price stability. The fact that central banks are unable to deliver a predictable monetary policy and that they at times signal mutually exclusive policy objectives may help to explain the perpetuation of an inflation bias in Central America.

While this chapter steps up the understanding of monetary policy in Central America, additional analytical work is needed to improve the effectiveness of monetary policy. Areas for further research include (1) analyzing how the transmission mechanisms of monetary policy work in the region; (2) identifying the most appropriate exchange rate regime applicable to the Central American countries, given their increasing openness and integration with the U.S. economy; and (3) defining the most suitable operational framework for monetary policy.

Appendix 6.1. Policy Reaction Function

The policy reaction function would work as follows: assume that within each operating period the central bank has a target for the interest rate, i_t^* that is based on the state of the economy. Let it also be assumed that monetary authorities care about stabilizing inflation and output, so we allow for the possibility that the central bank adjusts its policy response to anticipated inflation and output. Specifically:

$$i_t^* = \bar{i} + \beta(E[\pi_{t+n}|\Omega_t] - \pi^*) + y(E[y_{t+m}|\Omega_t] - y^*), \qquad (1)$$

where $\bar{i}$ is the long-run equilibrium interest rate, π_{t+n} is the rate of inflation between periods t, $t+n$, y_{t+m} is real output between periods t and $t+m$, and π^* and y^* are the targets for inflation and output, respectively. In particular, y^* is defined as the equilibrium level of output that would arise if wages and prices were perfectly flexible. Additionally, E is the expectation operator and Ω_t is the information available to the policymaker. The expression could include additional independent terms such as the exchange rate and international reserves.

To capture concerns about potentially disruptive shifts in the interest rate, it is assumed that the interest rate is adjusted only partially to its target level:

$$i_t = (1-\rho)i_t^* + \rho_{t-1} + v_t, \qquad (2)$$

where the parameter $\rho \in [0,1]$ captures the degree of interest rate smoothing. The exogenous random shock to the exchange rate, v_t, is assumed to be *i.i.d.* To define an estimable equation, let $\alpha = \bar{i} - \beta\pi^*$ and $x_t = y_t - y^*$, then equation (2) can be written as:

$$i_t^* = \alpha + \beta E[\pi_{t+n}|\Omega_t] - \pi^*) + \gamma E[x_{t+m}|\Omega_t]. \qquad (3)$$

So, combining equation (4) with the partial adjustment mechanism (3) and eliminating the unobserved forecast variables yields:

$$i_t = (1-\rho)\alpha + (1-\rho)\beta\pi_{t+n} + (1-\rho)\gamma x_{t+m} + \rho i_{t-1} + \varepsilon_t, \quad (4)$$

where the error term is a linear combination of the forecast errors of inflation and output, and the exogenous disturbance υ_t.

Let u_t be a vector of variables (set of instruments) within the policymaker's information set (i.e., $u_t \in \Omega_t$) that are orthogonal to ε_t. Possible elements of u_t include any lagged variables that help forecast inflation and output, as well as any contemporaneous variables that are uncorrelated with the current exchange rate shock υ_t. Thus, since $E[\varepsilon_t|u_t]=0$, the following equation can be estimated using the generalized method of moments (GMM) with an optimal weighting matrix:[39]

$$E[i_t = (1-\rho)\alpha - (1-\rho)\beta\pi_{t+n} - (1-\rho)$$
$$\gamma x_{t+m} - \rho i_{t-1}|u_t] = 0 \qquad (5)$$

Equation (5) is estimated over the sample period from 1999 to 2005 with year-on-year consumer price index (CPI) inflation, detrended output (using the Hodrick-Prescott filter) measured through the monthly index of economic activity (the so-called IMAE), and the nominal interest rate. Baseline elements of u_t are lagged values of CPI inflation, output, and the interest rate. The forward-looking horizons are varied (values n and m in the case of inflation and output, respectively) to assess the policy horizon.

[39]The use of an optimal weighting matrix implies that GMM estimates are robust to heteroscedasticity and autocorrelation of unknown form. It is worth noting that the GMM technique requires no information about the exact distribution of the error term, which, in general, is assumed to be drawn from a normal distribution.

Table 6A.1. Main Provisions of Central Bank Legislation as of 2005

	Costa Rica	Dominican Republic	Guatemala	Honduras	Nicaragua
Policy Mandate					
Central bank objective	The Central Bank of Costa Rica (CBCR) will have as its main objectives to preserve the internal and external value of the domestic currency and promote the normal functioning of the payments system.	Regulation of the monetary system, which includes the Central Bank of the Dominican Republic (CBDR) and the Superintendence of Banks, aims to maintain price stability, which is the necessary basis for the nation's economic development.	The fundamental objective of the Bank of Guatemala (Banguat) is to help create and maintain the most favorable conditions for the orderly development of the national economy. It should promote monetary, exchange, and credit conditions conducive to price stability.	The Central Bank of Honduras (CBH) will have as an objective to preserve the internal and external value of the domestic currency and promote the normal functioning of the payments system.	The primary objective of the Central Bank of Nicaragua (CBN) is the stability of the national currency and the normal functioning of the internal and external payments.
Political Autonomy					
Government body of the central bank	Board of Directors (BoD) comprises seven members, including its president, the minister of finance, and five other members.	Monetary Board (MB) comprises nine members, including the governor of the CBDR, the minister of finance, and the superintendent of banks (the last two ex-oficio members), plus another six members.	Monetary Board (MB) comprises nine members, including its president, the ministers of public finance, the economy, and agriculture, representatives of the Congress, the largest state-owned university, the banking association, and the private entrepreneurs' association.	Board comprises five members, including its president.	Board of Directors (BoD) comprises six members, including its president, the minister of finance, and four members in consultation with the private sector, including one nominated by the largest opposition political party.
Modality of appointment of members of the government body	The BoD president is appointed by the president of the country. He also appoints the other five members, but these are ratified by Congress.	The CBDR governor and six members of the MB are directly appointed by the president of the country.	The MB president is appointed by the president of the country, whereas the other members of the MB are appointed by the institution they represent.	All five members are directly appointed by the president of the country.	The president of the country directly appoints the BoD president and four members. The latter are ratified by Congress.
Term of appointment	The BoD president is appointed to the same term as the executive branch. The other five members serve for 90 months and are appointed every 18 months, one at a time.	The governor of the CBDR and the six members of the MB are appointed for two years. The term of the ex-officio members is according to the nature of the appointment.	The term of the MB president is four years, which does not coincide with that of the president of the country. MB members appointed by the private sector and the university for a one-year renewable term.	Two members of the board serve for the same years as the president of the country and the other three are appointed on a staggered basis.	The BoD president and the representative of the opposition political party serve for the same period as the presidential term. The other three members are appointed in the middle of the presidential term.
Dismissal	While the BoD president can be freely removed by the executive branch, the five members of the BoD are removed only under legal grounds, also by the executive branch.	The CBDR governor is fired by a unanimous decision of the MB or by a three-fourths vote of the MB under given legal grounds.	The MB president is removed only upon legal grounds, but Congress has the right to dismiss him—with a qualified majority—if its annual report to Congress is not found to be satisfactory.	Members of the board are dismissed following an investigation by the executive branch on legal grounds including "lack of professional competence in conduct of their duties."	BoD members are dismissed following an investigation by the BoD on legal grounds, including lack of professional competence in conduct of their duties. The president of the republic takes the final decision.

Economic Autonomy					
Formulation and execution of monetary policy	The CBCR's BoD is responsible for formulating and conducting monetary, exchange rate, and credit policies.	The MB is in charge of formulating monetary, exchange, and financial policies. It is responsible for approving the monetary program and monitoring its execution.	The formulation of monetary policy corresponds to the MB and the conduct of monetary policy to an Execution Committee. However, Congress has to approve Banguat paper that will be used in open market operations.	The CBH has the legal mandate to formulate and execute monetary policy.	The CBN is in charge of formulating and executing monetary policy in coordination with the government's economic policy, but subordinating this coordination to the CBN's observance of its primary objective.
Central bank lending to the government	The CBCR is allowed to buy treasury bills in the primary market at a market rate. The balance of treasury bills cannot exceed 1/20 of the government's expenditure at any given time.	The CBDR cannot extend credit directly or indirectly to the government except under emergency conditions as regulated in the central bank law.	The Banguat is not allowed to provide—directly or indirectly—credit to the government (constitutional mandate).	The CBH is not allowed to provide—directly or indirectly—credit to the government. However, it can provide advances to cope with seasonal liquidity shortages. These loans are limited to 10 percent of the previous year's tax revenue.	The CBN cannot provide credit—directly or indirectly—to the government. However, it can provide short-term advances in exchange for treasury bonds of up to 10 percent of the average tax revenues recorded in the previous two fiscal years.
Central bank role in public debt policy	The CBCR is informed about new issues of public debt.	No role.	The Banguat must issue a technical report every time the public sector issues debt.	The CBH provides a legal criterion before the government issues debt.	No role.
Lender-of-last-resort provisions (LOLR)	To safeguard financial stability, the BCCR can rediscount securities to financial institutions under specific conditions. It also provides emergency loans as defined in the law to institutions intervened by the financial authority.	The CBDR provides financial assistance to illiquid but solvent banks. The amount is capped at one and a half times the impaired bank's equity at a 30-day maturity. Financial conditions are defined by the CBDR.	The Banguat is empowered to provide lender-of-last-resort assistance only to illiquid but solvent banks. Amount of assistance limited to 50 percent of impaired bank capital. Liquidity assistance cannot be granted more than twice a year.	The CBH can provide financial assistance to banks facing liquidity problems and in light of situations that challenge the stability of the financial system.	Lender-of-last-resort only for liquidity purposes up to 30 days maturity without a maximum limit. The CBN defines the financial conditions of such loans.
Financial Autonomy					
Central bank's capital integrity	There is no legal provision requiring the government to compensate central bank losses.	The CBDR's losses must be compensated with Treasury bonds issued at market interest rates and at less than one-year maturity.	The Banguat must inform the Ministry of Finance should operational losses arise. The minister of finance has to incorporate these losses in the next fiscal year budget, to be covered with marketable government securities.	The CBH should register losses as receivables until agreement is achieved with the government about the mechanism and financial conditions to compensate such losses. This, in turn, has to be approved by Congress.	The government must restore the CBN's losses by transferring securities under market conditions.
Accountability and Transparency					
Accountability relative to its policy objective	The CBCR must publish its annual report within the first quarter of the year.	The CBDR governor reports annually to the executive branch and submits the CBDR annual report to Congress.	The MB president must appear before Congress twice a year to report on the policies implemented, with emphasis on the Banguat's objectives.	The board reports once a year to Congress and twice a year to the executive branch about the outcome of its activities.	Following a constitutional mandate, the CBN governor presents an annual general report to Congress.

Table 6A.1 *(concluded)*

	Costa Rica	Dominican Republic	Guatemala	Honduras	Nicaragua
Disclosure of a monetary policy or inflation report	Once a year, the CBCR must disclose the monetary program, and twice a year it must publish an analysis of its execution and prospects.	The CBDR disseminates a summary of the monetary program once a year and an update on a quarterly basis.	The Banguat must publish an explanatory monetary policy report twice a year.	No specific legal provision.	No specific legal provision.
Disclosure of income statements and certification	The CBCR discloses its detailed income statements certified by the internal auditor once a year. Income statements should be certified by the CBCR's internal auditor.	Audited income statements have to be disclosed once a year and certified by an internal auditor and also by an external audit firm.	At least once a year, the Banguat should disclose its income statement on an analytical basis. The Banguat's accounting practices are certified by an experienced and well-known external audit firm.	The CBH publishes its financial statements immediately after the end of the fiscal year. Accounting practices and the fidelity of income statements is done by the superintendent of banks, but an external audit firm may also be hired.	The CBN discloses its financial statements monthly. At the end of the fiscal year, it discloses financial statements certified by an internationally-known external audit firm.
Disclosure of policy decisions	The CBCR should publish the BoD's decisions on monetary policy.	Disseminates a bulletin containing the main policy/legal decisions.	The Banguat discloses a summary of the main MB decisions.	No specific provisions.	The BoD's decisions should be published.

Sources: Central bank laws and relevant constitutional provisions.

Table 6A.2. Main Features of Monetary Policy

Key Aspects	Costa Rica	Dominican Republic	Guatemala	Honduras	Nicaragua
Monetary policy regime	Real exchange rate targeting.	Monetary targeting.	Inflation targeting.	Real exchange rate targeting.	Real exchange rate targeting.
Exchange rate system	Crawling peg according to a pre-announced daily rate of devaluation. There is no foreign currency surrender requirement but market participants must sell existing remaining surpluses to the Central bank of Costa Rica (CBCR).	Flexible exchange regime.	Flexible exchange regime.	Crawling band of 14 percent width. The slope is the difference between domestic inflation and that of its main trading partners. There is a surrender requirement of foreign currency for export earnings (except within Central America).	Crawling peg based on a monthly announcement of the rate of depreciation aimed at maintaining a purchasing power parity. There is no foreign currency surrender requirement.
	The exchange rate is determined in the interbank market based on a reference exchange rate. The latter is calculated by the CBCR from a weighted average of market transactions in t–2, adjusted by the average change in t–1.	The exchange rate is determined by market supply and demand, but the Central Bank of the Dominican Republic (CBDR) may intervene.	The exchange rate is determined by the market's supply and demand, but the Bank of Guatemala (Banguat) intervenes to tame volatility according to a publicly known rule.	In practice, the Central Bank of Honduras (CBH) satisfies all demand of foreign exchange. Market participants make bids, taking as a reference the average exchange rate of the previous auction.	The exchange rate is determined by market supply and demand, but the Central Bank of Nicaragua (CBN) may intervene.
Financial programming	The Board of Directors (BoD) approves it every January and updates it by mid-year.	Approved annually by the Monetary Board (MB) and reviewed quarterly.	The Monetary Board (MB) approves a monetary program annually, and it is reviewed twice a year. The monetary program is not the key framework for policy formulation.	The CBH board approves the monetary program and conduct reviews on a quarterly basis.	The Board of Directors (BoD) approves it every year and conducts reviews not on a regular basis but as needed.
	The final objective is to address inflation. The intermediate targets are currency issue, money supply, and credit to the private sector.	The final objective is to address inflation. The intermediate targets are the money base and net domestic assets.	The final objective is to address inflation based on the forecasted inflation. Monetary variables are only indicative variables.	The final objective is to address inflation. The intermediate targets are CBH's net international reserves and net domestic assets.	The final objective is to address inflation. The intermediate target is the net international reserves.
Monetary policy decision	The BoD is in charge of adopting policy decisions, particularly those relative to monetary instruments.	The Open Market Operations Committee (COMA) decides changes on monetary policy.	The MB approves the formulation of monetary policy and the Executing Committee (EC) implements it, deciding on changes in the interest rate.	While the CBH board formulates monetary policy, the Open Market Operations Committee (COMA) is the executor.	While the BoD formulates monetary policy, the Open Market Operations Committee (COMA) is the executor.
	While the BoD meets regularly every week, decisions concerning the leading rate are not adopted on a regular basis during key meetings.	The COMA meets regularly every Wednesday, but the market is not aware of those meetings. There is no specific date when the COMA reviews the stance of monetary policy.	The EC meets regularly every week (generally on Fridays). The market is aware that decisions about the policy rate are considered during the meeting after the 15th of each month.	The CBH board meets regularly each Thursday, and the COMA meets once a month. The market ignores when the CBH board will adopt a change in the policy rate.	Both the BoD and the COMA meet separately once a week. The latter assesses the financial parameters to apply in the weekly auctions. There are no specific meetings to adopt key policy decisions.

Table 6A.2 ***(concluded)***

Key Aspects	Costa Rica	Dominican Republic	Guatemala	Honduras	Nicaragua
Monetary policy instruments	Reserve requirements: 15 percent on deposits in domestic and foreign currencies. Maintenance period of two weeks, with averaging provisions. Reserve requirements were changed once in 2004 (from 10 to 12 percent) and in 2005 (from 12 to 15 percent).	Reserve requirements: 20 percent for commercial banks and 15 percent for other financial institutions. Commercial banks have a daily and weekly maintenance period for domestic and foreign currencies, respectively. Other institutions have two-week and one-month maintenance periods.	Reserve requirements: 14.6 percent (0.6 percent remunerated) on deposits in domestic and foreign currency. The maintenance period is one month, with averaging provisions. Reserve requirements have not been modified since 1999.	Reserve requirements: 12 percent in domestic and foreign currencies. Maintenance period of 14 days, with averaging provisions. There is also a mandatory 2 percent remunerated investment at the CBH. In foreign currency there is another 38 percent requirement to be held in overseas.	Reserve requirements: 16.25 percent on deposits in domestic and foreign currencies. Maintenance period of one week without compensation within the period.
	Two modalities of open market operations: (1) Short-term investments in the CBCR at 7, 15, and 30 days; and (2) auctions of CBCR's zero-coupon securities (at 3, 6, 9, and 12 months) and coupon securities (at 2, 3, 5, and 7 years). Only banks and brokerage houses are authorized to participate in the auctions.	Open market operations are held weekly under multiple-price auctions of "certificates of participation," zero coupon, and long-term securities at 35, 91, 182, and 364 days. All economic agents can participate. The CBDR also offers short- and long-term deposit facilities that pay rates consistent with those resulting from the auctions.	The Banguat conducts open market operations at 7, 91, and 182 days, and at 1, 2, 4, 6, and 8 years. Only financial institutions participate. It also conducts auctions of time deposits at same maturities (except seven-day) in domestic and foreign currencies. All economic agents participate in the latter via brokerage houses.	The CBH conducts open market operations in domestic currency and a limited amount in foreign currency. It holds weekly auctions (at seven days) and bi-weekly auctions (at 90, 180, and 360 days). While in the former only financial institutions participate, the latter is open to other market participants.	The CBN calls for auctions once a week and offers securities at three-month and one-year maturities. Only banks can participate.
Liquidity management	The CBCR conducts liquidity forecasting every two weeks based on its financial programming. This is the basis for defining the absorption needed to observe monetary targets envisaged in the financial programming.	The CBDR conducts weekly liquidity forecasting based on the financial programming.	The Banguat conducts liquidity forecasting on a daily basis. The EC uses this information to plan weekly open market operations.	The CBH conducts weekly liquidity forecasting for each working day. It serves to define the amounts to be issued in open market operations.	The CBN carries out monthly liquidity forecasting on the basis of the financial programming after adjusting for seasonal trends.
	The CBCR uses its deposit facilities (at 7, 15, and 30 days) to drain liquidity. Most deposits concentrate on 30-day maturity. Interest rates are directly fixed by the CBCR.	The CBDR manages liquidity through the weekly open market operations.	The auctions at seven-day maturity are aimed at managing short-term liquidity.	The CBH uses the weekly auctions to handle short-term liquidity and biweekly auctions to manage structural liquidity.	The CBN plans and executes open market operations with the aim of observing its international reserves target in line with its monetary program.

	There is a shallow interbank market for overnight transactions of government and central bank securities.	There is a shallow interbank market based on certificates of deposit, which do not require pledging collateral.	There is an interbank market, mainly repo operations conducted through the stock exchange.	There are only limited transactions, which do not use collateral, as CBH and government securities are non-negotiable.	There is an interbank market. However, the CBN is in the process of ascertaining how significant this market is.
	The CBCR conducts overnight repo operations but no reverse repo transactions.	The CBDR does not conduct repo operations.	The Banguat holds repo transactions at seven-day intervals using government and its own securities as collateral.	The CBH does not conduct repo operations.	The CBN does not conduct repo operations at any maturity.
Policy signaling	The CBCR defines the 30-day interest rate paid in its deposit facility as its policy rate. This rate is not market-determined.	There is no specific policy signaling. Markets ascertain the CBDR's policy stance depending on its weekly open market operations.	The Banguat uses the seven-day interest rate as a policy rate. The EC adjusts this rate with the explicit intention of signaling Banguat's policy stance.	The CBH uses as a policy rate the seven-day interest rates resulting from the weekly auctions.	There is no specific policy signaling. Markets ascertain CBN's policy stance depending on the volume of weekly open market operations.
Standing facilities	The CBCR has not established daily standing facilities.	The CBDR has established standing facilities at up to seven days' maturity. The COMA sets interest rates and banks pledge the CBDR's paper as collateral in the credit facility.	There are no standing facilities available.	The CBH offers overnight deposit and credit facilities (pledging CBH's securities as collateral). As of end-2005, interest rates were +/– 4 percent of the policy rate, respectively.	There is only an overnight credit facility to be used at most four times a month, with at least two days in between. Banks pledge commercial paper as collateral at market rates.
Accountability and transparency	There is no specific legal provision for appearances before Congress by the CBCR governor.	The CBDR governor reports annually to the executive branch and submits the CBDR's annual report to Congress.	The Banguat president appears before Congress twice a year (January and July) to report on Banguat's policies.	The CBH board reports once a year to the legislative and twice a year to the executive branch.	The CBN governor reports annually to the president of the country. There is no legal provision for his appearance before Congress.
	The CBCR disseminates an inflation report twice a year. It also releases an economic report monthly and biannually.	The CBDR develops and disseminates a monetary policy report. It also releases a quarterly economic report.	The Banguat prepares and disseminates a monetary policy report twice a year.	The CBH does not prepare an inflation report but it develops a quarterly report about major developments of the Honduran economy.	The CBN releases a report on a quarterly basis—with a six- to eight-week lag—monitoring the monetary program.
	The CBCR publishes the decisions adopted concerning monetary policy, but not the minutes of the discussions behind such policy decisions.	The CBDR publishes the decisions adopted concerning monetary policy, but not the minutes of the discussions behind such policy decisions.	The Banguat discloses the minutes underlying the decisions adopted by the EC.	The CBH publishes the decisions adopted concerning monetary policy, but not the minutes of the discussions behind such policy decisions.	The CBN publishes the decisions adopted concerning monetary policy, but not the minutes of the discussions behind such policy decisions.

Source: Responses to monetary policy questionnaire.

References

Calvo, Guillermo A. and Carmen M. Reinhart, 2002, "Fear of Floating," *Quarterly Journal of Economics*, Vol. 68, No. 2, pp. 379–408.

Corbo, Vittorio, 2002, "Monetary Policy in Latin America in the 1990s," in *Monetary Policy: Rules and Transmission Mechanisms*, ed. by Norman Loayza and Klaus Schmidt-Hebbel (Santiago: Central Bank of Chile).

Cukierman, Alex, 1992, *Central Bank Strategy, Credibility, and Independence: Theory and Evidence* (Cambridge, Massachusetts: The MIT Press).

Eichengreen, Barry, 2002, "Can Emerging Markets Float? Should they Inflation Target?" Banco Central do Brasil Working Paper Series (February).

Goldstein, Morris, and Philip Turner, 2004, "Controlling Currency Mismatches in Emerging Economies: An Alternative to the Original Sin Hypothesis" (unpublished; Washington: Institute for International Economics).

International Monetary Fund, 2005, *Annual Report on Exchange Arrangements and Exchange Restrictions* (Washington).

———, 2006, "Developments in Domestic Fuel Prices, Taxes, and Subsidies in Selected Countries," Fiscal Affairs Department (unpublished; Washington: International Monetary Fund).

Jácome H., Luis I., and Francisco Vázquez, 2005, "Any Link Between Legal Central Bank Independence and Inflation? Evidence from Latin America and the Caribbean," IMF Working Paper 05/75 (Washington: International Monetary Fund).

Kim, Jun, and Laura Papi, 2005, "Regional Integration and Exchange Rate Arrangements," in *Central America: Global Integration and Regional Cooperation*, IMF Occasional Paper 243, ed. by Marcus Rodlauer and Alfred Schipke (Washington: International Monetary Fund).

Lybek, Tony, 1998, "Elements of Central Bank: Autonomy and Accountability," Monetary and Exchange Affairs Department Operational Paper 98/1 (Washington: International Monetary Fund).

McCallum, Bennett, 1988, "Robustness Properties of a Rule for Monetary Policy," Carnegie-Rochester Conference Series on Public Society, Vol. 29, pp. 173–204.

Papaioannou, Michael G., 2003, "Determinants of the Choice of Exchange Rate Regimes in Six Central American Countries: An Empirical Analysis," IMF Working Paper 03/59 (Washington: International Monetary Fund).

Parrado, Eric, 2004, "Singapore's Unique Monetary Policy: How Does it Work?" IMF Working Paper 04/10 (Washington: International Monetary Fund).

Rennhack, Robert, and Erik Offerdal, 2004, *The Macroeconomy of Central America* (Washington: International Monetary Fund).

Rodlauer, Markus, and Alfred Schipke, 2005, *Central America: Global Integration and Regional Cooperation,* IMF Occasional Paper No. 243 (Washington: International Monetary Fund).

Taylor, John, 1993, "Discretion versus Policy Rules in Practice," Carnegie-Rochester Conference Series on Public Policy, Vol. 39, pp. 195–214.

Recent Occasional Papers of the International Monetary Fund

257. Economic Growth and Integration in Central America, edited by Dominique Desruelle and Alfred Schipke. 2007.
256. Moving to Greater Exchange Rate Flexibility: Operational Aspects Based on Lessons from Detailed Country Experiences, by Inci Ötker-Robe and David Vávra, and a team of IMF economists. 2007
255. Sovereign Debt Restructuring and Debt Sustainability: An Analysis of Recent Cross-Country Experience, by Harald Finger and Mauro Mecagni. 2007.
254. Country Insurance: The Role of Domestic Policies, by Törbjörn Becker, Olivier Jeanne, Paolo Mauro, Jonathan D. Ostry, and Romain Rancière. 2007.
253. The Macroeconomics of Scaling Up Aid: Lessons from Recent Experience, by Andrew Berg, Shekhar Aiyar, Mumtaz Hussain, Shaun Roache, Tokhir Mirzoev, and Amber Mahone. 2007.
252. Growth in the Central and Eastern European Countries of the European Union, by Susan Schadler, Ashoka Mody, Abdul Abiad, and Daniel Leigh. 2006.
251. The Design and Implementation of Deposit Insurance Systems, by David S. Hoelscher, Michael Taylor, and Ulrich H. Klueh. 2006.
250. Designing Monetary and Fiscal Policy in Low-Income Countries, by Abebe Aemro Selassie, Benedict Clements, Shamsuddin Tareq, Jan Kees Martijn, and Gabriel Di Bella. 2006.
249. Official Foreign Exchange Intervention, by Shogo Ishi, Jorge Iván Canales-Kriljenko, Roberto Guimarães, and Cem Karacadag. 2006.
248. Labor Market Performance in Transition: The Experience of Central and Eastern European Countries, by Jerald Schiff, Philippe Egoumé-Bossogo, Miho Ihara, Tetsuya Konuki, and Kornélia Krajnyák. 2006.
247. Rebuilding Fiscal Institutions in Post-Conflict Countries, by Sanjeev Gupta, Shamsuddin Tareq, Benedict Clements, Alex Segura-Ubiergo, Rina Bhattacharya, and Todd Mattina. 2005.
246. Experience with Large Fiscal Adjustments, by George C. Tsibouris, Mark A. Horton, Mark J. Flanagan, and Wojciech S. Maliszewski. 2005.
245. Budget System Reform in Emerging Economies: The Challenges and the Reform Agenda, by Jack Diamond. 2005.
244. Monetary Policy Implementation at Different Stages of Market Development, by a staff team led by Bernard J. Laurens. 2005.
243. Central America: Global Integration and Regional Cooperation, edited by Markus Rodlauer and Alfred Schipke. 2005.
242. Turkey at the Crossroads: From Crisis Resolution to EU Accession, by a staff team led by Reza Moghadam. 2005.
241. The Design of IMF-Supported Programs, by Atish Ghosh, Charis Christofides, Jun Kim, Laura Papi, Uma Ramakrishnan, Alun Thomas, and Juan Zalduendo. 2005.
240. Debt-Related Vulnerabilities and Financial Crises: An Application of the Balance Sheet Approach to Emerging Market Countries, by Christoph Rosenberg, Ioannis Halikias, Brett House, Christian Keller, Jens Nystedt, Alexander Pitt, and Brad Setser. 2005.
239. GEM: A New International Macroeconomic Model, by Tamim Bayoumi, with assistance from Douglas Laxton, Hamid Faruqee, Benjamin Hunt, Philippe Karam, Jaewoo Lee, Alessandro Rebucci, and Ivan Tchakarov. 2004.
238. Stabilization and Reforms in Latin America: A Macroeconomic Perspective on the Experience Since the Early 1990s, by Anoop Singh, Agnès Belaisch, Charles Collyns, Paula De Masi, Reva Krieger, Guy Meredith, and Robert Rennhack. 2005.
237. Sovereign Debt Structure for Crisis Prevention, by Eduardo Borensztein, Marcos Chamon, Olivier Jeanne, Paolo Mauro, and Jeromin Zettelmeyer. 2004.
236. Lessons from the Crisis in Argentina, by Christina Daseking, Atish R. Ghosh, Alun Thomas, and Timothy Lane. 2004.
235. A New Look at Exchange Rate Volatility and Trade Flows, by Peter B. Clark, Natalia Tamirisa, and Shang-Jin Wei, with Azim Sadikov and Li Zeng. 2004.

234. Adopting the Euro in Central Europe: Challenges of the Next Step in European Integration, by Susan M. Schadler, Paulo F. Drummond, Louis Kuijs, Zuzana Murgasova, and Rachel N. van Elkan. 2004.
233. Germany's Three-Pillar Banking System: Cross-Country Perspectives in Europe, by Allan Brunner, Jörg Decressin, Daniel Hardy, and Beata Kudela. 2004.
232. China's Growth and Integration into the World Economy: Prospects and Challenges, edited by Eswar Prasad. 2004.
231. Chile: Policies and Institutions Underpinning Stability and Growth, by Eliot Kalter, Steven Phillips, Marco A. Espinosa-Vega, Rodolfo Luzio, Mauricio Villafuerte, and Manmohan Singh. 2004.
230. Financial Stability in Dollarized Countries, by Anne-Marie Gulde, David Hoelscher, Alain Ize, David Marston, and Gianni De Nicoló. 2004.
229. Evolution and Performance of Exchange Rate Regimes, by Kenneth S. Rogoff, Aasim M. Husain, Ashoka Mody, Robin Brooks, and Nienke Oomes. 2004.
228. Capital Markets and Financial Intermediation in The Baltics, by Alfred Schipke, Christian Beddies, Susan M. George, and Niamh Sheridan. 2004.
227. U.S. Fiscal Policies and Priorities for Long-Run Sustainability, edited by Martin Mühleisen and Christopher Towe. 2004.
226. Hong Kong SAR: Meeting the Challenges of Integration with the Mainland, edited by Eswar Prasad, with contributions from Jorge Chan-Lau, Dora Iakova, William Lee, Hong Liang, Ida Liu, Papa N'Diaye, and Tao Wang. 2004.
225. Rules-Based Fiscal Policy in France, Germany, Italy, and Spain, by Teresa Dában, Enrica Detragiache, Gabriel di Bella, Gian Maria Milesi-Ferretti, and Steven Symansky. 2003.
224. Managing Systemic Banking Crises, by a staff team led by David S. Hoelscher and Marc Quintyn. 2003.
223. Monetary Union Among Member Countries of the Gulf Cooperation Council, by a staff team led by Ugo Fasano. 2003.
222. Informal Funds Transfer Systems: An Analysis of the Informal Hawala System, by Mohammed El Qorchi, Samuel Munzele Maimbo, and John F. Wilson. 2003.
221. Deflation: Determinants, Risks, and Policy Options, by Manmohan S. Kumar. 2003.
220. Effects of Financial Globalization on Developing Countries: Some Empirical Evidence, by Eswar S. Prasad, Kenneth Rogoff, Shang-Jin Wei, and Ayhan Kose. 2003.
219. Economic Policy in a Highly Dollarized Economy: The Case of Cambodia, by Mario de Zamaroczy and Sopanha Sa. 2003.
218. Fiscal Vulnerability and Financial Crises in Emerging Market Economies, by Richard Hemming, Michael Kell, and Axel Schimmelpfennig. 2003.
217. Managing Financial Crises: Recent Experience and Lessons for Latin America, edited by Charles Collyns and G. Russell Kincaid. 2003.
216. Is the PRGF Living Up to Expectations? An Assessment of Program Design, by Sanjeev Gupta, Mark Plant, Benedict Clements, Thomas Dorsey, Emanuele Baldacci, Gabriela Inchauste, Shamsuddin Tareq, and Nita Thacker. 2002.
215. Improving Large Taxpayers' Compliance: A Review of Country Experience, by Katherine Baer. 2002.
214. Advanced Country Experiences with Capital Account Liberalization, by Age Bakker and Bryan Chapple. 2002.
213. The Baltic Countries: Medium-Term Fiscal Issues Related to EU and NATO Accession, by Johannes Mueller, Christian Beddies, Robert Burgess, Vitali Kramarenko, and Joannes Mongardini. 2002.
212. Financial Soundness Indicators: Analytical Aspects and Country Practices, by V. Sundararajan, Charles Enoch, Armida San José, Paul Hilbers, Russell Krueger, Marina Moretti, and Graham Slack. 2002.
211. Capital Account Liberalization and Financial Sector Stability, by a staff team led by Shogo Ishii and Karl Habermeier. 2002.
210. IMF-Supported Programs in Capital Account Crises, by Atish Ghosh, Timothy Lane, Marianne Schulze-Ghattas, Aleš Bulíř, Javier Hamann, and Alex Mourmouras. 2002.

Note: For information on the titles and availability of Occasional Papers not listed, please consult the IMF's *Publications Catalog* or contact IMF Publication Services.